Explore the World

NELLES

GW00703212

MALAYSIA

SINGAPORE · BRUNEI

Authors:
Karl-Heinz Reger, Albrecht G. Schaefer,
Gerd Simon, Dr. Martin Kehr

An Up-to-date travel guide with 134 color photos
and 24 maps

Second Revised Edition
1997

Dear Reader,

Being up-to-date is the main goal of the Nelles series. To achieve it, we have a net-work of far-flung correspondents who keep us abreast of the latest developments in the travel scene, and our cartographers always make sure that maps and texts are adjusted to each other.

Each travel chapter ends with its own list of useful tips, accommodations, restaur-ants, tourist offices, sights. At the end of the book you will find practical information from A to Z. But the travel world is fast moving, and we cannot guarantee that all the contents are always valid. Should you come across a discrepancy, please write us at: Nelles Verlag GmbH, Schleissheimer Str. 371 b, D-80935 München, Germany, Tel: (089) 3571940, Fax: (089) 35719430.

LEGEND

✳	Place of Interest	Lumut	Place Mentioned in Text	▦ National Border
▨	Public or Significant Building	⇥	International Airport	▬ Administrative Border
■	Hotel	✈	Airfield	▬ Expressway
▦	Shopping Center	🐘	Wildlife Reserve	▬ Principal Highway
○	Market	♣	National Park	▬ Main Road
✝ ⚲	Church, Buddhist Temple	🏖	Beach	▬ Provincial Road
		⑥	Route Number	▬ Secondary Road
☪ ☫	Mosque, Hindu Temple	G. Mulu 2371	Mountain Summit (Height in Meters)	╲18╱ Railway
				╲18╱ Distance in Kilometers

MALAYSIA–SINGAPORE–BRUNEI
© Nelles Verlag GmbH, 80935 Munich
  All rights reserved

Second Revised Edition 1997
ISBN 3-88618-902-3
Printed in Slovenia

Publisher:	Günter Nelles	**Translations:**	Ross Greville, Ginger Künzel, Robert Rowley, M. Radkai, Mariana Schroeder
Project Editor:	Karl-Heinz Reger Albrecht G. Schaefer		
Editors:	Berthold Schwarz Anne Midgette Marton Radkai	**Cartography:**	Nelles Verlag GmbH, Munich
		Color Separation:	Priegnitz, Munich
Photo Editor:	Heinz Vestner	**Printing:**	Gorenjski Tisk

TABLE OF CONTENTS

LIST OF MAPS

WHERE THE MONSOON
WINDS MEET

LAND AND PEOPLE

A Country of Many Faces

Brightly-colored kites soar in the air and rubber sap flows from trees. Temples and mosques are reflected in the mirrored windows of skyscrapers. While entire villages find shelter under a single roof, the Sultans still live in luxury, continuing their traditional, lavish way of life in grand palaces in the middle of huge, park-like estates. Expressway overpasses rise above extensive urban slums as if to bypass their problems, while elsewhere in the same cities shopping centers sprout like temples to a new god of prosperity, offering a glittering array of goods that only the rich can afford.

In Malaysia's big cities, young people love the sounds of pop and techno music; in the provinces of the east coast, modest veils and Islamic restraint – at least toward the outside world – are more the norm. Although Islam is the state religion, Malaysia's constitution guarantees religious freedom, and followers of the world's four major religions compete for the attention of their gods with a wide variety of traditional festivals.

Visitors and tourists are greeted with friendly smiles and welcomed with warm hospitality. But don't dare utter a word against the country's known environmental problems. Critics could face deportation. And – as the tourist brochures clearly warn – selling drugs is a capital offense. Offenders are hanged.

Preceding pages: Flying kites is a national pastime. An enchanting beach in the Langkawi Archipelago. Left: The Orang Asli are the descendants of the first inhabitants.

The beaches are a tropical paradise. The mountains hover over the palm-fringed landscape and the gods seem a lot closer on Mount Kinabalu in Sabah, the highest mountain in Southeast Asia. Orangutans still swing through the jungles and elephants and rhinoceroses roam the plains. And descendants of the Orang Asli, the region's original inhabitants, have not forgotten the art of hunting with a blowpipe.

At the same time, the ancient rain forests form the country's most fragile environment. Each day the forest shrinks as giant trees are felled to make way for progress and economic growth. Tropical lumber, tin, oil, rubber and palm oil products are Malaysia's chief exports. But tourism is rapidly becoming an important source of hard currency.

Malaysia is geographically split into distinctly different regions and demographically divided into several ethnic groups. The Malays see themselves as the elite amongst the *bumiputras* ("sons of the earth"), or native residents, and therefore claim their right to a home-court advantage. Neither the original, tribal inhabitants of the area – such as the Orang Asli in West Malaysia, the Kadazan in East Malaysia, or the Dayak from Borneo – nor the Chinese and Indians descended from immigrant laborers are able to contest these rights.

According to official accounts, the search for a national identity among the country's 19 million inhabitants of varied ethnic origin has been smooth and harmonious. In fact, social and ethnic conflicts continue to flare up, to greater and lesser degrees. The economic boom has leveled some differences, but poverty and unemployment in other areas have acted to fan the flames of old ethnic prejudices and rivalries.

The goal of ultimate unity is symbolized in the flag of the Malaysian Federation. Its 14 horizontal red and white stripes make way, in the upper left-

13

hand corner, for a blue field; this is emblazoned with a yellow crescent moon and a 14-pointed star. The number of stripes and points of the star symbolize the 13 federal states plus the federal territory of Kuala Lumpur, the country's capital.

The blue field stands for the unity of the diverse population, while the crescent symbolizes the state religion, Islam. The yellow color of the moon and stars honors the country's traditional rulers, the Sultans of Malaysia. Currently, these aristocrats are nine in number; every five years, one of them is elected to serve as the country of Malaysia's titular head of state.

Where the Monsoons Meet

Malaysia's geography is striking. From north to south, the country stret-

Above: Rice cultivation has long been the basis of Malaysian life. Right: Iban warriors in the rain forest of Sarawak.

ches between the eighth and first parallels north of the equator; from west to east, it lies between the 100th and 120th meridians. Encompassing the Malaysian peninsula and the two states on Borneo, Sarawak and Sabah, its territory covers 128,430 square miles (330,422 sq. km), an area larger than Poland.

The country's two sections are separated by some 434 miles (700 km) of the South China Sea, crisscrossed by trade routes since time immemorial. To the west, the country is bordered by the Straits of Malacca, a funnel for East-West shipping traffic. Time and again, the waterway has been a bone of contention between foreign powers seeking to safeguard their foothold on the Malaysian peninsula and thus gain control of Southeast Asia.

Malaysia has been uniquely singled out by nature; the monsoon winds create a distinctive climate. The north and south monsoons actually meet on the peninsula; both have an effect, to varying degrees, in the heavy rainfall and hot,

humid climate. These conditions are ideal for rain forests, which once covered the entire area, and for their singular fauna. Furthermore, it's this climate which, for thousands of years, has enabled human beings, in spite of floods and storms, to develop the science of rice-paddy cultivation. This autonomous, independent form of agriculture is the basis of the culture and civilization of many of the peoples and countries of Asia. Although rubber and oil-palm plantations have won Malaysia a place in the world's agricultural markets, rice cultivation – partly because of its time-intensive nature – remains the backbone of village life in Southeast Asia.

Tourists are still something of a rarity in the Sultanate of Brunei, the fossil-fuel-rich state between Sarawak and Sabah. Its wealth flows from the earth in the form of oil and gas. Foreigners are brought in to do the hard work of drilling for oil and running the wells; while the Bruneians sit back, take it easy, and pray to Allah that the oil keep gushing.

HISTORY

The Native Inhabitants

Although the first inhabitants of Malaysia settled the peninsula in the twilight of prehistory, it is possible to reconstruct the way they lived by observing their direct descendants. The Orang Asli (original people) are small-boned, dark-skinned jungle nomads who still live a neolithic existence even if their original stone tools have today been supplanted by modern ones made of plastic and metal. Orang Asli peoples, inclduing the Semang Negritos and the very similar Senoi, eked out a living by hunting with blowpipes and gathering fruit and roots in the rain forest. Typical dwellings were simple screens which afforded protection against the wind. Today, many cater to the tourists, but some still continue to live much as their prehistoric ancestors did.

Evidence of still earlier inhabitants who roamed the peninsula prior to the arrival of the Semang and the Senoi has

15

been found in various Stone Age sites. Burial sites 35,000 years old have been uncovered in the state of Perak. The skull of a *homo sapiens*, believed to have lived 40,000 years ago, was discovered in Sarawak's Niah Caves. Early tools testify to the activities of nomadic hunters and gatherers in prehistoric times.

Around 3,000 years ago, scientists estimate, the first proto-Malays left their South Chinese homeland of Yunnan, the "mother of many peoples," and began their migration across the mainland to the East Indies. Supported by their superior agricultural techniques of crop cultivation in fields which they cleared by burning in the jungle, they pushed the local nomads back into the mountains and peripheral areas of the rain forest. They cultivated yams, mountain rice, bananas and other food plants, and traveled along the

Above: Members of Malaysia's Indian population around 1900. Right: Roof decorations on the clan house of the Khoo family in George Town.

rivers in dug-out canoes. The sedentary proto-Malays lived in small village communities of rectangular pile houses.

The Malaysian Migration

The inhabitants of the Southeast Asian archipelago who call themselves Malays trace their ancestry back to the so-called Deutero-Malayans who arrived around 300 B.C. from the inland regions of mainland Asia and settled down as farmers and fishermen. They brought iron tools and weapons with them, organized their villages into defensive units, and established a working system of government led by the *datos*, a hereditary aristocracy.

On the island of Borneo, in what are today the states of Sarawak and Sabah, as well as Brunei, dwell the large ethnic groups of the Dayak and Kadazan. The ancestors of the third ethnic group, the nomadic hunters and gatherers of the Punan people, had settled Borneo even before the Dayak.

The Influence of India

In the West Malaysia of today, Islam seems to have affected every aspect of life; but Malay culture was strongly influenced by India before Islam ever arrived. A close look at the marriage ceremony today reveals traces of Hindu tradition. The shadow puppet plays of the *Wayang Kulit* often tell stories drawn from the Indian *Ramayana* epic. The Malaysian language contains many words borrowed from Sanskrit, and the country's cuisine would be unimaginable without Indian spices and curries.

The spur of land of the Malaysian peninsula has always acted as a bridge between the Asian continent, Oceania and Australia. Since the dawn of man's history, therefore, it has seen mass migrations of many peoples. Trade routes established a channel between China and

India; in the same way, a cultural exchange took place between these two great powers of Asia, following in the wake of the ships sailing from west to east. So powerful was the fascination exerted by Indian civilization that even on the Mekong river, which was under the jurisdiction of the Chinese Empire, centers of Indian culture came into being.

Malaysia's location on the Straits of Malacca, at the crossroads of all the shipping routes between India and China, made it an ideal base for players in the arena of east-west trade.

India did not colonize with fire and the sword. It relied on trade and its superior culture. Even if Indian ships did sail with military as well as civilian goals, the temptations of sea trade and the fascination of the country's culture made it easy for the empire to create a whole network of vassal states with a minimum of bloodshed.

India's veiled desire for power showed its purely political face in the early 11th century, when the Chola Empire of south India, led by Virirajendra I, attacked the flourishing kingdom of Kedah (also known as Kalah) and wiped it out completely. Kedah, which along with Palembang on Sumatra formed the axis of the Srivijaya kingdom, had controlled the narrow bottleneck of the Straits of Malacca, the link between east and west, since the 7th century. The increase in the state's wealth and power, a thorn in India's side, represented, from a cultural standpoint, the advance of Malay power and the development of the interior of the peninsula. Kedah was sacked for resisting India's authority, but in the course of the ensuing centuries the city of Melaka rose out of its ashes. In the 14th century the Malay-Hindu kingdom of Majapahit, based on Java, controlled the Malay archipelago.

Contact with China

Until this point in the history of Southeast Asia, China, the Empire of the Sun, isolated itself behind the Great Wall and sought contact with other nations only for the purpose of exacting tribute. Buddhism, however, exerted such a powerful attraction that pilgrims began traveling from China to India. Those who stopped off to visit the Malay peninsula on the way were among the most important chroniclers and historians of events in Malaysia 1,000 years ago.

The Straits of Malacca were another major route along which Chinese travelers journeyed to explore the West. Cheng Ho, an imperial eunuch of the Ming Dynasty, led the biggest of the seven expeditions China sent out between 1403 and 1433. By the 15th century, Chinese fleets were often anchoring at Malacca, which had become an important stop along the Chinese-Indian route.

The Advance of Islam

By converting to Islam, Admiral Cheng Ho paved the way for the religion of Mohammed to conquer virtually all of Southeast Asia. Certainly, there had already been contacts between the insular, Indian-influenced culture and Moslems as early as the 7th century, when Persian and Arab merchants sailed the Straits of Malacca on their way to Canton. The travel journals of one Abu Dulaf from the 10th century mention important harbors between Malaya and Sumatra.

But Islam only truly began to spread after the destruction of the Srivijaya Empire in the 11th century. Marco Polo, on a mission from the Chinese Emperor, wrote about two Moslem settlements in Perlak and Pasai on Sumatra. Until the 15th century, Buddhism and Hinduism continued to hold spiritual sway over the area. But when Melaka (Malacca), a region open to the new, Islamic way of thinking, began its ascendancy, crowding out the Madjapahit empire and its Indian

Right: The mosque in the old royal city of Pekan.

influence, Islam also began its steady spread throughout the peninsula. Leaders who had theretofore been known as rajahs began to call themselves Sultans and Shahs.

Melaka, strategically placed on the narrowest part of the Straits, began its expansion in the years between 1446 and 1488 under the Shahs Muzaffar, Mansur and Riayat. On the peninsula, the states of Johor and Pahang were annexed; Siar, Kampar and Indragiri on the coast of Sumatra followed. Brunei also wanted to profit from the lucrative China trade and intensified its relationship with Melaka. It, too, showed no opposition to the green flag of Mohammed. Kedah followed suit, and soon the entire region, with a few exceptions, such as Hindu Bali and Buddhist Siam, had become Moslem.

Islam and Language

The history of the country of Malaysia gives clear evidence of the relationships between power, religion and language. The Terengganu stone from 1380, found near Kuala Berang, is the oldest known example of Arabic script yet found in Malaysia. The fact that Arabic had replaced Sanskrit, which had until then been commonplace, clearly shows that Islam was well on its way to becoming the dominant religion by the 14th century.

The *Jawi*, or Arabic alphabet of the Malaysian language, was used until the 1920s; and it is still used today in some conservative Moslem circles. Koran schools gave instruction in Arabic until the 19th century; evidently the Malay language, a branch of the Austronesian linguistic family, was not deemed worthy of expressing the Koran's teachings. The historic linguistic research of Melaka-born Munshi Abdullah, known as the "Luther of Malaysia," led to his compiling the first grammar of the Malay language in the 19th century.

By thus claiming the right to a linguistic identity, the region had effectively declared war on the resident colonial powers. England and Holland favored the simply-structured vernacular of Bazaar Malayan (*melayu pasar*), and tried to establish it as the country's *lingua franca*. The key discussions about knowledge or power could therefore be held as usual in English or Dutch. Today, *bahasa melayu* is a living language; its scope, expressiveness and usefulness have been increased through the adoption of words and terms from Sanskrit, Arabic and European languages.

Malacca, Hub of Colonialism

An old handbook of the British colonial administration enumerates the advantages of the narrow waterway between Malaysia and Sumatra, with Melaka (malacca) perched on the choicest spot: "The Malay peninsula is bordered on the west by a narrow passage of water, the Strait of Malacca, which is no wider than the peninsula and in some areas not more than 40 miles across, so that, for several hundred miles, it can be easily closed off from land through the use of cannon, all the more so as its waters are quite shallow... Because of this, the entire southern part of the peninsula has particular strategic importance."

In 1398, the Malay Prince Parameswara from Palembang in Sumatra found shelter in a tiny fishing village and pirates' nest. Under his rule, the village known as Malacca (or Melaka) grew, in the words of one enthusiastic Portuguese sailor, into "the richest harbor in the world." The vast territory of the original city-state extended to both sides of the Strait.

Thanks to the monsoons, all trade routes led to Malacca. The North Monsoon in the spring brought the Chinese junks, while the Southwest Monsoon filled the sails of Arabic and Indian ships. Contact between Malacca and the Ming Dynasty began with the visit of Cheng Ho's fleet. Even when this largely symbolic relationship ended in 1433, the re-

19

ligious zeal of Cheng Ho, the Moslem convert from the east, increased the already wide-ranging influence of the Arab merchants from the west. In 1414, Prince Parameswara converted to Islam, gave up his Hindu beliefs, and changed his name to Megat Iskandar Shah with the title of Sultan.

Malacca continued to prosper under European colonial rule. Only when its harbor silted up and Panang and Singapore overtook it in importance for the British did Malacca begin to lose significance as a cosmopolitan metropolis. But even today, the city remains a meeting point between east and west. Malay, Arab, Indian, Chinese and European influences have left their mark. Eurasian descendants live next to *peranakan*, the descendants of "Straits Chinese" who intermarried with Malayans. Members of this group also call themselves *Baba-Nyonyas*, people descended from

Above: Porta Santiago, part of the ruins of A Famosa. Right: Alfonso d'Albuquerque.

Chinese men (*babas*) who married Malayan women (*nyonyas*).

The Portuguese in Malaya

Treasure and spices: it was for these wares, so sought-after in Europe, that the Portuguese developed their footholds in Southeast Asia. Although they often ascribed their presence to the draw of the biblical Star of the East, greed for gold and spices was what really that brought the Portuguese and Spanish to the Far East in the late 15th and even more in the 16th centuries. The conversion of Moslems by fanatic Christian missionaries was intended to boost trade. And business, regardless of its motives, proved highly profitable: a sack of East Indian pepper brought 40 times its purchase price in Europe. Through overseas trade, the Portuguese crown could raise four times more money than by raising taxes at home.

Malacca appeared especially valuable to the Portuguese. The city was the chief port for spices from the Indonesian spice islands, especially from the Molucas. Pepper, gold and ivory came from Sumatra, camphor and batik from Java, and tin from Perak. From the Far East came porcelain and silk. Best of all, everything in Malacca could be bought with Indian cotton from Goa.

The Portuguese wanted to supplant the Venetians as leaders in trade between Asia and Europe, true to the then-contemporary saying, "whoever is master of Malacca has his hands around the throat of Venice." In April, 1511, Alfonso d'Albuquerque, Portugal's colonial strategist in Asia, left Goa and sailed to Malacca with 18 ships and 1,400 men.

At first the Sultan took no notice. He trusted the merchants of Malacca to act in their own self-interest, failing to realize that the non-Muslim merchants would join the enemy. The Portuguese, furthermore, had the advantage of greater fire power and aimed their cannons more accurately. On August 15, 1511, the city fell to the Europeans. The Empire of Malacca, with its Sumatran possessions, was drawing near its end. The states of Johor and Perak became independent.

Characteristically for the Portuguese throughout their history, the new rulers limited their conquest to establishing bases from which to carry on trade and exact customs duties. Even in Melaka, the Portuguese entrenched themselves behind the walls of their fort. *A Famosa*, probably the first stone building in the city, was a heavily armed "little Portugal" which eventually contained a cathedral, three churches, two hospitals and a school.

Nonetheless, the Portuguese were able to maintain their city as a sea power until 1635, when the Dutch fleet sank Portugal's ships off Melaka. Their continued power before this occurance owed more to happenstance than strategy, as they had no support whatsoever from the interior of the country. Their only lifeline

was the sea, and this could all too easily be cut off. The religious zeal of the Portuguese made them unpopular with the non-Christians in Malaysia, and their policy of taxing all ships that passed through the Straits of Malacca made them unpopular with everyone else. Holland first attacked Malacca in 1597, but it wasn't until 1641, after they besieged the city for six months, that they could celebrate their final, decisive victory over the Portuguese.

The Protestants from Holland

In 1606, almost 100 years after the Portuguese settled in Malacca, a Dutch merchant named Heemskerck arrived in Johor on the southern part of the Malaysian peninsula. The business ambitions of the Protestant Dutch were, unlike those of the Portuguese, untempered by religious missionary zeal. Sultan Ala'uddin of Johor (1597-1615) gave them a warm welcome, hoping, rightly, that the Dutch would set limits to Portugal's strict con-

trol over Malacca, even drive them out altogether.

After the Dutch made short, exploratory visits to Kedah in 1602 and to Batu Sawar in 1603, the two powers formed an alliance against the Portuguese, formalized by a treaty in 1606. The Dutch were to take over Malacca, while the Sultan would have a free hand to rule in the interior. This goal was not fully realized until 1641, when the *Vereenigde Oostindische Companie* (VOC or United East India Company) signed an exclusive treaty with Johor, which gave the Dutch the monopoly on Malaccan trade.

The Dutch and English presence in the East Indies was the result of political changes in Europe. In 1580, Philip II of Spain, a Catholic, conquered Portugal; in 1594, he denied all of Europe's non-Catholic nations access to the port of Lisbon, the main trade center for goods from the Far East. This Spanish-decreed

Above: A relic of colonial times: Seri Rambai cannon at Fort Cornwallis, George Town.

"Council of Portugal" indirectly sealed the fate of that country's colonies by forcing the English and Dutch to move toward the sources of the East Indies trade and bring it under their own control.

The Dutch conquest of Malacca also began a long-term shift from trade-motivated conquests to a brand of expansionist colonialism that saw territorial increase as its true goal. This also signaled an end to the relative freedom of trade enjoyed by the Sultanate of Johor and Aceh, the power center on northern Sumatra.

The Dutch moved the headquarters of their United East India Company to Batavia (later called Jakarta) and thereafter used Malacca more as a garrison town and military base from which to control the Straits. Trade shifted first to Aceh and then to Johor. The strife between the Malay and Sumatran states weakened their resistance to the new brand of European colonialism. This paved the way for the British, who were waiting in the wings with yet another modern variant of colonial rule.

British Malaysia

Once England had defeated France in the Seven Years' War in 1763, its economic power increased. At first, its colonial interests were limited to trade. The search for markets for home products and sources for raw materials came in the wake of the Industrial Revolution a century later.

The *East India Company*, which had controlled Britain's Asian trade since 1600, extended its field of operations in the second half of the 18th century from India eastwards to China. The tea trade, embodied in fast China clippers like the *Cutty Sark*, rapidly increased in importance. The Malay peninsula and Borneo lay on this vital trade route, and Britain soon secured the area with military bases in Penang, Singapore and Balambangan in North Borneo.

While this phase of its Far Eastern operations was rather superficial, the real beginning of British territorial expansion in the area was marked by Francis Light's seizure of Penang in 1786. The East India Company had commissioned Light to negotiate with the Sultan of Kedah about the purchase of Penang. Instead of money, the Sultan accepted assurances of British protection against an attack by neighboring Siam.

This deal demonstrated the contradictions inherent in Britain's colonial policy in Malaysia and Borneo. What started as a policy of establishing bases to secure sea routes and outposts for overseas trade soon became blatant British intervention in the region's domestic affairs. Despite the treaty he had signed, Francis Light declined to help the Sultan when Siam attacked Kedah. The Sultan retaliated by attacking the British garrison in Penang, and the British defended themselves – by turning their guns on their one-time ally.

Penang was declared a free port in 1787, a move equivalent to a declaration of war on the tax-happy Dutch. With the foundation of Singapore in 1819, Penang's importance as a trade center was diminished; but the move also increased the pressure on the obstreperous Netherlanders. The British had already made a clear advance on the mainland by buying a strip of land opposite Penang's east coast from the Sultan and naming it Wellesley Province.

The British arrived in Malacca in 1795. Holland had become entangled in the wars and upheavals that followed in the wake of the French Revolution; occupied by France, it was accordingly treated as a French ally and "partner" in colonial affairs, as well, by the Treaty of the Hague. By agreement with the Dutch government in exile in England, the British occupied Malacca, which then numbered some 15,000 inhabitants, on the understanding that they would return it to the Dutch government once Holland had regained its sovereignty. The first thing the British did was raze what was left of the old fort, *A Famosa*. This later proved unnecessary because, although Malacca did return to Holland in due course, it was given back to England by the Colonial Treaty of London in 1824.

At the dawn of the 19th century, a new kind of colonial emissary arrived on the promising territory of the Malay peninsula in the person of Sir Thomas Stamford Raffles. A tenacious bureaucrat, Raffles also showed an avid interest in nature and ethnic cultures, and even spoke the Malay language. His academic achievements and training ultimately served colonial ambitions: Raffles envisioned a large colonial territory under the jurisdiction of an all-British East Indies. Decisions about Southeast Asia's future, however, continued to be made in Europe, where the Congress of Vienna in 1815 had just sealed the end of the Napoleonic Wars. In London, there were calls for the help of strong European nations to help keep France in check. One of these "strong" countries was Holland,

which, without its colonies, would have been hopelessly weak. So the decision was made to let Holland keep its colonies, and Raffles's dreams remained unfulfilled.

This did not keep him from founding Singapore on the sparsely-populated island of the same name south of the Malay Peninsula. The advantages of the site, which was intended to become the economic heart of the region, were undeniable: it was located at the intersection of several vital sea routes, it had an excellent harbor, and it was free of the Dutch. Raffles took advantage of hereditary disputes among the successors of the Sultan of the "Lion State" (*singha pura*), and bought land for the settlement and harbor on behalf of the East India Company.

The island quickly grew into a bustling, powerful city at the cost of the other

Above: Raffles Square, Singapore at the end of the 19th century. Right: "Running amok in Malaysia:" European depiction of the effects of opium on the natives.

"Straits Settlements," Penang and Malacca. In the 1824 Treaty of London, which delineated the colonial territories and interests of Holland and England, Singapore was awarded to England.

Yet British colonialism in Southeast Asia was still, at that point, limited to the policy of establishing trade bases in a region eventually meant to deliver raw materials, provide land for plantations and become a market for products made at home. A change in this strategy first became evident in 1874, when, with the attack on the island of Pangkor, Britain began to seriously meddle in Malaysia's internal affairs.

One result of Britain's presence in Malacca was maintenance of the political status quo in the interior; Siamese expansionist efforts in Kedah, Kelantan and Terengganu were held in check. This uneasy balance was maintained by a "hands-off" policy backed up by the continued British presence and such clever tactical negotiations as the Anglo-Siamese Treaty of 1826.

However, the British also abandoned their "hands-off" policy when it suited their purposes. One such instance occurred in 1831, when the Minangkabau on the tiny island of Naning refused to pay tribute to the Crown. The latter struck back with a punitive military expedition into the jungle, and forcibly annexed Malacca's neighbor into their city-state. In 1862, there was further military action against the mainland. From the sea, the British opened fire on Kuala Terengganu on the mainland to frighten the Siamese, who time and again intervened in Malayan territory, violating the provisions of the Anglo-Siamese Treaty. With this incident, the British policy of non-intervention, of allowing its colonies administrative autonomy, seemed threatened with imminent collapse.

The Private Colony on Borneo

The colonies located on present-day East Malaysia were shaped in the 19th century by James Brooke, the Lord of Sarawak. A colorful character, this first of the "White Rajahs" was an anachronistic and at the same time avant-garde colonialist. By the middle of the 19th century, a private explorer, conqueror, and man with a mission such as James Brooke seemed like a holdover from a bygone era. On the other hand, he was far ahead of his British contemporaries in that he practiced a policy of territorial expansion that wasn't officially implemented for some years to come. Brooke followed Raffles in his vision of a British colonial empire that included all of the East Indies. Convinced of his purpose, and armed with an inheritance of £30,000, he left England in 1835 and sailed to Southeast Asia to make his fortune, landing on Kuching in 1840.

He got off to a good start. Thanks to his dashing appearance and aura of adventure, he was offered the position of Governor of Sarawak by the local ruler, Rajah Muda Hassim, the uncle of the Sultan of Brunei. In return for the post, all Brooke had to do was put down an upris-

ing of the native Dayak and Malays, who had rebelled against the repressive Sultanate of Brunei. The English were able to quell the rebellion; in thanks, the Sultan awarded them the vast tribute-paying region of Sarawak, which Brooke and his descendants were to rule for the next 100 years.

James Brooke, the founder of the dynasty of the "White Rajahs," was at once an emissary of the British Empire and an arbiter of local conflicts. He resisted the idea of forcing Sarawak to adapt to the norms of European civilization, and held that "the activities of European governments should serve the development of local native interests and capabilities, rather than merely the greed to conquer and to possess."

Since he received no financial support from the East India Company, Brooke in-

Above: Chinese coolies toiling in a mine near Taiping. Right: A street scene in the British Crown Colony of Singapore around 1900.

vested his own capital in his plans for Sarawak. In 1886, however, he did request the help of the British navy, which had a base in Singapore. When his ally and supporter, the Rajah Muda Hassim, fell victim to an intrigue in Brunei, Brooke used British cannon to force Brunei's Sultan to grant Sarawak complete autonomy and release it from its previous tributary obligations.

The New Colonial Policy

Around the mid-19th century, colonization of the Malay archipelago began to move in a new direction. The idea was to create an economic system that was both efficient and extensive, based on free trade and administered on colonial terms. The Spanish in the Philippines, the Dutch in Indonesia and the French in Indochina had already taken steps in this direction. By 1844, Singapore newspapers were urging London to follow suit.

The opening of the Suez Canal in 1869 accelerated the move toward new colo-

nial policies. First of all, the new, shorter sea route to Asia gave a whole new importance to the Straits Settlements; shipping traffic to Australia and New Zealand increased dramatically, as well. And in England, the mother country, the Industrial Revolution was in full swing. For the Malay peninsula, the growing need for raw materials led to an increasing demand for cheap labor. Chinese immigrants streamed into Perak and Selangor where tin was abundant and jobs plentiful. Ultimately, this brought about fundamental changes in colonial Malaysia's traditional economic and ethnic structures.

The Colony Needs Immigrants

The pattern for Malaysia's ethnic mosaic had been established well before the 19th century by the internal movements of various Malay peoples and the development of international communities in the port cities. But the massive migration of Chinese, and later Indians, only set in with the redefinition of the country's economy.

The Malay interior was "upgraded," by means of resettled immigrant laborers, in two stages. First, Chinese miners and farmers, who had generally come to the country on their own initiative, acted as pioneers by opening up and settling the interior. Then the British brought in Indians – mainly Tamils – to work as coolies on the plantations that resulted from the Chinese agricultural efforts.

The peninsula's doors were thrown open to the immigrants. In 1836, the sparsely-populated Malay peninsula had approximately 250,000 inhabitants. Most of these lived at the edges of the territory – along the coast or in settlements at the mouths of rivers – rather than inland. Because the population was mainly on the water, the economy was also water-based, centering on rice-paddy cultivation, fishing and piracy.

To the landless peasants of South China, this country without people must have appeared – much as it had to the proto-Malayan groups from Yunnan who were the very first wave of immigrants – like a promised land. But this time the migrants came not overland on foot, but by ship from Canton (Guangzhou) and Amoy (Xiamen), overpopulated areas where hunger, drought and frequent flooding provided more than enough incentive to leave.

The Chinese began migrating to the Straits Settlements after around 1820. From there, they moved inland for two purposes. Small and mid-sized Chinese investors who were already established in the cities provided the capital for the development of the tin industry in the West and the establishement of plantations in the south; these funds also attracted the necessary work force. This twofold pioneering work on the part of the Chinese, resulting in the clearing of forests, building towns and roads, and settling the interior, ultimately paved the way for the advance of British colonial rule.

Tin had always been profitable and easily obtainable through sluice mining in Malaya. Long before colonial times, it was mined and brought to the west coast of the peninsula, where it was used to fashion jewelry and other small objects. But it was the demand for tableware in Europe and America that unleashed the tin boom in Malaya. Chinese coolies trudged through the jungle to build sluice mines. Very soon, their traditional secret societies, strictly organized by family and origin, took over the organization of the all-male labor camps. Law and order, as interpreted by the societies, was brutally enforced at gunpoint.

Rivalry between the Chinese clans, or *Kongsi*, soon developed into violent, war-like feuds. At the same time, disputes between the societies and the Malay rulers regarding mining rights and taxes were escalating in a similar fashion.

Right: William Jervois (center) during an inspection tour of Perak in 1875.

This supplied the British with a perfect excuse to step up colonial demands. By 1867, fighting in the Chinese sections of Selangor and Lamut had spread to the secret society headquarters in Penang, and therefore directly affected British interests.

British entrepreneurs, who had invested heavily in the tin trade, began calling loudly for intervention. In 1870, cannon were even brought in to settle disputes, as the country threatened to dissolve into chaos.

The Waning Power of the Sultans

About this time, the Colonial Office in London began to re-think the Malayan situation. The Suez Canal was fully functional by now, and jingoism was on the rise in Britain. The young politicians of the ruling Liberal party began wondering if the colonies did not owe something for the benefits of being kept out of the free trade system. Having first declared the Straits Settlements Crown Colonies in 1867, the British government began extending the area under its control, adding Perak, Selangor, Negeri Sembilan, Pahang and Johor to its system of "protectorates."

Andrew Clarke, acting Governor of the Straits Settlements since 1873, exceeded his authority and forced the Chinese secret societies Gihin and Haisan to lay down their weapons. In 1874, Clarke interfered unexpectedly into Malay internal affairs in Pangkor, and appointed a British Resident for the area.

Setting up what was in effect an acting governor marked the beginning of Britain's direct authority over the Malay mainland. As the Residents were ostensibly there to "advise" the Sultans, the institution of the office was supposed to enable local governments to go along voluntarily with British demands and interests. If a Sultan did not voluntarily follow the Resident's "advice," however, the

veil of "indirect rule" dropped to reveal naked desire for power.

In 1875, Clarke was replaced by the even stricter Governor William Jervois. Fearing that British interests in Perak were in danger, he forced the Sultan to accept Resident Birch as his immediate superior. Birch, in turn, proved overly conscientious in the exercise of his duties. He so humiliated the Sultan – so one hypothesis – that nothing short of murder could restore the Sultan's face and standing with his people. Birch was indeed assassinated in 1875, a short time after taking office.

Jervois retaliated immediately. Ordering reinforcements from the British colonies of Hong Kong and India, he marched into Perak to bring the Sultanate back into the British idea of line. Another consequence was a change in the powers of the Residents, who thenceforth acted less as "advisors" and more as authorized administrators of the Sultanate. They controlled the treasury, while the Sultans had to content themselves with a salary.

One exception was Johor, which was in any case under Singapore's authority. The Sultan of Pahang held on to autonomy the longest; he didn't see his power significantly curtailed until 1888. Finally, in 1895, the British created the "Federated Malay States" with a General Resident appointed from London at its their head.

Settling of the Peninsula

While the British continued to gain political and economic power, not shrinking from using force to secure their interests when necessary, immigrants continued to pour into the country. In 1860, approximately 122,000 Chinese lived in Malaysia, 95,000 of them in the port cities. By 1871, 12,000 Chinese were recorded in the mining area of Selangor; 20 years later the number had climbed to 50,000.

The Sino-Malaysian population continued to grow in fact until World War II. According to the country's first census in

1939, 25 percent of the population was Chinese. Besides making a living in mining – as entrepreneurs or workers –, they also toiled in the plantations of Johor, or in city-based trade or service industries (the so-called bazaar economy). The one occupation the Chinese settlers rarely took up was cultivation of rice paddies in the east; and they were generally slow to settle Sabah and Sarawak.

Indian immigration was considerably smaller. Tamil workers from the south of India were brought in large numbers to Malaya. They were meant to act as an ethnic counterweight to the rapidly growing Chinese. In addition to being willing workers and accepting lower wages, the Indians unlike the Chines, did not organize into mafia-like secret societies.

Indians were principally occupied working on public projects, such as building roads and railroads, or cultivating the large, European-owned plantations. By 1891, approximately 20,000 Indians had migrated to Malaya; during the first big rubber boom, between 1908 and 1913, their numbers increased from 49,000 to 118,000. By 1921, an estimated 470,000 Indians were living in the country. At the beginning of the 20th century, the Indians were allowed to immigrate with their entire families. In 1930, in response to a world economic recession, a law was passed limiting immigration to the wives, but not the children, of workers.

By this time, the colorful ethnic makeup of present-day Malaysia had already been set in stone. Equally established were the obstacles to harmony between the divers various groups: The immigrants tended to retain their focus on their own cultures and countries of origin. Ghettoes and segregation, religious intolerance, discrimination and the concentration of certain ethnic groups in certain economic sectors played their part in keeping such differences alive.

New Forms of Agriculture

The change from a traditional economy based on subsistence agriculture to one that produced raw materials for export to Europe and North America at the heighth of the colonial era did not occur without opposition. The economy, now oriented toward a world market, influenced the regional infrastructure and changed the social organization of the country. Newly-built roads and railroads from the tin mines to the port cities cut through the rural landscapes of traditional villages and rice paddies.

Previously, the autonomous rural culture centered on rice cultivation, fishing, gardening and handicrafts had produced only a limited amount of surplus products, which were brought to local markets to be sold. Malay peasants were hardly involved in a money-based economy. They sowed only what they needed to feed themselves. Subsistence farming gave them a measure of independence and security. Traditional rice-paddy cultivation also meant several months of leisure each year, which made for a pleasant lifestyle.

Only later, as the rice paddies began to diminish in size while the growing population developed a preference for industrial products, did the market economy finally reach the peasants. Smallholders, family farms of less than 100 acres (40 ha), entered into the market system and profited from it. While the plantation system revolved around a single crop, smallholders usually divided their land between traditional crops needed to feed their families and cash crops, marketable produce such as coconut and sugar cane, later also rubber and oil palms. When market prices fell, they simply stepped up their traditional subsistence farming. And

Right: A meeting of Sultans and representatives of the colonial government in 1903 in Kuala Lumpur.

when prices rose, they planted what was in demand.

Things were different with the Chinese of Johor, who had long planted spices and other cash crops. Along with the immigrant plantation workers, they became the agents of a major economic change throughout the country. Interestingly, too, they became very significant agents in the struggle for independence from Great Britain.

The dual agricultural system with the smallholders in Malaysia also created two new forms of urban development: trade centers and collection sites for raw materials on the one hand, and port cities for international export on the other. In both types of settlement, Chinese bazaar economy played an important part.

The Japanese Occupation

On the eve of World War Two, Malaysia was still a colony, but one with an fascinating cultural and ethnic mix. Inchoate moves towrd independence had hardly caused a ripple on the political surface. The British ran the country in orderly fashion, and to their credit goes the eradication of such illnesses as malaria and beriberi. The war turned everything upside down.

Orang puteh lari! ("The whites are running away!") – Malaysians watched in amazement as the British fled before the invading Japanese in 1942. The colonial power's unceremonious ouster by the Japanese caused the British to lose face once and for all in the eyes of their erstwhile vassals.

Because of its overseas territories, Great Britain, in the war, was caught in the vise of the German and Japanese Axis. Its military resources were tied up in the West, where Hitler's *Luftwaffe* strafed English cities, German U-boats threatened the Royal Navy, and Rommel's troops advanced to the Suez Canal. In the East, the war was about raw materials. The Japanese war machine was put into high gear by the American embargo; itself lacking in natural resources,

Japan was drawn by the tempting booty of the resources of Southeast Asia.

After their surprise attack on Pearl Harbor on December 7, 1941, the Japanese started moving into Southeast Asia, bombarding Singapore and landing on the coast of Kelantan. The British, who had made the costly mistake of expecting an attack by sea, were easily defeated on land, and even lost their only two battleships off the coast, the *Prince of Wales* and the *Repulse*. On February 8, Singapore fell into Japanese hands; by that time they controlled all of Malaysia.

Despite their propaganda claiming that their only goal was an "Asia for Asians" and the "creation of a common sphere of well-being," the Japanese occupation soon revealed its true colors. These came in the form of repression, beatings, rape and deportation to forced labor camps.

Above: Japanese soldiers with a captured British airplane following their landing in December 1941. Right: Declaration of Malaysia's independence on August 31, 1957.

In domestic affairs, the invaders proceeding according to the classic motto of *divide et impera* – divide and conquer. In Malaysia, they practiced this by antagonizing various ethnic groups and pitting them against each other. While Malays enjoyed official favor, the Nanyang Chinese had to endure brutal repression.

But this also gave them twice as much motivation to resist the Japanese occupation. The Chinese-led Malaysian Communist Party (MCP) with its huge organization of the Malayan People's Anti-Japanese Union and its military fraction, the Malayan People's Anti-Japanese Army (MPAJA), formed the backbone of the guerilla resistance. It had already been formed before the war, and now received its baptism by fire in the fight against the Japanese. This strong commitment to the Malayan cause foremed the basis for the Communist Party's later claims in Malaysian politics, and was the reason they tried to take control of the country after the Japanese capitulation in 1945.

Malaysia Becomes a Federation

At the end of World War II, the political constellation in Asia changed rapidly. The confrontation of super-powers along new fronts in the Cold War made bitter enemies out of former allies. When China went Communist in 1949 after a bitter civil war, the balance of power shifted heavily to the "Red" camp in Asia. The anti-colonial message of the Communists was finding fertile ground, and the West was divided over the colonial issue.

Malaysia remained loyal to the British, but nevertheless had to wait until 1957 for *merdeka* or independence. Colonial power lingered on largely due to two factors: the heterogeneous make-up of Malaysia's population and the country's wealth of natural resources. Britain had emerged from the war victorious but virtually bankrupt. Because of the British national debt and depleted gold reserves, Malaysia's tin mines and rubber plantations became tremendously important for this European power.

In 1947, rubber production alone in Malaysia yielded a total of US $200,000,000: more than Britain's total exports for the same year, which amounted to only US$ 180,000,000. The following year, Malaysia supplied nearly 46 percent of the world's rubber and 28 percent of its tin. The outbreak of the Korean war in 1951 brought a dramatic increase in the demand for both of these raw materials, and again underlined the importance of Britain's colony.

While this situation should have spurred Malaya's peoples on to throw off the colonial yoke, the ethnic tensions within the population slowed progress toward *merdeka*.

How much the country's potential strength was hobbled by inner discord became particularly evident with the idea of the "Malay Union" that the British, acting in their own interests, wanted to set up right after the war. In July, 1945, the British Labour party, led by Clement Attlee (1883-1967), had won the British elections. This "anti-imperialist" party now found itself in something of a dilemma. On the one hand, ideology impelled Labour leaders to end colonialism; as adminstrators of an impoverished country, however, they wanted to make use of Malaysia's wealth.

The idea for the Malay Union grew out of this contradiction. It was certainly progressive in that it was a step toward unifying the various Sultanates into a single, national entity. It was also positive in that it treated all of Malaysia's ethnic groups equally. However, it was a historical step backwards in that it separated the Borneo states and Singapore from the peninsula, making them Crown Colonies and denying their Sultans any autonomy.

The Malay aristocracy, which had been denied participation in discussions over the Union, vigorously opposed the plan. After protest from the United Malays National Organization (UMNO), founded by Dato Onn Bin Ja'afar in 1946, a new plan for a Federation was presented in 1948 that largely anticipated the Constitution still in effect today.

Creating the Federation, however, didn't fundamentally affect the nature of British control. Sultans were given a merely representative role. Ethnic Malays were supported in their administrative and economic ambitions by legislation granting them special rights. For Chinese and Indians, on the other hand, becoming a citizen was made even more difficult; requirements included 15 years' residence in Malaysia and mastery of the English or Malaysian language. These strict new citizenship laws sharpened Indian and Chinese opposition; strikes and acts of sabotage were the result.

Guerillas Without a Chance

Britain's losses at the hand of the Japanese during the war, and their subsequent attempts to force the country to adopt a political system it didn't want, intensified nationalist sentiment rather than mollify it. Moreover, the British also tried to maintain their rule by the old "divide and conquer" system, which made matters more tense.

Nonetheless, the first elections took place in Kuala Lumpur in 1951. A coalition of the UMNO and MCA (the anti-Communist Malay Chinese Association) emerged as the winner. It later expanded to include the Malaysian Indian Congress (MIC). Paradoxically, however, the coalition also came to symbolize the country's division along ethnic lines. In 1951, Dato Onn stepped down as the leader of the UMNO, having proved unable to make the UMNO a truly national party equally accessible to all of Malaysia's ethnic groups. He was replaced by Tunku Abdul Rahman who, as the brother of the Sultan of Kedah, represented the Malay "establishment."

The elections tookplace in part because the British could no longer cope with the pressure from the Malan people, and in part to coopt another important political power, namely the Malayan Communist Party (MCP), which promulgated a radical anti-colonial position. But because of its ethnic – that is to say, Chinese – roots, it failed to win the hearts and minds of the general population. In addition, it could not ideologically capture the support of a major socio-economic stratum in Malaysia, namely its many smallholders and peasants.

The MCP therefore remained a minority party. In 1939, the party had an estimated 37,000 armed guerillas; by 1945, the number had dropped to 8,000. The foundation of the Malaysian Races Liberation Army (MRLA) on February 1, 1949, was meant to cover up the failure of the Communist resistance. Although Malay and Indian names appeared on the lists from time to time, the party never rallied enough support to spark the

Right: The British heritage: a bagpipe band in Kuala Lumpur.

desired revolution. Furthermore, between 1948 and 1960, Malaysia became a kind of Asian testing-ground for counterinsurgency, the suppression of rebels through military and economic pressure.

Though small, the MCP was capable of inflicting considerable damage. In June, 1948, after the murders of three European planters in Perak and numerous attacks against mines and plantations, Britain declared a state of emergency. A short time later, 24,000 soldiers were called in to defend against the MRLA. In a forced migration, about half a million Chinese were relocated from the area where the guerillas were active into new villages; this partly succeeded in weakening the liberation movement, which by this time was receiving support from newly Communist China.

In 1951, the Communists murdered the British High Commissioner Gurney. He was just one of some 2,500 victims of the MCP. His death caused Britain to again step up its fight against the MCP, which forced the Communist leadership to real-

ize that they could not win militarily. Thereafter, they switched their emphasis to the political arena, hoping to gain power within the framework of a national democratic revolution against the colonial might. They made enough progress to bring about a meeting in 1955 between MCP leader Chin Peng and the Prime Minister Tunku Abdul Rahman. The meeting, however, was unsuccessful; and from that point, the Communists were effectively in retreat.

The Emergency lasted until 1960, three years after Malaysia had become independent. Ironically, it probably did more to delay independence than anything else, which was not the intention of the Communists originally. In fact, their war never really ended: Although the colony of North Borneo remained outside the conflict, occasional clashes continued to plague the peninsula into the 1980s. In the end Chin Peng, over 70 and described as the world's oldest guerilla fighter, surrendered, along with 1,200 exhausted followers: at the end of 1989.

Merdeka for Malaysia

Steering a dangerous course between military intervention against the Communists and slowly granting independence, the British paved the way for autonomy by setting up national elections in 1955. It turned out to be a spectacular victory for the coalition of MCA, UMNO and MIC, and led to the creation of a partially autonomous Malaysian government. The Conference of London in 1956 promised full independence in 1957, while seeing to it that Malaysia remained in the "Sterling Zone."

In June, 1957, agreement was reached over the special privileges demanded by Malays. Malayan was recognized as the official language and Islam the state religion, but religious freedom was guaranteed to other faiths. Other guarantees, such as preference given to Malays in agrarian matters, civil service jobs and education, were also written into law and promptly caused riots in Kuala Lumpur. Tunku Abdul Rahman, the *Bapa Malaysia* (father of Malaysia) and first president, declared Malaysia's independence on August 31, 1957.

As the head of state of an elected monarchy, the *Yang di-Pertuan Agong*, "the great one made master," is chosen every five years by the nine Sultans of Malaysia from among their own ranks. (In April, 1994, the 72-year-old Prince Tunku Jafaar Abdul Rahman, ex-diplomat and lawyer, became the tenth king of this elective monarchy).

The Federation of Malaysian States was proclaimed in 1963. The former Straits Settlements of Penang and Melaka joined quickly. A short time later Singapore, still a British crown colony, decided to join, but left in 1965 owing to ethnic tensions between Malays and Chinese that were exacerbated by the

Right: In the heart of the capital city: Merdeka Square.

Federation's ethnic laws. In the late 1960s, the inclusion of the Sultanate of Brunei, North Borneo (later Sabah) and Sarawak were also discussed. Brunei declined to join tbecause it did not want to share the revenues from its oil fields.

Each of the 13 federal states and the federal territory of the capital city Kuala Lumpur, created in 1974, has its own elected parliament. The Parliament of the Federal Government consists of two chambers: the Senate (*Dewan Negara*) and the House of Representatives (*Dewan Rakyat*). The *Basiran Nasional*, the ruling National Front, is a coalition comprised of about a dozen parties, the strongest of which is the UMNO Baru (New UMNO), founded in 1988. The National Front was able to preserve its long-standing majority in the House of Representatives in the parliamentary elections in 1990. Along with the MCA and the MIC, political parties of Sabah and Sarawak are also members of the coalition.

In Borneo, the victory of the Pasok Momogun (an alliance of Kadazan and Murut) meant the rise to power of one of the main opposition coalitions. Within this group, the greatest influence is that of the Democratic Action Party (DAP) composed largely of disgruntled Chinese, and the Pan Malaysia Islamic Party (PAS). The PAS wants to create an Islamic state subject to Islamic law, and demands strict adherence to the teachings of the Koran. They accuse the government of fostering a western-style, non-Islamic, consumer society. In Kelantan, the PAS achieved an absolute parliamentary majority in the 1990 election.

Malaysia, the Little Tiger

Datuk Seri Dr. Malhathir bin Mohammed has headed the country's government since 1981. Malaysia, like Thailand, is known as a "little tiger." But in an epoch that's been dubbed "the Pacific Age," Malaysia has a good chance of fol-

lowing hard on the heels of the four "big tigers," Singapore, Hong Kong, South Korea and Taiwan.

The average per-capita income of US $3,115.00 (figures of October 1993) puts Malaysia at the level of a developing industrial country. 22 percent of the population is illiterate. The average life expectancy for men is 66; for women, 71. The gross national product rose from US $3.13 billion in 1965 to US $136 billion in 1993; in the same year, inflation was only 3.7 percent, thanks to a steady increase in exports. Meanwhile Malaysia, traditionally an exporter of raw materials, has increased its export of manufactured goods so they now make up one-half of all exports; in 1965, by contrast, manufactured goods accounted for a mere six percent.

Whether or not Malaysia can keep up this brisk pace of development into an industrial power will depend largely on the dynamics of the continuing process of democratization and improvements in the country's social structures. The bloody riots of May 13, 1969, in Kuala Lumpur, a result of clashes between *bumiputra*, the Malay "sons of the earth," and non-*bumiputra*, descendants of immigrants, have not been forgotten. The trouble began when the MCA lost most of its mandate in the election. As Maoist students celebrated the results, a racist mob of Malays swept through the streets of the capital, setting fires and killing at random. Indian and Chinese shop owners struck back. After four days of rioting, hundreds of people from every ethnic group were dead. Martial law was declared, and Parliament dissolved.

Not until 1971 was the democratic Constitution revived. Out of this dark chapter in Malaysia's history, the Malays once again emerged the winners. Their privileged status was re-confirmed, and criticism of it was to be punished.

The acceleration of the country's Islamization, hastened by various political forces, could further augment the inequities of Malaysian society. Although the Constitution is democratic, it is

37

limited by a number of emergency measures, which have taken their toll on freedom of speech, freedom of the press, labor unions and political opposition.

The political power of the Sultans is severely limited, but they continue to enjoy their traditional privileges, living in unimaginable splendor and enjoying immunity from prosecution, even for illegal activities. Symbols of their traditional power, such as the *kris*, musical instruments surrounded by popular legends, and palaces laden with historical significance, are still widely honored. For celebrations, the royal color, yellow, used to decorate the Sultans' clothing and palaces is a reminder and emphasis of their status. They are supported by the Islamic religion, as they are believed to embody the continued presence of the teachings of Mohammed; and they are influential in

Above: An Iban warrior with blowpipe, quiver, and headdress adorned with hornbill feathers. Right: Modern times in Kota Bharu.

seeing to it that religious duties are properly observed. In many places, these royal guardians of the faith advocate purely Moslem marriage ceremonies, and have adulterers arrested. Furthermore, the Sultans are still always consulted in questions of land concessions and grants, which guarantees the preservation of at least a part of their former power.

Malaysia's rapid economic progress and significant social changes have not had much of an effect on the Sultans, nor do they pose a threat to them. Still, their repeated squabbles with local politicians do sometimes escalate into open strife.

One example of this took place at the end of the 1970s when the Sultans of Johor and Perak, both candidates for the rotating elective monarchy, used their authority to pressure a minister out of office. In order to prevent such abuse of power in the future, the government passed a law in 1983 under which the Sultans had two weeks in which to approve laws regarding national and state affairs. The King and the other eight Sul-

tans saw the amendment as an insult to their dignity and refused to sign the new law. A national crisis was narrowly averted when the government backed down; however, one result was a compromise giving Parliament the right to enact laws which have not been authorized by the King.

In 1993, there was another dispute between the monarchs and the politicians over naming the successor of the Sultan of Kelantan. Accusations of meddling in other parties' internal affairs flew back and forth between both sides, and the issue remained unsettled until the Prime Minister Dr. Mahatir bin Mohammed stepped in to restore order.

The positive outlook for Malaysia's economy is overshadowed by the country's ecological and social problems. The extended families of the peasants are disintegrating, and migration into the cities has increased: 44 percent of all Malaysians now live in urban centers. A lower class of working urban poor is developing apace; the cities are plagued by

an unemployment rate of 10 percent, while poverty and growing slums are widely visible.

The rain forests, moreover, are being plundered and destroyed to the point of near-eradication to support unchecked industrial and agricultural (palm plantations, for example) growth. Their disappearance threatens both the rare animal species and the tradition lifestyles of the native tribes who make their home in the jungle. The creation of new, tourist-attracting nature parks cannot begin to check the pace of destruction.

In 1992, tourism rose to become the third most important source of revenue. In September, 1993, Datuk Sabruddin Chik, the Minister of Culture, Art and Tourism, stressed that Malaysia's natural resources were of vital importance – to the tourist industry. Just in time for the 1994 tourist year, the government pledged to increase its protection of Malaysia's natural resources, but don't be overheard criticizing the government's way with the rain forests.

AT THE HEART OF
A MELTING POT

WEST MALAYSIA
KUALA LUMPUR
AROUND
KUALA LUMPUR

WEST MALAYSIA

With the Andamen Sea to the west, the Straits of Malacca to the southwest, the South China Sea to the east, Thailand to the north and Singapore to the south, West Malaysia grows out of the Asian continent and thrusts boldly into the island world of Indonesia. Although its area of 51,319 sq. miles (131,587 sq. km) makes up only 40% of the country's total (128,865 sq. miles / 330,422 sq. km), West Malaysia dominates the nation by virtue of its economic and political importance. Approximately 400 miles (650 km) of sea separate East and West Malaysia, forming a geographic barrier that has given rise to cultural differences and intense rivalry between the two states, particularly from the side of the Borneo provinces.

West Malaysia, the "thick" end of the Malaysian Peninsula, extends from a latitude somewhat north of 6° to just short of 1° N; it is at a longitude of between 100° and 105° E. From the peninsula's southernmost point to the Equator is just over 62 miles (100 km); from the same point

Preceding pages: Colonial and modern splendor in the capital city of Kuala Lumpur. Left: The Sri Mahamariamman temple in Kuala Lumpur stands out in the traffic.

to the Thai border, 465 miles (750 km), while peninsular Malaysia boasts a total of 1,197 miles (1,930 km) of coastline. A near neighbor is the Indonesian island of Sumatra, about 25 miles (40 km) away across the narrowest point in the Straits of Malacca. This narrow, heavily-traveled waterway is still vital to West Malaysia's trade; but it's also brought the threat of environmental catastrophe right up to its doors (not least through the spectacular tanker accident and resulting oil spill in early 1993).

The peninsula boasts a rich and varied landscape. To the east and west, it is framed by alluvial plains. Two nearly parallel mountain ranges of different lengths run north-south through the interior of the peninsula. They are part of the continental shelf and composed of sediment and granite, a rocky sub-soil rich in tin deposits. Heavy tropical rains and erosion have washed the minerals into the valleys and low-lying plains creating a stratified crust – known as "soap" – of ore deposits and silt. But there are also numerous limestone formations, which create the peninsula's striking, steep, mostly wooded conical hills of chalk. As well as brown iron ore and ilmenite, the limestone conceals the rich deposits that have made Malaysia the world's leading producer of tin.

43

WEST MALAYSIA

0   50   100 km

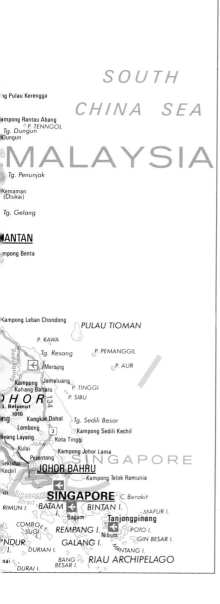

SOUTH

CHINA SEA

ng Pulau Kerengga

ampong Rantau Abang
P. TENNGOL
Tg. Dungun
Dungun

MALAYSIA

Tg. Penunjak

Kemaman
(Chukai)

Tg. Gelang

ANTAN

mpong Benta

Kampong Leban Chondong
PULAU TIOMAN
P. RAWA
Tg. Resang   P. PEMANGGIL
Mersing   P. AUR
Kampong Jemaluang
Kahang Baharu   P. TINGGI
OHOR   P. SIBU
i. Belumut
1010
ng   Kangkar Dohol   Tg. Sedili Besar
Lombong   Kampong Sedili Kechil
yang Layang   Kota Tinggi
Kulai   Johor
Pelentong   Kampong Johor Lama
SINGAPORE
Sekudai
Kechil   JOHOR BAHRU
Kampong Telok Ramunia

Singapore
SINGAPORE   C. Berakit
RIMUN I.   BATAM   BINTAN I.
Bagam   MAPUR I.
Tanjongpinang
COMBO
SUGI   REMPANG I.   POTO I.
Nibum   GIN BESAR I.
NDUR   GALANG I.
I.   DURIAN I.   MANTANG I.
nai   BANG   RIAU ARCHIPELAGO
DURAI I.   BESAR I.

Banjaran or Barisan Titiwangsa (the Great Titiwangsa Chain), is the longest of the two mountain ranges that run through West Malaysia. Stretching from Thailand down to Negeri Sembilan, it reaches its highest altitude of 7,138 feet (2,183 m) at the peak of Gunung Korbu near the mining town of Ipoh. Malaysia's capital city, Kuala Lumpur, also lies at the foot of the Titiwangsa chain; some of the range's best-known areas are the Cameron and Genting Highlands.

The smaller Bintang chain takes its name from the peak of Gunung Bintang, which dominates the chain at 6,089 feet (1,862 m). It stretches from Perak in the northwest to Kedah in the south. East of the Titiwangsa mountains, the Gunung Tahan range, named after West Malaysia's highest mountain (Gunung Tahan: 7,151 ft/2,187 m), extends nearly to the coast. It lies in the northwest of the Taman Negara National Park, one of the last stands of the virgin forest which until recently covered most of the peninsula.

In the northeast of the Tahan mountains, Gunung Lawit soars majestically to an altitude of 4,967 feet (1,519 m), forming the center point of the eastern Banjaran Timur chain. In the southwest, is a smaller range named after the 6,893 foot (2,108 m) Gunung Benom.

Southwards, the mountains give way to a landscape of gentle hills and swampland. The countless rivers that meander through the countryside, flowing into the Straits of Malacca or the South China Sea, keep the coastal areas provided with deposits of fertile silt. The longest river in West Malaysia is the 295-mile (475 km) Sungai (meaning river) Pahang; it is followed by Sungai Perak (248 miles/400 km) and Sungai Kelatan, respectively.

The peninsula's largest lakes are the result of human labor, dams and flood control. Water supplies are ensured, in the northern Perak region, by the lakes of Tasek Temengor and Tasek Kesind; in Terengganu, they're provided by the

45

such as the Jakun, a settled people who today are the largest of the proto-Malay ethnic groups. Ultimately, the Malays form the elite of the *bumiputras* and remain the majority on the peninsula with roughly 8 out of 15 million inhabitants. They make up 48 percent of Malaysia's 18.7 million people.

Among the non-*bumiputras* are the Chinese, who first arrived on the peninsula 2000 years ago; massive immigration, however, occurred in the mid-19th century when they arrived to work in West Malaysia's tin mines. Today they represent approximately five percent of the population. Indians (Tamils, Sikhs and Malayalees), imported as labor by the British, are twice as numerous, accounting for approximately ten percent of the population of West Malaysia.

KUALA LUMPUR: BEGINNINGS IN THE MUD

The skyscrapers of Kuala Lumpur make it hard to imagine that this city of 1.5 million inhabitants began with a few wooden shacks. In 1857, 87 Chinese from the mountains sailed down the Kelang River. At the place where the Kelang joins the River Gombak, where the town of Ampang still lies, they discovered a rich tin deposit. They built their settlement on the muddy confluence of the two rivers and gave the place the descriptive name of *Kuala Lumpur*, which means "muddy confluence of rivers." Only 18 of the original pioneers lived to enjoy the fruits of their discovery; the rest succumbed to malaria.

By 1860, Kuala Lumpur was a boom town, center of a "tin rush" with all that that implied. Disputes over water rights and mining claims, murder and gang fights between Malays and Chinese characterized the city's early history. In 1870, Yap Ah Loy, also known as "Captain China," took matters into his own hands and made order out of chaos. His efforts

enormous Lake Kenyir created by the Kenyir Dam. In the south, Tasek Bera and Tasek Dampar have been joined to form a huge reservoir.

Rice paddies dominate the coastal areas; while rubber plantations, coconut and palm oil plantations stretch into the uplands of the interior, gradually pushing back what is left of the virgin tropical forest.

The population of both East and West Malaysia is roughly divided between *bumiputra* and non-*bumiputra* inhabitants. Among the *bumiputra*, the "sons of the land" native to the Malaysian peninsula, are the Orang Asli. Composed of the nomadic people known as the Semang Negritos and the Senoi, an agricultural people who probably arrived somewhat later, the Orang Asli are probably descended from the first, indigenous inhabitants of the peninsula. They were gradually pushed back by proto-Malays,

Above: Orang Asli mother and child in Taman Negara. Right: A street stand in Kuala Lumpur's Chinatown.

made him the effective ruler of the settlement and its mine. At the time of his death in 1885, some 80 percent of the mine's profits were pouring into his coffers.

The friction between Chinese and Malays came to a head in 1879, resulting in a fire that destroyed much of the settlement. Captain China rebuilt Kuala Lumpur, beginning with the opium dens, bordellos, jails and hospital. At first it was a city of wooden houses, tinder for subsequent fires. But in 1880, Frank Swettenham, the representative of the British crown, moved his office from the royal city of Kelang into the booming settlement on the muddy riverbanks. With his support, Yap Ah Loy expanded the city with new structures in brick, some of which survive to this day in the Jalan Hang Lakui district of Kuala Lumpur.

A Capital Built on Tin

As tin prices rose, Kuala Lumpur expanded rapidly. In 1886, British engineers built a railroad link to the port city of Kelang. Colonial rule replaced that of the Sultan of Selangor, elevating "K.L." – the English nickname for this tin town – to the status of new capital of the sultanate. Under Islamic influence the gambling dens and Chinese secret societies had largely disappeared by the turn of the century. By 1888, the one-time jungle settlement could boast of having a botanical garden; two years later, it had added a British school and was important enough to warrant a royal visit from the King of Siam.

In 1896, K.L. was named capital of the newly formed Federation of the Straits Settlements, which included Malacca, Penang and Singapore. Kuala Lumpur has been the capital ever since, through the years of British military rule and even after Malaysian independence in 1957.

Playground for Builders

Kuala Lumpur's architecture is a rich mix of styles. Most of the buildings completed before 1930 were built in the

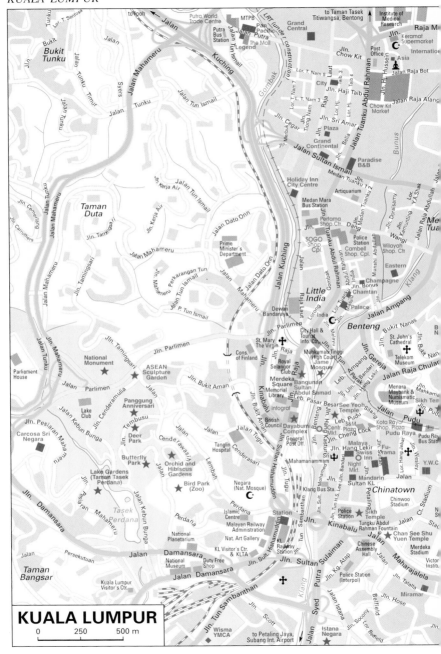

KUALA LUMPUR

0   250   500 m

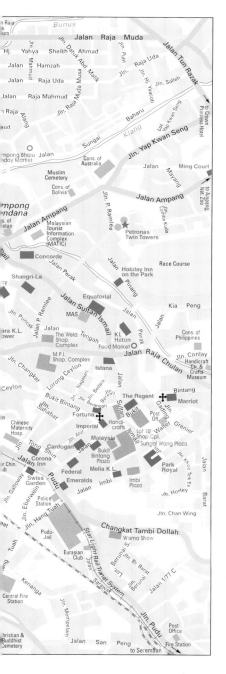

classical, renaissance or some form of the Indian "Mogul" style by the British architects A. C. Norman and A. B. Hubbock. After that, colonial architecture predominated until 1972, when K.L. expanded into a real "city," a business center as well as a political capital.

When the city was separated from Malaysian state of Selangor in 1974 and made a Federal Territory with its own political administration, its territory grew from 36 to 95 square miles (93 to 244 sq. km). The uncontrolled building boom gave rise to many futuristic foibles. Since then, the skyscrapers of the 1970s have yielded to new extravagances, palaces of stone and glass which critics have dubbed "white elephants." One popular and still controversial style, especially favored by banks and airline offices, employs Islamic elements superimposed on "Malaysian" ornamentation.

Some buildings which combine Oriental playfulness with actual aesthetic integrity can be found between the clumsy skyscrapers and glittering department stores. Façades copied from Singapore or Manhattan reflect the growing self-confidence of Malaysia as an emerging power. Kuala Lumpur derives much of its charm from the contrasts of its architecture, but its main energy comes from the close juxtaposition of many different cultures. Officials would have it that the various races and nationalities live in perfect harmony; in reality, the tensions that led to violent race riots in 1969, turning the city into a battlefield, are not so quickly forgotten.

Wide highways, overburdened by too-heavy traffic, crisscross the Federal Territory, linking tropical forest to asphalt jungle and high-rise developments to suburbs. A showcase of modern urban development, and at the same time living proof of the ecological imbalance it creates, is the Kelang Valley. Thousands of acres of forest were destroyed to build the Federal Highway connecting Kuala

Lumpur to the port city of Kelang. Rapid industrial growth sparked a mass migration into the cities, where people traded rural country life for squalid slums. In the 1980s, 40,000 slum dwellings housed more than 250,000 people; in the nineties they have been partially replaced by modern housing schemes.

Although Kuala Lumpur is not really a tourist city and lacks a well-defined center, many attractions are within walking distance of each other. But the sweltering climate makes touring by air-conditioned car or taxi preferable.

Stone Witness to History

A good place to start in any case is **Benteng**, where Kuala Lumpur began – as described above – at the confluence of its rivers.

Above: Bangunan Sultan Abdul Samad, the former Selangor government building. Right: The colonial main post office with the Kompleks Dayabumi in the background.

Today the rivers' flow is harnessed by concrete and the water polluted by urban filth, but on the shore is one of the city's most important sites, the impressive **Jamek Masjid** (also spelled Jame Masjid), or Friday Mosque. This mosque, built to resemble the Moti Masjid (Pearl Mosque) in Fort Delhi, India, was constructed in 1909 of red brick trimmed with white. Until the completion of the Masjid Negara (National Mosque) in 1965, it served as the religious center for West Malaysia's Moslems. Jamek Masjid now stands in the shadow of K.L's skyscrapers, a reminder of how quickly the city has expanded since the 1960s; back then, this elegant building was a prominent element of the city's skyline.

Close by on the other side of the park, which was re-named **Merdeka Square** (Freedom Square) in 1989 by Prime Minister Dr. Mahatir bin Mohammed, is a Tudor-style building housing the **Royal Selangor Club**. The half-timbered building was expanded in 1910 and remains a bit of old England in Malaysia. Because of its black and white construction, members dubbed it the "spotted dog." It was *the* meeting place for Orang Putih, the white colonial aristocracy; today, it's a hangout for the Malaysian elite. On the veranda overlooking the *Padang*, or Green Belt, characters of the type immortalized in the novels of Joseph Conrad and Somerset Maugham – planters, officers and merchants – ordered their gin or whiskey at the long bar, sipped their drinks, discussed the price of rubber, and drank a toast to the Queen or King. For decades the Padang served as the playing field for the club's polo, rugby and cricket matches.

In August, 1957, the Union Jack was lowered for the last time from the world's tallest flagpole in front of the club and a new era began for the Royal Selangor. The Malaysian flag now flies from the 330-foot (100 m) pole high above Merdeka Square. On Sundays, a brass band sometimes plays; families of all races and religions spread out on the lawns; while Malaysian soldiers in polished boots parade smartly by. The square is crowded late into the evening, when decorative lamps on neighboring buildings light the way home. Since 1990, the official "Visit Malaysia Year," this "Garden of Lights," as its tourist office calls K.L., is illuminated with thousands of electric bulbs. The "Visit Malaysia" concept was repeated in 1994, and the tourist office expected an influx of at least seven million tourists.

On the other side of the square, separated by Jl. Raja, the spectacular **Bangunan Sultan Abdul Samad** sparkles in the sun. It was built in 1898 to be Selangor's government office by the architectural firm of A. C. Norman. This jewel of a building is decorated with Moorish arabesque arches. A copper onion dome tops its 130 foot (40 m) clock tower. Today the building houses the office of the state Attorney General. The prosperity of the tin mines stamped this, one

of Kuala Lumpur's oldest buildings, with a touch of Victorian pomp translated into a blend of western and Islamic building styles.

Further down on Jl. Raja, just before the bridge over the Gombak River, is another noteworthy building: **Mahkamah Tinggi**, the Supreme Court. The court, and other colonial buildings, are dwarfed by the surrounding skyscrapers. You can hardly make out the **Church of St. Mary the Virgin**, at the northern end of Jl. Raja. Also built in 1894 by Norman, it is the oldest Anglican brick church in Malaysia. This prolific architect also designed the **Dewan Bandaraya** (City Hall), the **Jabatan Penerangan** (State Information Office), the former **Pejabat Pos Besar** (main post office) and the present **Jabatan Kerja dan Bank Pertanian** (Office of Public Works and Agricultural Bank).

Every now and then it is worth craning your neck for a view of the Islamic-style **Kompleks Dayabumi**, which cost 600 million M$ to build and which now

towers over the historic district as a symbol of modern Kuala Lumpur. From the 34th floor of this building, you have a spectacular view over the city.

Things are more down-to-earth at the **Pasar Seni** (Central Market), which Malaysians like to compare to London's Covent Garden. The market building on Jl. Hang Kasturi at the edge of Chinatown, designed in Art Deco style in 1936, was transformed into a shopping and cultural center in 1986. Young artists sell their work here, restaurants offer a wide choice of foods, and the cookshacks, or "hawker stalls," tempt passers-by with delicious snacks. The forecourt is often the scene of dance performances, Chinese opera, shadow plays and the like.

One notorious sight is the "world's longest painted prison wall" surrounding **Pudu Jail** (corner of Jl. Pudu and Jl. Imbi). This tableau of rivers, forests,

Above: Pasar Malam, the Night Market in Kuala Lumpur's Chinatown. Right: Incense spirals in the Chinese See Yeoh Temple.

lakes and mountains was painted by the prisoners in 1983 using their bare hands and rags. The 852-ft (266 m) façade took all of a year to complete.

The **Kuala Lumpur City Center** (KLCC) is rising a short distance away on the grounds of the former race track. The latter was moved to Sungai Besi at the gates of the city. The KLCC has two towers of 84 stories reaching a height of 1346 ft (451,9 m), making it one of the tallest office buildings in the world.

A good place to visit on a rainy day is the newly-opened **Telekom Museum** on Jl. Raja Chulan.

Chinatown

K.L.'s lively, if steadily shrinking, Chinatown occupies the area between Jl. Petaling, Jl. Sultan and Jl. Sultan Mohamed. Chinatown used to be much larger, but whole streets were sacrificed in the seventies to build shopping centers and banks. In re-developing the area, Kuala Lumpur seemed bent on following

Singapore's example. What remains of Chinatown comes to life in the late afternoon when the streets fill up and business is as lively as in any East Asian city. The **Pasar Malam** (night market) on Jl. Petaling is open every evening, a labyrinth of stalls and food shops. Fabric merchants squeeze in next to fortune tellers; exotic fruit juices are sold next door to shops crammed with audio cassettes; a Peking duck seller operates alongside a stand of fake designer watches.

A host of Chinese medicines promise to cure every imaginable illness. The smell of spices wafting through the air mingles with the scent of freshly baked buns. Parrots screech from perches, autos and rickshaws add their own notes to Chinatown's nightly cacophony. A pet market at the intersection of Jl. Petaling and Jl. Sultan sells birds in brightly-colored cages.

Most of the Chinese, who now make up one-third of the Malaysian population, are the descendants of immigrants who arrived in the 7th, 15th, 19th and 20th centuries. Many have become prosperous. The Hokkiens from the hinterland of Amoy and Guangzhou (Canton) were especially adept at the export and wholesale business. The Henghus from Fukien have traditionally pursued technical professions. There are also many Cantonese, Kheh and Hainanese in Malaysia, who have become well-to-do mainly by running coffee- and teahouses.

Religions and Street Festivals

Chinatown is not limited to the Chinese. Malaysians and Indians add to its vibrant mix. Everyone benefits from the restriction of car traffic in some of its streets. One such is Leboh Pudu, a tiny side-street near Jl. Bandar and the Central Market, where, hidden behind the warehouses and food-stalls, you come upon **See Yeoh Temple**, one of the oldest Chinese places of worship in the country.

It was finished in 1883 and dedicated to the goddess Sen Sze Ya, patroness of pioneers, whose statue from 1864 predates the temple. The great incense spirals that adorn the courtyard of the old building convey a sense of mysticism. The building was financed by "Captain China," Yap Ah Loy, whose portrait hangs over one of the rear altars.

Another Buddhist temple worth mentioning is the **Chan See Shu Yuen Temple** in the southern part of Chinatown, on Jl. Petaling near Merdeka Stadium. It was built in 1906 as a house of worship for three of K.L.'s Chinese clans. One of the clan's houses, incidentally, still stands on Jl. Petaling near the **Tungku Abdul Rahman fountain** and continues to serve as a meeting place for a family clan numbering several hundred members. Relatives of the Chan, Chin and Tan families still flock to honor their ancestors in the haze of countless sticks of burning incense within the **Chan See Shu Yuen Temple**, with its beautiful glazed decorations and sweeping roof.

Scenes from Chinese mythology decorate the walls and propagate the traditions of the past, while visitors piously probe the future with "luck" sticks and contributions of money.

Honoring the dead and worshipping ancestors creates a brisk business for many small shops in the narrow streets of Chinatown. They sell money, miniature houses, luxury autos, televisions, airplanes – all made of paper, painstaking imitations of the real thing. These paper status symbols are cremated together with the bodies of the dead, who are accompanied by female mourners right up until the very last minute. In this way, loved ones enjoy the comforts of this world in the next.

In the southern part of Jl. Bandar, between Jl. Hang Lekir and Jl. Sultan, is the **Sri Mahamariamman Temple**, a Hindu shrine built in 1873. It is the oldest, largest and most lavishly decorated house of worship of this kind in all Malaysia. Dedicated to the god of rain, Mahamariamman, it is especially impressive for the six-storey "mountain of gods" above the entrance. The famous *Thaipusam* festival kicks off here every year in January and February; the temple is therefore of central importance to the Hindu community in Malaysia. One of the temple's rooms contains the largest silver carriage in the country, on display.

Kuala Lumpur also has a red-light district, albeit a rather hidden one. In front of the **Masjid India** (Indian Mosque) on the Jl. Masjid India and in the side streets around the Jl. Tungku Abdul Rahman, the *pondan*, transvestites, come out at twilight. This area known as **Little India** is the place for small shops selling wares and foods typical of the sub-continent. Massage parlors on the Jl. Bukit Bintang advertise a full range of services, of the sort that kept the first tin miners who settled in this muddy town smiling despite their grueling work.

Above: Mountain of gods adorns a Hindu temple. Right: Apartment building on the outskirts of Kuala Lumpur.

Recreation and National Pride

Taman Tasek Perdana, also known as **Lake Gardens**, lies southwest of the city center and offers natural and generally accessible recreation for everyone. Extending over 16 acres (6.5 ha), it's one of the largest and most popular parks in all of Asia. Rowing on **Tasek Perdana** (Lake Perdana) is lovely way to spend a relaxing afternoon. Visitors to the botanical section of the park can view plants indigenous to the Malay Peninsula's tropical rain forest, an orchid garden in the eastern part of the park, the **Mousedeer Park** and a bird sanctuary. The wonderful **Butterfly Park** is also not far away. There is also a zoo and collection of rare birds, plus ample opportunity to discover the hibiscus or *bunga raya*, Malaysia's national flower.

The northwest side of the garden's green hill is adorned by **Carcosa**, a picturesque British-Malay villa which the Governor of the Malay Federation of States moved into in 1896. Most recently tenanted by the British High Commissioner, it now belongs to the Malaysian government. On the northern bank of Lake Perdana is the **Lake Club**, founded in 1900 by some "defectors" from the Royal Selangor Club.

A bit further north is the **National Monument**. The bronze statue, cast in Italy, is dedicated to all those who died fighting Communism during the time of the "Emergency" in the 1950s. The names of the British, Australians, Fijians, Maoris and Malaysians who lost their lives are engraved on the monument's base. The monument was designed by the American sculptor Felix de Weldon and officially unveiled in 1966. Below the monument is the **ASEAN Sculpture Garden**, where prize-winning works by Asian sculptors have been set in an attractive garden.

A skein of highways separates the monument from the **Parliament House**.

18 storeys high, this shining tower with its strict geometric form was built in an open meadow in 1963. The House of Representatives (*Dewan Rakyat*) and Senate (*Dewan Negara*) are housed in a flat, three-storey building nearby.

The **Muzium Negara** (National Museum) is well worth an afternoon. It is on Jl. Damansara, at the southeastern corner of Lake Gardens. Built in 1963 in a manner reminiscent of the old Malayan Minangkabau style, its façade is covered with mosaics depicting historic events in the style of modern Malaysian batik painting. It is divided into several departments of natural history, ethnography, and history, giving the visitor an unparalleled overview of Malaysia's history and culture

The exhibit about the Orang Asli is especially interesting. There are also symbols of modern technology like a tin dredger, a Rolls-Royce, and the first locomotive of the "Malayan Railway." In addition, you'll find rotating exhibitions, an impressive collection of jewelry in the

Gold Gallery, and a well-stocked bookstore to round out the museum's offerings.

From the National Museum it is only a short distance to the contemporary art displayed in the **National Museum of Arts**, next door to the **Kuala Lumpur Visitors Center** a bit further south on Jl. Sultan Hishamuddin. The building itself recalls another era: it was built in 1932 as the art-deco Hotel Majestic, an establishement which was, in its day, Kuala Lumpur's best hotel.

The **Railway Station** is a work of art in itself and undoubtedly one of the most beautiful stations in the world. Construction on this Indo-Islamic-style building began in 1892 and went on until 1911; further additions continued until 1971. With its many towers, onion domes, minarets and arches, the station that architect Hubbock created seems more appropriate for a journey into the world of the Arabian Nights than for modern railway

Above: Architecture out of the Arabian Nights: the railway station in Kuala Lumpur.

travellers. Practically enough, this fairy-tale station includes a **Station Hotel**; unfortunately, this facility is long overdue for a thorough renovation. Across the street, the railway is run equally decoratively from the colonial building which houses the **Malayan Railway Administration**.

Rich in Islamic symbolism is the architecture of the National Mosque or **Masjid Negara** near the station, which cost millions to build in 1965. A 245-foot (75 m) minaret rises out of one of the many pools surrounding the building. The 18-sided central dome symbolizes the 13 states of Malaysia plus the five pillars of Islam; while the 48 smaller domes resemble those on the mosque in Mecca. The mosque, with room for 6000 worshippers, is open every day to visitors. The head-covering and robes which everyone is required to wear inside are available at the entrance for a small charge.

The white palace of **Istana Negara** (National Palace) lies south of the Railway Station and the National Mosque. Visitors can glimpse the official residence of King Duli Yang Maha Mulia Seri Paduka Baginda Yang di Pertuan Agung (as his official name runs in full). The white palace, which is surrounded by a huge park, lies to the south of the train station and the national mosque. The only time the common folk can come to revere the king in the Istana Negara, is during the Moslem new year's festival *Hari Raya Puasa*.

On the way to **Subang International Airport** 13.5 miles (22 km) away, is the Thean Hou temple standing to the left of the Federal Highway. It is the largest Chinese temple in Kuala Lumpur. A visit is worthwhile, also for the terrific view of the city's skyline from here.

While building the new bypass on the way to the highway to Seremban, planners had to take the large Chinese cemetery complex into account.

Attractive Outskirts

Anyone spending a weekend in Kuala Lumpur should not pass up the opportunity to visit the **Pasar Minggu**, the Sunday Market in Kampong Baru, the northernmost section of the city, on the right bank of the River Kelang. In Malaysian usage, the evening is named after the day that follows it, which means that the Sunday Market is actually held on Saturday evening. Here, between Jl. Raja Muda Musa and Jl. Sungai Baharu, you can find virtually every local product imaginable, including a huge selection of Malay culinary specialties. Antiques are also on sale in this area.

A favorite destination for day-trippers from K.L. lies on the other side of the beltway Jl. Tun Razak and the northern city limit: the recreational park **Taman Tasek Titiwangsa**. Here, a selection of restaurants plus a variety of sports and recreation are available to residents and visitors alike. Also north of the city, an-

other pleasant outing is the 260 foot (80 m) wooded hill of **Bukit Nanas** (Pineapple Hill). One of the world's tallest TV towers (1348 ft/421 m) was erected here in 1996. The tower with its revolving restaurant and a panoramic platform – in good weather you can see the road from Melakka – is already one of the favorite attractions in Kuala Lumpur. To the west, toward Petaling Jaya and the airport, is the university district on Jl. Universiti, with the **International Islam University** and the nearby **Museum of Asian Art**.

AROUND KUALA LUMPUR

Just 9 miles (15 km) from the center of the city, animal lovers get their due at the **National Zoo and Aquarium**. Near the town of **Ampang**, this is easily reachable by public bus. The zoo features Malaysian fauna and underwater creatures, including members of species which have been driven into far corners of the country, such as tigers and elephants. On the way there is a typical Malay dwelling, **Pa' Ali's House** (6.25 miles down Jl. Gombak). The guide is a descendant of the original builder and has a great deal to say about how the house was built. (Open daily from 9 a.m. to 6 p.m.)

The **Royal Selangor Pewter Factory** at 4 Jl. Usahawan Enam, Setapak Jaya, is not far off. Pewterware is displayed for sale there, and the factory also has demonstrations of tin-working.

Templer Park is a showcase of pristine nature just 13.6 miles (22 km) north of Kuala Lumpur, where the road branches off toward Ipoh and Penang. Its creator, British High Commissioner Sir Gerald Templer, created the 3,000-acre (1,200 hectare) park for the inhabitants of Kuala Lumpur. Not far away is **Bukit Takun**, a 1,150-foot (350 m) limestone formation that is sure to delight amateur climbers and botanists. More than 200 varieties of plant grow on its cliffs, none of which is too difficult to climb.

The **Forest research Institute of Malaysia** (FRIM) in Kepong is the place to go for documentation on Malaysia's flora. The institute has a small museum for its visitors.

Staying on the B9 beginning in **Sungai Buloh**, one arrives soon at a **lepers' camp** that lies off to the side of a large grounds. The inhabitants work as gardeners and sell plants at fairly low prices. The **Natural Rubber Museum** is also very close by. It is open Monday through Thursday and Saturday from 10:00 am to 4:00 pm, free of charge.

Further south, some 7.5 miles (12 km) north of K.L., the **Batu Caves** lure visitors with their air of mysterious adventure. Giant limestone formations, rising out of the nearly flat landscape, conceal hollows up to 1,300 feet (400 m) long, under a limestone dome as high as 390 feet (120 m). Since they were discovered by William Hornaby, an American, only about twenty of the caves have been explored. In 1892, a shrine to the Hindu god Murugan was built in the uppermost chamber, called "Light Cave," today, this is the annual goal of a spectacular procession during the festival of *Thaipusam*. Laboriously and painfully, the hordes of pilgrims have to climb the 272 steps to the cave with their *kavadi*, wooden structures decorated with fruit and flowers and fastened to their bodies with sharp hooks.

The "Dark Caves" are supposed to be especially mysterious, giving onto narrow passages leading deep into the earth. Unfortunately, falling stalactites forced officials to close them to the public some time ago. A "Museum Cave" at the beginning of the cave system houses an exhibit of miniature plaster copies of all the gods in the Hindu pantheon.

A few miles to the east, along the feeder road to the Karak Highway, is a **batik factory** with a sales room. A 30-minute tour free of charge permits visitors to learn more about the production techniques.

The **Orang Asli Department** concerns itself with Malaysia's Negritos; it runs a clinic as well as the **Muzium Orang Asli**, filled with crafts and cult objects of the people called *Mah Meri*.

Some 31 miles (50 km) northeast of Kuala Lumpur, the visitor seeking refuge from the city's heat and bustle suddenly steps into a perfectly artificial world. A well-improved road winds its way partly around tight hairpin turns by the **Chin Swee temple** pagoda – with a superb view of the plain and Kuala Lumpur in good weather – and the lower station of a cable car, before reaching the **Genting Highlands**, which lie at an altitude of 5,560 feet (1,700 m).

This resort is the only place in Malaysia where gambling is legal. Moslems are prohibited from coming here. It was the dream of a Chinese businessman who wanted to build a pleasure palace high above the misty jungle. For several years now, his "Genting Highlands, Ltd." has consisted of a glittering city of five hotels, an 18-hole golf course, shops, an amusement park and the aforementioned "Casino de Genting," which Malaysians are forbidden to enter. Shows by international artists are presented in the same building. The program changes every 2-3 months.

The climate provides for coolness; during the rainy season, the temperature drops to as low as 55°F (13°C). Gamblers are less interested in the clean crisp air outside than in the smoke-filled rooms where they play the blackjack and roulette tables. They stack their chips and feed the one-armed bandits until late into the night, while their children enjoy the artificial lake and the indoor swimming pool, or while away the hours in front of the television set.

It's hard to escape the modern world of technology in **Petaling Jaya**, a former suburb south of the city which is now almost indistinguishable from Kuala Lumpur itself. This community, which grew

up out of the rice terraces in the 1950s, is today surrounded by a ring of domestic and international industrial concerns.

An archway commissioned in 1981 by the Sultan of Selangor marks the border between the Federal Territory and the state of **Selangor Darul Ehsan**. The Arabic inscription reads, "The land of good intentions."

About 3.5 miles (5 km) from Petaling Jaya on the way to Port Klang is **Sunway Lagoon**. This newly-built recreational park, which combines swimming with a theme park, lies off the Federal Highway.

The first things to catch the eye in **Shah Alam**, the capital of Selangor, are the **Istana Bukit Kayangan** (Sultan's Palace) and the **State Mosque** or Masjid Sultan Salahuddin Abdul. A 300-foot (91 m) aluminum dome which cost 160 million M$ adorns the impressive building. It was a cost that the Sultan could well afford. He receives 300 million M$ a year in compensation for use of the land he owns in Kuala Lumpur and for the residence he agreed to move to Shah Alam. Non-Moslems can only admire the mosque from the outside.

Another of the country's status symbols also originates in Shah Alam: The national car brand EON's Proton line, which is manufactured here using 70 per cent local materials. Another auto manufacterer is located on the east coast, the one building the Kecil, a compact car at a bargain basement price.

The sports stadium in the shape of an oyster was opened in 1994. It has space for 80,000 spectators. The Commonwealth Games will be held here in part in 1998. In the immediate vicinity is the **Shah Alam Racing Circuit**, where runs for the motorcycling world cup are held each year; local authorities are trying to get Formula 1 racing going here too. When the temperature along the track gets too hot, you can drop in on a show in the **Taman Pertamian Malaysia** at the Bukit Cahara Sri Alam: The "four seasons – unknown to the tropics – including snowfall are presented here from 9 a.m. to 5 p.m.

7.5 miles (12 km) west of Selangor lies the former royal city of **Kelang** (also called Klang) with more than 200,000 inhabitants. Sights here include the royal mosque and the **Istana Alam Shah**, the royal palace. **Gedung Jaja Abdullah**, a museum housed in a former warehouse built in 1857, is a reminder of the city's pioneer past; while **Fort Raja Mahadi** is evidence of the strategic value the city placed on protecting its tin mines. It's ideally situated to watch over both natural mineral resources and traffic on the Kelang River.

Port Kelang, formerly known as Port Swettenham, has become Malaysia's most important port. It's worth visiting the city to sample its delicious fish delicacies. **Pulau Ketam**, Crab Island, is only a short boat trip away and is also known for excellent seafood restaurants.

Indigenous people of the Mah Meri tribe live on the island of **Pulau Carey**,

Above: Outlet store of a factory producing batik.

south of Kelang. These Orang Asli are renowned for their ritual wooden masks and other wood carvings.

Beach lovers should head for **Morib**, an island 28 miles (45 km) south of Kelang, where the sand is fine and the water still relatively unpolluted.

North of Kelang is the former royal city of **Kuala Selangor**, at the mouth of the Selangor River. The narrow road leading to the city passes through rubber and coconut plantations. Old fortifications here and in **Jeram** are reminders of the days when the Bugis from Sulawesi, and, later, the Europeans, controlled the whole area.

The Dutch-Malaysian **Fort Altingsburg**, for example, was built in the reign of Sultan Ibrahim (1778-1826) on the hill of Bukit Melawati. Visitors can enjoy the marvellous view from the ramparts, while shuddering at the sight of the wooden block where victims were beheaded.

Ornithologists can have a field day at the **Taman Alam Kuala Selangor** (Kuala Selangor Nature Park) and at the **Pulau Angsa** just off shore. The 625-acre (250 ha) park contains 130 different species of birds, including long-tailed macaws as well as other rare species. Also well worthwhile is a climb up **Kuala Selangor Hill** with its impressive rain forest, which leads to an old lighthouse at the summit. This is a terrific vantage point for a plunging view of **Sungai Selangor**.

Kajang, 12.5 miles (20 km) south of Kuala Lumpur on the road to Seremban, offers culinary adventure. *Satay*, the tiny meat kabobs in a spicy peanut-chili sauce so famous throughout Malaysia, have put the town on the map since Haj Tasmin invented *satay kajan* in 1917. His followers in Kajang are still doing a brisk trade in these delicacies. Local Chinese, meanwhile, are prouder of the beautiful temple **Shen Sze She Yar** on the Jl. Tukang, nearly 100 years old.

KUALA LUMPUR
Telephone code: 03

Getting there / Getting Around

BY AIR: **Subang Airport** has three terminal buildings. The first is International, Terminal 2: domestic flights; Terminal 3: shuttle service between Kuala Lumpur and Singapore. If you are planning to fly on further on a domestic flight, plan for at least one hour transit time.

The terminals are accessible by bus from the Klang bus station (near the train station). Taxi rides between the airport and the city are for a fixed fare and with tickets from the taxi counter. (at the exit of the arrivals building).

BY BUS: Buses for the **north** and **south**leave from the **Perhentian Bas Pudu Raya** (Central Bus Station Pudu Raya), Tel: 2300145. Buses for **Pahang** leave from the **Central Pahang Bus Station**, Jl. Tun Razak; buses to the **east coast** depart from the **Dewan Bandaraya Car Park** next to the Putra World Center.

Important bus lines: **National Express**, Tel: 2388185; **K. L.-Singapore-Express**, Tel: 2327553; **K. L.-Melaka-Express** ("Jebat Express"), Tel: 2380202. *TAXIS* (car pools only) also depart from the **Pudu Raya Bus Station**.

MINIBUSES: Throughout the whole city, with conductor, 60 c, stop on request.

GROUP TAXIS: Departure is also from the **Pudu Raya bus station**.

BY TRAIN: Kuala Lumpur is on the **Singapore-Butterworth** train line, with connections to Bangkok. Timetable information (in Malayan: *Jadual Waktu*) from the Malaysian Railroad (*Keretapi Tanah Melayu*): Tel: 2747442.

RENTAL CARS: **Avis Rent a Car**, 40, Jl. Sultan Ismail, Tel: 2417144. **Hertz Rent a Car**, Lot 214 A, International Complex, Jl. Sultan Ismail, Tel: 2433433. **Budget Rent a Car**, 29, Jl. Yap Kwan Seng, Tel: 2425166 u. 2425006 (Central Reserv.) **National Car Rental (Europcar),** Head Office, Shop 9, Ground Floor, President House (next to the Parkroyal Hotel), Jl. Sultan Ismail, Tel: 2480522. The companies listed have offices at the airport that are open during business hours. If flying in at night, you should reserve a car in advance. **Important note**: Remember to drive *on the left-hand side* of the road.

LIGHTRAIL TRANSIT: An express railway system, the Ampang-Pudu Raya-Sentul line is currently under construction.

Accommodations

LUXUS: **Carcosa Seri Negara**, Taman Tasek Perdana, Tel: 2306766, the top hotel of the country, for presidents kings and very VIPs, former residence of the British High Commisioner, on a hill overlooking the Lake Gardens. **Kuala Lumpur Hilton**, Jl. Sultan Ismail, Tel: 2422222. **The Regent**, 160 Jl. Bukit Bintang, Tel: 2418000. **Parkroyal Kuala Lumpur**, Jl. Sultan Ismail, Tel: 2425588. **Shangri-La**, Jl. Sultan Ismail, Tel: 2322388. **Pan Pacific**, Jl. Putra, Tel: 4425555. **Hotel Istana**, Jl. Raja Chulan, Tel: 2441445. **Crown Princess**, Jl. Tun Razak, Tel: 2625522. **Holiday Inn City Centre**, Jl. Raja Laut, Tel: 2939233. **Holiday Inn on the Park**, Jl. Pinang, Tel: 2481066. **Ming Court Hotel**, Jl. Ampang, Tel: 2618888. **The Legend**, 100 Jl. Putra, Tel: 4429888.

MITTEL: **Federal Hotel**, 35, Jl. Bukit Bintang, Tel: 2489166. **Equatorial Hotel**, Jl. Sultan Ismail, Tel: 2617777. **Concorde Hotel**, 2, Jl. Sultan Ismail, Tel: 2442200. **Imperial**, 76-80, Changat Bukit Bintang, Tel: 2481422. **Mandarin Hotel Kuala Lumpur**, 2-8, Jl. Sultan, Tel: 2303000. **Micasa Hotel Apartements**, 368-B, Jl. Tun Razak, Tel: 2618833. **Grand Central Hotel**, Jl. Putra/Jl. Raja Laut, Tel: 4413011. **Malaya Hotel**, Jl. Hang Lekir, Tel: 2327722. **Pudu Raya Hotel**, 4th Floor, Pudu Raya Station (central bus station, Chinatown), Tel: 2321000. **Plaza Hotel**, Jl. Raj Laut, Tel: 2982255. **Subang Airport Hotel**, Subang International Airport, Tel: 7462122. **Swiss Garden**, 177 Jl. Pudu, Tel: 2413333.

BUDGET: **Coliseum Hotel**, Jl. T. Abdul Rahman, Tel: 29266270, unique atmosphere, favorite of the rucksack crowd, usually no vacancies. **Station Hotel**, Bangunan Stesen Keretapi (train station), Jl. Sultan Hishamuddin, Tel: 2741433. **The Lodge**, 2, Jl. Sultan Ismail, Tel: 2420122. **YMCA**, Jl. Tun Sambathan, Tel: 2741439. **YWCA**, Jl. Hang Jebat, Tel: 2383225. **Malaysian Youth Hostels Ass.**, 21, Jl. Kg. Attap, Tel: 2306870/71. **Diamond City Lodge**, 74 B, C, D, Jl. Masjid India, Tel: 2932245. **Paradise Bed & Breakfast**, 319-1, Jl. Tuanku Abdul Rahman, Tel: 2932322. Numerous cheap hotels are located in Jl. Tuanku Abdul Rahman.

Restaurants

*MALAYAN:***Ahamed**, Merdeka Stadion, 1st floor, open-air with roof, excellent *Fish-Head-Curry*, closes evenings. **Bunga Raya Restaurant**, Level 2, Putra World Trade Center, Tel: 4422999. **Rasa Utara**, Tel: 2488639. **Satay Anika**, Tel: 2483113 (both in the Bukit Bintang Plaza, Jl. Bukit Bintang). **Yazmin Restaurant**, 6, Jl. Kia Peng, Tel: 2415655. **Nelayan Floating Restaurant**, Lake Titiwangsa Gardens, Jl. Temerloh, Tel: 4228400. In **Kajang: Satay Terkenal Sejak 1917**.

CHINESE: **Hakka Restaurant**, 231, Jl. Bukit Bintang, Tel: 9858492. **Mak Yee Restaurant**, 32, Jl. Sultan Ismail, Tel: 2486036. **Marco Polo**, 1st.

Floor, Wisma Lim Foo Yong, Jl, Raja Chulan, Tel: 2425595. **Overseas**, in the Central Market, good, inexpensive *dim sum*. **Regent Court Chinese Rest.**, Jl. Sultan Ismail, Tel: 2422232. **Restaurant Teochew**, 270, Jl. Changat Thambi Dollah, Tel: 2483452. **Shang Palace**, Shangri-La Hotel, Jl. Sultan Ismail, Tel: 2322388. **Ming Court Hotel**, Jl. Ampang, Tel: 2618888. **Golden Phoenix**, Equatorial Hotel, Jl. Sultan Ismail, Tel: 2612022.

INDIAN: **Bangles**, 60-A, Jl. Tuanku Abdul Rahman, Tel: 2983780. **Bilal**, 33, Jl. Ampang, Tel: 2380804. **Devi Annpoorna**, 94, Lorong Maaroof, Tel: 2823799. **Shiraz Restaurant**, 1, Jl. Medan Tuanku, Tel: 2910035. **Yussoof**, Merdeka Stadium Tel: 2307411. **Omar Khayam Restaurant**, 5, Jl. Medan Tuanku, Tel: 2911016. **Bombay**, 388 Jl. Tun Razak, Tel: 2454241.

ITALIAN: **Modesto's**, No. 1D Lorong Perak, Tel: 9841625. **Chiao Coffee Ristorante**, 428 Jl. Tun Razak, Tel: 2485487.

RUSSIAN: **Troika**, Jl. Raja Chulan, Tel: 2616734, Specialty is *Borscht*.

THAI: **Cili Padi**, 2nd Floor, The Mall, Jalan Putra, Tel: 4424319. **Sawasdee Thai**, Holiday Inn on the Park, Jl. Pinang, Tel: 2481066, ext. 147.

JAPANESE: **Chikuyo-tei**, Plaza See Hoy Chan, Tel: 2300729. **Edogin Japanese Restaurant**, 207 A, Jl. Tun Razak, Tel: 2610522. **Hoshigacka**, 2nd Floor Lot 10, Jl. Sultan Ismail, Tel: 2442585.

KOREAN: **Koryo-Won**, Kompleks Anatarabangsa, Jl. Sultan Ismail, Tel: 2427655. **Seoul Garden**, 37, Jl. Sultan Ismail, Tel: 2420425.

WESTERN: **The Smokehouse**, 11 Jl. Yap Kwan Seng, Tel: 2412720, *Beef Wellington* (for 2 or more) should be tried, pre-ordered! **Carcosa Seri Negara**, Taman Tasik Perdana, Tel: 2821888, a place for kings, not cheap but worth seeing. **Castell Grill**, 81, Jl. Bukit Bintang, Tel: 2428328. **Decanter Restaurant**, 7, Jl. Setiakasih 5, Tel: 2552507.

Esquire Kitchen, 1st Floor, Sungai Wang Plaza, Jl. Bukit Bintang, Tel: 2485006. **Le Coq D'or**, 121, Jl. Ampang, Tel: 2429732. **The Ship**, 40/1, Jl. Sultan Ismail, Tel: 2418805. **Coliseum Café and Restaurant**, Jl. Tuanku Abdul Rahman, Tel: 2926270. **40 Carrotts**, 2nd Floor, The Mall, Tel: 4424319.

COOKSHOPS: in Chinatown along Jl. Petaling, Jl. Bukit Bintang, and in the Pudu Raya bus station; the first floor of the **Central Market**, Jl. Hang Kasturi; 4th floor of the **Mall** in Jl. Putra.

Note: Tipping is not expected, but welcome.

Pubs

Hardrock Café, Jl. Sultan Ismail, live bands from 11 pm on.

T.G.I. Friday's, Jl. Sultan Ismail.
Ronny 'Q', Jl. Telawi 2, Bangsar.
A German beer cellar on the ground floor of the **Wisma Haw Par**, Jl. Sultan Ismail, specialties such as *Bitburger*, *Alt*, as well as Bavarian *Erdinger* wheat beer.
Many hotels operate a pub or a bar, happy hour is Mon-Fri from 5:00 pm to 7:00 pm.

Discos

Tin Mine, K.L. Hilton Hotel, Tel: 2422222.
Blue Moon, Hotel Equatorial, Tel: 2617777.
The Musictheque, Hotel Istana, Tel: 2419988.
Tsim Sha Tsui Disco, Jl. Kia Peng, Tel: 2414929.
The Jump, Jl. Tun Razak, Tel: 2450046, terrific cocktails.

Folklore

Restaurant Sri Melayu, 1 Jl. Conlay, Tel: 2451833. **Yazmin Restaurant**, 6 Jl. Kia Peng, Tel: 2415655.
Nelayan Floating Restaurant, Taman Titiwangsa, Tel: 4228400, the dining room is on a platform in the lake.
Tuanku Abdul Rahman Hall, shows are Tue, Thu, Sat and Sun at 3:30 pm.

Museums / Mosques / Markets

Muzium Negara, Jl. Damansara, near Lake Gardens, open daily 9:00 am-6:00 pm, closed Fri 12:00-2:00 pm, Tel: 2381067.
National Art Gallery, Jl. Hishamuddin, open daily 9:00 am-6:00 pm, closed Fri 12:15-2:15 pm, Tel: 2300157.
Telekom Museum, Jl. Raja Chulan, Tel: 2019966, 8:30 am-4:45 pm.
Natural Rubber Museum, Sungai Buloh, Mon-Thu and Sat 10:00 am-4:00 pm.
Bank Negara Money Museum, Jl. Dato Onn, Mon-Fri 9:00 am-4:00 pm, Sat till 5:00 pm, free.
Artiquarium, Jl. Medan Tuanku, a private museum with paintings and Asian art.
Masjid Negara, open daily 8:00 am-6:00 pm, Fri 3:00-6:00 pm.
Masjid Jamek, open daily 9:00 am-12:30 pm, 2:45-4:30 pm, Fri 8:30-10:30 am, 2:45-4:30 pm.

Shopping

Kuala Lumpur has large shopping centers where prices are lower than in Singapore: **Wang Plaza**, **Bukit Bintang Plaza**, **Lot 10**, **The Mall**, **The Weld** and **SOGO**. Hours: 10:00 am-10:00 pm.
Crafts are not only sold at the **Central Market**, but also in the state-controlled stores **Karyaneka**, on Jl. Conlay, or the **Infocraf**, Jl. Sultan Hishamuddin near the main Post Office.

The **Night Market** in **Chinatown** is a colorful place and cheap, opens at 5:30 pm (watches, electronic items, cosmetics, clothes, etc...).

You can buy batik, silverware and pewter (a compound of tin and copper) directly from manufacturers, such as the **Royal Selangor Pewter Factory**, 4, Jl. Usahawan 6, Setapak (a suburb of Kuala Lumpur). Visitors' center and showroom are open Mon-Sat 8:30 am-4:45 pm, Sun 9:00 am-4:00 pm, Tel: 4221000.

The **market in Jl. T. Abdul Rahman** (clothing, leather, batik, basketware) and the **market in Jl. Sungay Baharu / Kampong Baru** (fresh foods, native products, cookshops) are open Saturdays only at 5:30 pm.

TAYLORS: **Spark Manshop**, Kuala Lumpur Hilton, Tel: 2414535. **The Master Tailor**, MiCasa Shops, MiCasa Hotel Apartements, Tel: 2612108.

Cinemas
Cathay, Jl. Bukit Bintang.
Cathay, The Mall.
Sungai Wang, Jl. Bukit Bintang.
Rex, Chinatown.
Federal, Jl. Bukit Bintang.
International films in original version with Malaysian subtitles are generally shown earlier than in the Europe and the USA.

Hospitals
Hospital of the University of Malaya, Jl. Universiti, Petaling Jaya, Tel: 7564422 ext. 2500. **General Hospital**, Jl. Pahang, Tel: 2921044 (both are state-run and offer free medical care). **Pantai Medical Center**, 8, Jl. Bukit Pantai, Tel: 7575077 (private, therefore relatively expensive).

Post Office / Telephone / Amex
Postal Headquarters (Pos Besar), Kompleks Dayabumi, 50670 Kuala Lumpur, Tel: 2741122. **Telephone information Kuala Lumpur:** 103. **American Express**, Wisma Lim Foo Yong, Tel: 2444988.
Card- or coin-operated booths can be used for making local calls, cards only for international calls. Or use the Telecom offices around the city. Most hotels are equipped with IDD service (surcharge).

Police / Emergency Numbers
Tourist Police, Tel: 2425522. **Police, Ambulance, Fire**: Tel: 999.

Tourist Information
Malaysian Tourist Promotion Board (MTPB), 24-27th Floor, Menara Dato' Onn, Putra World Trade Center, 45, Jl. Tun Ismail, Tel: 2935188, Fax: 2935884.
Malaysia Tourist Information Complex (MATIC), 109, Jl. Ampang, Tel: 2423929.
K. L. Tourist Association (KLTA) and **K. L. Visistors Center**, 3, Jl. Hishamuddin, Tel: 2381832.
Tourist Information Center, Jl. Parlimen, Tel: 2936664.
Subang Airport, Teminal 1, Arrival Hall, Tel: 7465707.
Information Counter Railway Station, Tel: 2746063.
Putra World Trade Centre, Level 2, 45, Jl. Tun Ismail, Tel: 4411205.

Local Festivals
In addition to religious celebrations such as the **Thaipusam Festival** (beginning of February) or **Christmas,** Malaysia celebrates **Federal Territory Day** (February 1) and **National Independence (Merdeka) Day** (a particularly beloved event) on August 31. The latter is celebrated in grand style, with athletic events throughout KL, and other activities.

Other important addresses
Department of Fisheries, Ministry of Agriculture, Wisma Tani, Jl. Mahameru, Tel: 2982011.
Wildlife and National Park Department, K. L. Km 10, Jl. Cheras, Tel: 9052872.
Malaysian Society of Marine Science (Info about protected marine areas) P.O. Box 250, Jl. Sultan Post Office, 46730 Petaling Jaya (Selangor).

AROUND KUALA LUMPUR
Area code: 03
Selangor Darul Ehsan
LUXURY: **Hyatt Saujana Hotel & Country Club**, Subang Internat. Highway, Tel: 7461188. *MODERATE:* **Petaling Jaya Hilton**, 2, Jl. Barat, Tel: 7335211. **Merlin Subang**, Jl. 12/1, Subang Jaya, Tel: 7335211. **Crystal Crown**, Tel: 7584422 *BUDGET:* **S. Pacific**, Petaling Jaya 7, Jl. 52/16, Tel: 7569922. **Resthouse**, Kuala Selangor Hill.

In and around Port Kelang Accommodations
BUDGET: **Embassy Hotel**, 2-8 Jl. Kem, Pelabuhan Kelang, Tel: 386901/2. **Morib Guesthouse**, with a 9-hole golf course and cookshop.

Genting Highlands
LUXURY: **Genting Hotel**, Tel: 2112345. **Highland Hotel**, Tel:2111118. **Awana Golf and Country Club**, Tel: 2113015.

SILVER-PLATED TIN STATE

PERAK
HILL RESORTS
IPOH
PANGKOR ISLAND
KUALA KANGSAR
TAIPING

PERAK

The name of West Malaysia's second-largest state, Perak, actually means "silver," but the metal that turned the 8,190-square-mile (21,000 sq. km) state into the richest area of the country was in fact tin. The state's economy received a severe setback in 1983 when the world market price dropped. But a hundred years previously, Malaya, already the world's foremost tin producer, controlled 60 percent of the global market. Center of production, then as today, was the **Kinta Valley**. Tin mining, which started there around 1,500 years ago, is still the region's most important industry; today, it again accounts for approximately one-third of the world's total production.

Perak Darul Ridzuan, "the land of grace," is one of the oldest states of the peninsula. In 1528, the eldest son of the last ruler of Malacca founded the Perak dynasty in Beting Bras Basah on the Perak River. His kingdom survived, through successive attacks from Sumatra, the Dutch, the Bugis and the kingdom of

Preceding Pages: Tea harvesters in the Cameron Highlands going about an ancient and hard business. Left: The Orang Asli live between two worlds.

Siam, into the 19th century, when pirates and warring Chinese clans finally weakened Perak and opened the way for colonial rule.

The British were quick to take advantage of the situation, and under the 1874 "Contract of Pangkor" took over the administration of Perak. But the colonial government was not without opposition: James Birch, the first governor, was murdered in 1875. Although the assassins were caught and hanged, the British blamed Sultan Abdullah and forced him into exile.

Under Governor Hugh Low, the first white man to climb Mount Kinabalu, better times returned to Perak. The tin mines attracted tens of thousands of immigrants, mainly from China, and the population rose from 81,000 in 1879 to 214,000 in 1891. Today the population is over two million, comprised almost in equal measure of Malays (45%) and Chinese (41%); Indians make up the difference.

In addition to tin mining, there are rice and pineapple plantations in the north of the state. Broad rubber and oil palm plantations extend through the south, while lumber comes from Upper Perak (Hulu-Perak).

The 248-mile-long (400 km) River Perak, the second-longest river in West

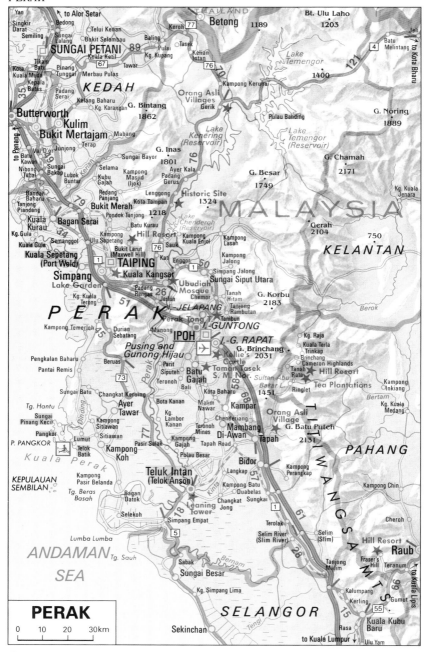

PERAK

0   10   20   30km

Malaysia, flows through the entire state. In 1987, archaeologists discovered an important site near **Kota Tampan**, along the river's upper course: a Stone Age workshop, estimated to be some 35,000 years old.

HILL RESORTS

Before the new North-South highway was built, anyone traveling from Kuala Lumpur to Ipoh had to pass through the city of Kuala Kubu Bharu. Even today, many travelers come this way. Branching off from the city is State Road Number 55, which turns into Number 8 at Raub as it continues toward Kota Bharu on the northeast coast.

Fraser's Hill

Following Number 8 until just before Teranum, in the state of Pahang, you come to the "Gap," a break in the mountains around the narrow road. From there, it's about 5 miles (8 km) to Fraser's Hill (Bukit Fraser), a mountain resort where the temperature fluctuates around a cool 10-20°C. (One-way regulation applies, changes hourly).

What is today a favorite weekend retreat for heat-weary tourists and city dwellers began in 1916 with a man of the cloth. The Singapore Bishop Ferguson-Davie was looking for a Scottish adventurer by the name of Louis James Fraser, who was known to live in the mountains and transport tin ore from Kuala Lipis to Kuala Kubu Bharu. Rumor had it that Fraser smuggled opium as well, which was the reason for the Bishop's interest, and for the fact that he had a police officer accompanying him.

What they found resembled a den of thieves rather than a tin depot; Fraser himself was nowhere to be seen. The Bishop and other officials, however, were captivated by the beautiful mountain landscape and climate as they ex-plored the area. The first of Malaysia's many "Hill Resorts" was born. By the 1920s, guests were already arriving to enjoy a rest and respite from the peninsula's tropical summers in what had once been an outlaw's hideaway: Fraser's Hill.

Numerous hotels and chalets, many in neo-Tudor style, have sprung up since then, and Fraser's Hill now does a brisk business cashing in on the romance of colonial times. Sport and leisure activities keep visitors fit, and cozy fireplaces add a touch of home to the chilly evenings. Fraser's Hill also has modern hotels for visitors who prefer less expensive and less Anglicized accommodations. Although many of the newer structures obstruct some of the views, the panorama is still worth the trip. The fifteen-minute walk to **Jeriau Waterfall**, while lovely, can be spoiled if the picnic-grounds are too crowded when you get there.

The Cameron Highlands

West Malaysia's other favorite hill region also lies in the state of Pahang, but, like Fraser's Hill, it can only be reached by way of Perak.

After Kuala Kubu Bharu, the North-South highway passes through the town of **Slim River**, where Japanese and British tank divisions fought a bitter battle during World War II. **Bidor** has a gentler claim to fame: it is known for the vitamin-rich guavas and other tropical fruit sold from stands along its streets.

In **Tapah**, a narrow road with breathtaking views turns off into the highlands named after the British map-maker William Cameron. He discovered the region that begins about 112 miles (180 km) north of the capital in 1885, and immediately fell in love with its beauty. During the 1930s, Communist guerillas used the Cameron Highlands as their hiding place, making it dangerous for tourists. It remained closed until the early sixties when the "Emergency" ended.

The climate changes noticeably along the curving 55-mile (90 km) road to the Highlands, which rises to an altitude of 7,520 feet (2,300 m). Along the lower part, cool air wafts down from the Titiwangsa Mountains, ruffling the fronds of banana trees and palms. Higher up, ferns and bamboo frame the view. Seven miles (11 km) up the road, the roar of rushing water marks the site of the **Lata Iskandar Waterfalls**. There are also many Orang Asli villages along the way where visitors can get a quick lesson in the art of using the blow gun.

After **Ringlet**, an unprepossessing town just beyond the border between Perak and Pahang, **Sultan Abu Bakar's Lake** provides an inviting place to rest. The lake was created by a dam on the Sungai Bertam. Fruit, flowers and vegetables are sold along its shores. Anyone who wishes can have them shipped to

Above: A hotel in the Cameron Highlands' picturesque landscape. Right: Working in a tin mine near Ipoh.

Kuala Lumpur or Singapore and be confident they will arrive in good condition. Because of the cooler temperatures, farmers can cultivate many exotic varieties; unfortunately, they are more and more frequently resorting to the use of pesticides to increase their crops.

Tea also grows in the highlands on extensive plantations that dominate the landscape. The **Boh Tea Estate**, a plantation started in 1926 in the valley of the Sungai Boh, is open to visitors every day except Monday. You can get there on Road C 168, which branches off a few miles after the dam. **Gunung Emas Tea Estate** (turn off about a mile further down the road toward Tanah Rata) is open daily except Friday. **Bharat Tea Estate** (3 miles/5 km south of Tanah Rata) is also open to visitors.

English settlers brought tea from Assam to the Malaysian peninsula; they also imported Tamil workers from the south of India to tend the plantations. Their descendants still work here for pitifully low wages The Chinese also tapped

the agricultural possibilities of Camerons; it was they who built the first road
to the highlands so they could bring their
produce to market. They were followed
by well-to-do businessmen, who built
weekend homes in the heights.

Tanah Rata, a resort and the major
town of highlands, is 8.5 miles (14 km)
from Ringlet. Groomed estates make this
a pleasant place to stay; it's also an ideal
base for excursions into the surrounding
area. **Robinson Waterfall**, for instance,
is close by; from here, there's a trail leading to the Boh Tea Estate. Several other
trails wind to the summit of the 6,020
foot (1,841 m) **Gunung Beremban**.

Gunung Jasar (5,346 feet/1,635 m)
and **Gunung Perdah** (5,150 feet/1,575
m) offer unforgettable excursions for experienced hikers. If you'd rather explore
by car or taxi, take West Malaysia's highest road up to **Gunung Brinchang**
(6,641 feet/2,031 m). Walking up the
mountain, through tea plantations, farms
and dense jungle to the summit, takes
about two hours. At the top, you're re-
warded by a superb view: you can look
out over a seemingly endless expanse of
forest to the east, and glimpse the distant
sea to the west.

Ye Olde Smokehouse Hotel, an inn in
typical English country style, is located
in the village of **Brinchang**. This pretty
hotel with restaurant has few rooms,
however, so advanced booking well
ahead of time is necessary. Even if not
staying overnight, you should drop in for
a cocktail around the open hearth or
around tea-time – the scones are excellent. The Camerons otherwise have any
number of cheaper accommodations, as
well as a number of inviting restaurants.
Many of these latter feature a typically
English dessert, which one would hardly
expect to find in these tropical surroundings: strawberries and cream.

On the outskirts of Brinchang, a rather
overdeveloped tourist spot, is the **Sam
Poh Temple**. An outstanding feature of

the temple are the huge gold-colored
statues that stand guard outside. A 13-
mile (21 km) road connects Brinchang to
Tringkap, Kuala Terla, Kampong Raja
and the **Blue Valley Tea Estate**. Unfortunately, the farmers selling their produce along the roadside are no longer as
interested in bargaining as they may have
been before the Europeans' mass arrival.
Even the Orang Asli have adapted to the
tourist industry. Among other things,
they sell butterflies and insects mounted
on pins – many of which are endangered
species.

Nature lovers can hire a guide at the tea
plantation and climb the mountain of **Gunung Siku** (6,265 feet/1,916 m) or go to
the border between the states of Pahang
and Kelantan to conquer the 6,020-foot
(1,841 m) **Peak**. It would take at least
four days to climb **Gunung Chali Pon-
dok** (6,278 feet/1,920 m) and **Gunung
Yong Blair** (7,131 feet/2,181 m); but at
the end of this, you would have covered
all of the "high points" of the Cameron
Highlands.

IPOH: THE TIN CAPITAL

Passing through the very Chinese city of **Kampar**, a resort town 12.5 miles (20 km) northwest of Tapah which is proud of its restaurants and recreational parks, the old North-South Highway comes to Ipoh. Perak's capital since 1937 is also Malaysia's second-largest city, with 450,000 inhabitants. Until tin was discovered in 1884, Ipoh was just a sleepy Malay settlement in the valley of the Kinta, a tributary of the Perak. It was then called Paloh, meaning "standing water," because the inhabitants had dammed the stream to create a fishpond.

"Tin fever" brought streams of newcomers to the Kinta Valley, and the town was soon dubbed "City of Chinese Millionaires." By 1900 the population had grown to more than 12,000. Although the boom is long over, business is still brisk in this metropolis on the Kinta, even, by Malaysian standards, frivolous: Ipoh's night life keeps alive some more questionable traditions of the days when tin, or "white gold," determined the pace of life. Fortunes were quickly made and quickly spent, and people weren't shy about displaying what they had. The buildings of the period are appropriately showy; many of the edifices in the **Old Town** are a vivid reminder of the era.

Moorish style characterizes the **Ipoh Railway Station**, built in 1917; the **Dewan Bandaraya** (City Hall), with the tourist office on the ground floor; and the **High Court**. Tudor was the choice for the **Royal Ipoh Club** on the Padang, as well as **St. John's Church** and **St. Michael's Mission School**. Nearby are **Masjid India** (Indian Mosque) and **Masjid Negara** (National Mosque). The nearby **Clock Tower** commemorates the first British governor, James Woodford Wheeler Birch, murdered in 1875.

Right: A Hindu god watches sternly over one of the cave temples of Ipoh.

Victorian charm is very much in evidence in the old shops of Chinatown between Jl. Sultan Yususf and Jl. Treacher in the New Town. **Pasar Besar** (Central Market) on Jl. Lakasamana has everything for the Chinese kitchen, including the juicy pomelos for which Ipoh is justly famous. Further south, near the banks of the Kinta River on Jl. Datuk, is the venerable **Masjid Paloh** (Paloh Mosque), built in 1912, and renowned for its richly ornamented pulpit.

At the recreational park **Taman D.R. Seenivasagam**, you'll find answered the question of where the city got its name. Here, you can still see live Ipoh trees (*Antiaris toxicaria*), a relative of the rubber tree. From its white resin, the Orang Asli used to extract the poison used in their blowpipes.

Cave Shrines

Some of Ipoh's most interesting attractions lie outside the city limits. The **Japanese Gardens**, a gift of the Japanese government to the Perak Turf Club, are about half a mile (1 km) away on Jl. Tambun, east of the city. Horse races are held here every weekend, and half of Ipoh seems to turn out to place bets.

The only geological museum in Malaysia lies east of the city on Jl. Harimau Ipoh, also known as Tiger Lane. The **Muzium Geologi** opened in 1957 and has exhibits of more than 600 minerals, precious gem stones, fossils and, of course, plenty of tin ore.

If you follow Jl. Tambun out of the city, a bumpy dirt road leads off after about 3 miles (5 km); this will bring you to the first prehistoric cave-paintings ever discovered in West Malaysia. A British soldier looking for Communist insurgents stumbled on the drawings in 1958. They depict hunting scenes, and are estimated to be 5,000 years old.

The bizarre limestone cliffs to the north and northeast of Ipoh also contain a

few surprises. Buddhists and Hindus built temples in the chalk caves within the cliffs. On the other side of Tambun is **Om Sai Ram**, an Indian cave shrine. A thermal spa nearby makes a restful stop along the way. Further northeast, toward the town of Tanjung Rambutan, the eaves of a pagoda peeking out of a cliff mark the entrance to a Chinese temple.

The most spectacular of the cave temples is on Jl. Kuala Kansar, about 3.5 miles (6 km) north of Ipoh. The Chinese built the **Perak Tong Temple** in the gigantic cave of **Gunung Tasek** in 1926. It is dedicated to Buddha, who is depicted laughing in the entrance and again as a 42-foot (12.80 m) sitting figure in the main hall. The walls are adorned with paintings by various artists; from here, 385 steep steps lead to a second entrance and a stunningly beautiful view of the landscape. A Thai temple lies on the return route, 2.5 miles (4 km) from Ipoh. Notable in **Wat Meh Prasit Sumaki** is the sculpture of worshippers paying homage to a reclining figure of Buddha.

Sam Poh Tong, another cave temple, lies 3 miles (5 km) south of the city in Gunung Rapat. Numerous statues of Buddha peer out between the stalagmites and stalactites. Visitors can feed the temple turtles, symbols of a long life; wish for a better future at the fountain; or enjoy a vegetarian meal at the restaurant at the neighboring temple **Nam Thain Tong**.

Haunted Castle and Stone Elephants

Construction on **Kellie's Castle**, 12.5 miles (20 km) south of Ipoh at the town of **Batu Gajah**, was begun sometime before World War I and never finished. The rubber baron William Kellie-Smith dreamed of building a castle at least as grand as the governor's residence in Kuala Lumpur. Because it was to be so large and grand, it took a long time to build. Kellie was in Europe, buying an elevator for one of the towers when he died. His dream castle was only half-finished and remains in that state to this day. A romantic ruin that would be more at

home on the Scottish moors than in the tropics, it is now the setting for dozens of popular Malaysian ghost stories. Kellie's portrait still hangs over the altar of the Indian temple he had built for the workers on his plantation.

Batu Gajah itself has slipped into obscurity. At the height of the tin boom, this place, today a sleepy little backwater, was more important than Ipoh, and served the British as their administrative headquarters in Perak. Supposedly, stone (*batu*) elephants (*gajah*) were once found here; hence the town's name.

Apart from being the birthplace of the current Sultan, Batu Gajah's main claim to modern fame is **Taman Tasek S.M. Nor**, a zoo featuring snakes and crocodiles, located about half a mile (1 km) out of town in the direction of Kellie's Castle. A swimming pool and lake on the grounds make it a popular resort spot.

Above: Still life on the River Perak. Right: Beach fun and a variety of water sports on Pulau Pangkor.

74

Down the Perak River

West of Batu Gajah, the city of **Parit** nestles in the fertile valley of the Perak River. It was the river that first attracted settlers, whose numbers grew through the centuries until the area between the coast and the rich tin mines of upper Perak was densely populated; and because of the river, it was fiercely defended against invaders and ruled by mighty Sultans whose graves – some dating from the 16th century – poke out of the dust at the roadside. Tradition dictates that every newly-crowned king has to travel down the river from his residence in Kuala Kangsar aboard his houseboat to pay his respects to these ancient graves.

The terrapin or river turtle breeding center at **Bota Kanan** is a livelier attraction, providing a rare glimpse of these remarkable creatures.

Further south along the Valley of the Kings, near Kampong Gajah, the village of **Pasir Salak** lives off its warlike past. In its **Historical Complex** you can see

typical, traditional Malayan houses with beautifully carved decorations. It also is the site of another monument to James Birch, the Resident who was murdered in 1875. Curiously enough, while the obelisk commemorates the murdered white colonial governor, a large *kris* on the monument honors the memory of the assassins of the Maharaja Lela, Dato Sagor and Si Puntum, both of whom were hanged by the British in 1875. Birch's grave can still be visited in **Pulau Besar**, south of Kampong Gajah.

The only tin refinery in the Kinta valley is at **Telok Intan**, also known as Telok Anson, which you can reach by a spur on the north-south train line. Except for the fruit and vegetable market the only noteworthy sight here is the **Leaning Tower**. The 82-foot (25 m) tower was built in 1885 by the Chinese settler Leong Choong Choong as a water tank.

Traveling south from Perak, you soon reach **Sabak** on the River Bernam, which forms the border between Selangor and Perak.

THE ISLAND OF PANGKOR

Pulau Pangkor is an island for swimming near Kuala Lumpur with good recreational value. The water in the coves is clean, the amenities on the beach are more than satisfactory. Besides the eastern coast, the island offers the only clean beaches, which are additionally accessible by highway from Kuala Lumpur as a day trip. Busses shuttle regularly from Ipoh, Taiping and even from Singapore via Kuala Lumpur to **Lumut**, the ferry port on the mainland. This fishing village lies on the banks of the Dinding River, 51 miles (84 km) south of Ipoh. Lumut is also a naval station of national importance. In the **Government Resthouse**, a museum displays old weapons and tools along with a collection of shells and coral.

The best time to visit Pangkor is during October and November when the village of **Telok Batik**, 3.5 miles (6 km) further down the coast, celebrates the festival of *Pesta Laut* (Lake Festival) with water

sports and traditional folklore performances. For the exact date, contact the Perak Tourist Information Center.

If you'd rather be alone, there are always the nearby **Kepulauan Sembilan** (Nine Islands). On these, would-be Robinson Crusoes can enjoy an idyllic holiday swimming, fishing, bird-watching, snorkeling and diving, and camping under the stars. The only catch is that you have to bring in your own food, equipment, mosquito nets, and, of course, drinking water.

Pangkor's place in Malaysia's history was assured in 1874, when an agreement was signed on the island to subordinate the Sultan of Perak to a representative of the British Crown and to turn the Dinding region of Lumut and Pangkor over to the Straits Settlements. They were not returned to Perak until 1935.

The island was a popular anchorage for European ships even earlier than that.

Above: The daily catch is sorted and sized up on Pangkor.

They filled their holds with rice, lumber, and most important of all, clean drinking water for the long voyage north. When Holland controlled the tin mines, Pangkor was often the scene of bloody fighting between the Europeans, the natives of Perak and the seafaring Bugis from Sulawesi.

An ancient legend tells of a princess from Sumatra who, searching everywhere for her lover, sailed to Pangkor in hopes of finding him there. He had become a warrior to prove himself worthy of her love, and died in a battle on the island. When she saw his grave, the grief-stricken princess decided to join him, and promptly leapt from the cliff to her death. **Pantai Puteri Dewi**, "the beach of the love-lorn princess," now belongs to the Pan Pacific Resort; it lies in the northeast of the island, on Golden Sands Bay. Here, as on nearby **Coral Beach**, the beaches and water are clean, but there is little to attract divers. The island does, however, boast a number of lovely nature walks.

The ferry from the mainland stops first in the shipbuilding and fishing port of **Sungai Pinang Kecil**, then sails south to the village of **Pangkor**. The lighthouse is open to visitors; while the houses on stilts built out over the water are a picturesque sight. From there it is another mile and a bit (2 km) by bus or taxi to **Pasir** (beach) **Bogak** on the west coast, where hotels and cottages line the shore. On weekends and during school holidays it can get crowded here, and it pays to travel a bit further north to **Pasir Ketapang**. From May to July the beach is a breeding ground for sea turtles; hence its nickname of "Tortoise Bay."

After the village of **Telok Nipah**, the road winds north through thick jungle. With luck you can spot hornbills, monkeys and eagles; and you are certainly assured of magnificent views of the coast and neighboring islands. Even the exclusive **Pan Pacific Resort** with its 161 rooms, its own ferry to Lumut, its wide selection of sports facilities and its golf course is a starting point for paths through the dense jungle.

If you'd like a taste of island history, stop off at **Telok Gedung**, 2 miles (3 km) away from Kampong Pangkor. Here, you'll find the ruins of **Kota Belanda**, a fort that the Dutch used to defend their tin merchants from pirates when they (the Dutch) controlled the area (1680-90, and again in the mid-18th century). Further south, there's further evidence of the Dutch presence on the cliffs of **Batu Berserat**. A Dutch inscription here dated 1743 records that, among other news, a child has been eaten by a tiger.

Except for Sungai Pinang Kecil in the north, the other towns on the island are also worth a visit: **Kampong Telok Dalam** to the north, for example, or **Kampong Telok Kecil** to the south of Pangkor. All told, the islands have a population of around 25,000 people – Malays, Chinese and Malabar fisherman from India – who live primarily off of the sea and tourism.

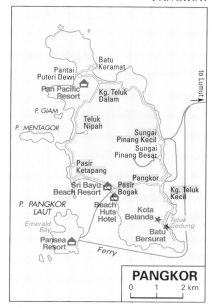

PANGKOR

0   1   2 km

One shouldn't overlook the small island of **Pulau Pangkor Laut**, which claims the best strip of beach in the entire region. **Emerald Bay**, on its east coast, is a truly beautiful spot for snorkeling and swimming, with four small beaches side by side. It's the place for glorious sunsets, and with a little bit of luck you will see shooting stars darting through the night skies, especially in April and May. The **Pansea Resort**, set against a backdrop of thick jungle on the east coast, is impressive indeed. The resort has its own ferry system for guests.

Pulau Pangkor Laut is entirely in the hands of a Chinese gentleman, who ecologically opened the island to the public. Unfortunately, excursions onto the islands are not possible, even private yachts seldom get permission to moor. Guests can stay in the wooden houses amidst lianas and flowering orchids. Some of the bungalows are built un stilts over the sea. Luciano Pavarotti stayed here once, and he even gave a little concert for a hand-picked audience.

THE ROYAL CITY OF KUALA KANGSAR

If, as you travel north, you're willing to allow a little more time for a detour to Kuala Kangsar, rather than taking the highway from Jerlun directly to the city, then you should take the old state road from Ipoh. It runs parallel to the railroad, and leads through **Chemor**, where you can glimpse a number of caves in the limestone cliffs.

Further on in **Enggor**, you can buy inexpensive local crafts in the **Perbadanan Kemajuan Kraftangan Malaysia**. In the village of **Labu Sayong**, just past the Iskandariah Bridge over the Perak, talented potters exhibit and sell the black glazed pottery typical of the area.

Although the small city of **Kuala Kangsar** only has 25,000 inhabitants, it has a veritably regal flair. For since 1876, the city has been home to the Sultan of Perak. About 2-3 miles (3-4 km) from the city, southeast of the confluence of the River Kangsar with the Perak, there are several buildings that warrant a look near the **Istana Iskandariah**, or royal palace, built in 1933. The immense ornate building with its six onion domes was again enlarged in 1984. The old palace, the **Istana Kenangan** or Istana Lembah, built in the traditional Malay style of wood and wattle, without nails, seems modest in comparison. Today, it houses the **Perak Royal Museum**, which charges visitors no admission to peruse its collection of royal memorabilia, including photographs, art and personal belongings of the Sultans of Perak.

The main tourist attraction of Kuala Kangsar is about half a mile (1 km) further toward the city, on Chandan Hill. This is the **Ubudiah Mosque**, considered one of the most beautiful Islamic houses of worship in all of Malaysia. An architectural masterpiece, it is crowned with a gilded dome and myriad smaller gold onion domes atop its many minarets. At the behest of the former Sultan Idris Shah, the Indian architect Timor Tengah completed this structure – with some help from the English – in 1917. Next to the mosque is the Mausoleum, where members of the royal family were interred. Halfway between the mosque and the main street is the State Resthouse, which boasts a view of the River Perak, and stands next to an old Chinese cemetery.

In the city itself, one of the most interesting buildings is **Malay College**, which was built in 1905 as a private school for the Sultan's children. Today it is where Perak's future leaders pore over their books. A relic of Malaysian history grows in front of the **District Office** on Jl. Chulan: one of the first rubber trees *(Hevea brasiliensis)* to reach Malaysia. Sir Henry Wickham smuggled the trees from South America to London in 1876. No less a personage than Hugh Low, the governor of Perak from 1877-89, planted 12 of the rubber trees in the garden of his residence as an experiment. The second surviving tree still grows there.

The North of Perak

Since the new highway was completed, Kuala Kangsar has stood outside of the mainstream flow of North-South traffic; it remains, however, a hub for traffic from the east coast to the west. Just west of the city, State Road 76 passes the first of two of the upper Perak's *(Hulu Perak)* most important lakes, both formed by dams.

The smaller one, **Tasek Chenderoh**, is near the town of Sauk and is fed by the Perak. The surrounding mountains are overgrown with dense rain forest. Water lilies crowd the lake's surface and local fishing boats float silently among them, assured of a plentiful catch.

Near the larger **Lake Tasek Temen-**

Right: Chinese storefronts in Taiping.

gor is the town of **Gerik** or Grik. Orang Asli, Senoi and Negrito tribes live in the area around the town. You can organize trips to the native villages, as well as fishing trips on the lake, at the Pulau Banding Rest House, approximately 22 miles (35 km) east of Gerik.

The East-West Highway climbs steadily to an altitude of 3,270 feet (1,000 m) for spectacular views of Perak and Thailand. Until 1990, guerilla activists made the region unsafe, and driving at night – indeed, venturing out at all at night – was forbidden; military police still patrol the road. The East-West Highway is the only place in Malaysia where there are signs warning against elephants, who still roam free in the region. A few years ago, allegedly, a rampaging elephant trampled a car killing all inside.

From Gerik, State Road 76 runs north into Thailand. In the border town of **Keroh** it crosses the East-West Road 76 from Penang; which means you can also take in this area as a detour on the way from Kuala Kangsar or Ipoh to Penang.

TAIPING: CITY OF ETERNAL PEACE

Taiping is one of the oldest cities in Malaysia. Before the tin rush, it was known as Larut; it later served as the first capital of Perak. Even before 1848, Chinese workers were streaming to Sungai Larut to work the mines. By 1861, they had organized secret societies, the Hai San and Ghee Hin, and the feuds of these groups soon spread violence throughout Perak. Worried about the future of its colony, England blockaded the state and pressured the Sultan to take action. But it wasn't until the Treaty of Pangkor in 1874 that peace returned to the area and the "Larut Wars" were ended. Larut was re-christened with a Chinese name – unusual in Malaysia – and called Taiping, "the city of eternal peace."

Chinese shop houses and elegant colonial buildings in the northeastern section of the city testify to the economic boom that followed. The country's first train

tracks were laid here to bring tin to **Port Weld**, now known as Kuala Sepetang. Mosques are set throughout the city; **Masjid India** and **Masjid Lama Tandar Taiping**, built in 1893, are among the loveliest. The Chinese temple is **Seng Tong Temple**, while the Indian population worships at **Sri Nagamuthu Mariammam Temple**, dedicated to the Hindu rain god. Taiping has the highest rainfall of any West Malaysian city, proof perhaps of this god's effectiveness.

By 1883, Hugh Low had already founded the country's first museum. Opposite the jail on Jl. Muzium, the **Muzium Perak** is rich in historical documents and interesting collections that shed light on Malayan culture and the crafts of the Orang Asli who live in the region. Other colonial buildings of note are the **New Club**, built in 1894; the wooden **All Saints Church**; **King Edward School**; and **St. George's School**.

Above: Blossoms in the Lake Gardens of Taiping.

Lake Gardens, laid out in an abandoned tin mine east of the city center, was a popular spot as early as 1890. The 155-acre (62 ha) park is abloom with color and has a lovely lake full of fish as well as the small but beautiful **Taiping Zoo**. Animal lovers shouldn't miss the **Kuala Gula Bird Sanctuary**, 15 miles (24 km) out of Taiping. As well as rare birds, the park has monkeys, snakes, and dolphins.

Malay and Chinese fishermen have divided the small coastal village of **Kuala Gula** into two halves, each representative of its distinct culture. The last sight to greet the visitor on the Perak side of the border is the **Masjid Tinggi**, a tower-like wooden mosque built in 1877, near the village of Bagan Serai.

Kuala Sepetang, once named Port Weld, made headlines in 1988 when the Malaysian archaeologist Dr. Nick Hassan Shuhaimi unearthed the ruins of a 10th-century island settlement of pre-Islamic Malays in a mangrove swamp near the city. **Pulau Buloh** had first been mentioned in 1932 by an English member of the Royal Asiatic Society.

Maxwell Hill

Maxwell Hill is the oldest fresh-air spa in Malaysia. Located 6 miles (10 km) northeast of Taiping on the Gunung Hijau (Green Mountain), it was developed in the late 19th century by William Maxwell, a British resident of Perak. Japanese prisoners of war had to build the hairpin road that curves up to the resort at an altitude of 3,600 feet (1,100 m); even today, this road can only be navigated in a vehicle with four-wheel drive. Once you get to the top, you find that **Bukit Larut**, as it is now officially named, is a simple, not-too-luxurious recreation compound with bungalows, lodges, a golf course, and tasty meals in its restaurant. And you can't overlook the fabulous panorama out over Taiping, Penang and Pangkor.

HILL RESORTS
Accommodations
FRASER'S HILL: *MODERATE*: **Fraser's Pine Resort**, Fraser's Hill, Tel: 09-3622122. **Merlin**, Jl. Lady Guillemard, Tel: 09-3622300. **Ye Olde Smokehouse**, Tel: 09-3622226. *BUDGET*: **Puncak Inn**, Tel: 09-3622055.
CAMERON HIGHLANDS: *MODERATE*: **Fosters Lakehouse**, Ringlet, Tel: 05-4956152. **Ye Olde Smokehouse**, Tanah Rata, Tel: 05-4911215. **Strawberry Park**, Tanah Rata, Tel: 05-4911166. **Golf Course Inn**, Tanah Rata, Tel: 05-4911411. *BUDGET*: **Brinchang**, 36, Brinchang Town, Tel: 05-4911755. **Highland**, 29-32, Brinchang, Tel: 4911588. **Hollywood**, 38, Main Road, Tanah Rata, Tel: 05-4911633. **Lutheran Bungalows**, Tanah Rata, Tel: 05-4911584.
MAXWELL HILL: *BUDGET*: **Bukit Larut Resthouse**, **Speedy Resthouse**, **Bungalows**, Bukit Larut, Tel: 05-8077241 (Hill Superintendent in Bukit Larut, Taiping).

IPOH, KUALA KANGSAR, TAIPING
Getting there
There are **express buse**s from Kuala Lumpur **to Ipoh** (Medan Kido Terminal) and **Taiping** (Jl. Panggong Terminal), via **Kuala Kangsar** (Jl. Bendahara Terminal). All three towns are on the **K. L.-Butterworth** train line. **Kuala Kangsar Station** is on **Jl. Sultan Idris**, on the edge of the city. **MAS** has daily flights to Ipoh.

IPOH
Accommodations
LUXURY: **Royal Casuarina**, 18, Jl. Gopeng, Tel: 05-2555555. **Excelsior**, Clark St., Tel: 05-2536666. **Tambun Inn**, 91, Jl. Tambun, Tel: 05-2577211. **Meridien**, 2, Simpang Rd., Tel: 05-2551133. *MODERATE:* **City**, 79 Chamberlain Rd., Tel: 05-2512911. **Winner**, 32-38 Jl. Ali Pitchay, Tel: 05-2515177. **Perak**, Jl. Ali Pitchay, Tel: 05-2515011. **Diamond**, Jl. Ali Pitchay, Tel: 05-2513644. **New Kowloon**, Jl. Yang Kalsom, Tel: 05-500924. **Hollywood**, 72-76, Chamberlain Rd., Tel: 05-2415404. **Mikado**, 86-88, Jl. Yang Kalsom, Tel: 05-2555855. **Station**, Club Rd., Tel: 05-2512588. *BUDGET:* **Cathay**, 92-94, Jl. Chamberlain, Tel: 05-2513322. **New Ipoh**, 163, Jl. Sultan Idris Shah, Tel: 05-548663. **Mayflower**, 62, Jl. Raja Ekram, Tel: 05-2549407. **Casplan**, 6, Jl. Jubilee, Tel: 05-2542324. **YMCA of Ipoh**, 211, Jl. Raja Muda Aziz, Tel: 05-2540809.

Restaurants
CHINESE: **Public Seafood**, Pusing. **Overseas Restaurant**, opposite the Excelsior Hotel: **Moon Gate**, Jl. Datoh. **Ipoh Jaya**, Green Lane.

INDIAN/VEGETARIAN: **Sayur Sayuran**, Jl. Chung Thye Pin. **Restoran Krishna Bhawan**, Jl. Laxamana.

KUALA KANGSAR
Accommodations / Restaurants
BUDGET: **Tin Heong Hotel**, 34, Jl. Raja Chulan, Tel: 05-7662066. **Double Lion**, Hotel und Restaurant, 74, Jl. Kangsar, Tel: 05-7661010.
Kassim Restaurant, Jl. Doomg Setiti; the street also boasts a number of cookshacks.
Museums
Muzium Diraja Perak, Sat-Wed 9:30 am-5:30 pm, Thu 9:30 am-12:45 pm.

TAIPING
Accommodations
MODERATE: **Miramar**, 30, Jl. Peng Loong, Tel: 05-8071077/8. **Oriental Hotel**, 14, Jl. Berek, Tel: 05-8075433. **New Rest House**, Jl. Sultan Mansur, Tel: 05-8072571. *BUDGET:* **Kwong Onn Hotel**, 50, Jl. Eastern, Tel: 05-8073000. **Cheong Onn**, 24, Jl. Iskandar, Tel: 05-8072815. **Peace Hotel**, 30-32, Jl. Iskandar, Tel: 05-823379. **Wah Bee Hotel**, 62-64, Jl. Kota, Tel: 05-8072065.
Restaurants
Numerous restaurants & cookshacks on **Taman Selera** (Market), **Jl. Sultan Abdullah**, or the **Night Market** on Jl. Panggong Wayang.
Museums
Perak Museum, Mon-Sun 9:30 am-5:30 pm, Fri 9:30 am-12:15 pm and 2:45-5:00 pm.

PULAU PANGKOR
Getting there
Pelangi Air has several flights a day to Pangkor from K.L., Singapore and Penang.
Ferries run between **Lumut** and **Pangkor** daily every 20 minutes until 7:30 pm; and several times a day (until 6:30 pm) between **Lumut** and **Pansea Pangkor Laut**. Overnight stay in Lumut is cheaper than on the islands.
Accommodations
PANGKOR: *LUXURY:* **Pansea Pangkor Laut Resort**, Tel: 05-6851320. *MODERATE:* **Royal Bay Resort**, Pulau Pangkor Laut, Tel: (K. L.) 03-2423654. **Pan Pacific Resort**, Teluk Belanga, Pulau Pangkor, Tel: 05-6851399. **Sri Bayu Beach Resort**, Pantai Pasir Bogak, Pulau Pangkor, Tel: 05-6851929. **Sea View Hotel**, Pantai Pasir Bogak, Tel: 05-6851605. **Beach Huts Hotel**, Pantai Pasir Bogak, Tel: 05-6851159. *BUDGET:* **Government Rest House**, Pantai Pasir Bogak, Tel: 05-6851236. **LUMUT**: *LUXURY:* **The Orient Star**, Tel: 05-6834199, good Western cuisine. *BUDGET:* **Indah**, 208, Jl. Iskandar, Tel: 05-6835064

TEMPLE RUINS AND RICE FIELDS

KEDAH
PERLIS
LANGKAWI ARCHIPELAGO

The highway that connects Perak's cities to Butterworth and George Town passes through the southwest tip of Kedah. The state, with its 3,676 square miles (9,426 sq. km) of mostly flat land, is called the "rice bowl" of Malaysia. Malays predominate, making up 72 percent of the 1.2 million inhabitants; of the rest, 19 percent are Chinese, 8 percent Indian.

Kedah is the oldest state in the country. Its royal family traces its ancestry back more than 1000 years, to the days of Hindu rule. Ruins dating from this epoch have been found in the Bujang Valley; they are unique in Malaysia for their age alone. Located on a number of main trade routes, the Kedah region attracted settlers and conquerors very early in its history.

Today, it's the Langkawi Archipelago that attracts tourists. Politically, the archipelago belongs to Kedah; geographically, it lies off the coast of Perlis, closer to Thailand. This tiny state, the smallest in Malaysia, has had a turbulent history. It was handed back and forth between the Sultans of Kedah, Thailand (Siam), Britain and Japan, before finally becoming a part of the Malaysian Federation.

Left: The cupola of Balai Besar in Alor Setar shows Thai influence.

KEDAH: INDIA'S BRIDGEHEAD

India's involvement in Malaysia's history has its roots at the foot of the 3,980-foot (1,217 m) **Gunung Jerai**. Both Chinese and Sanskrit records from the 4th century A.D. recount that here, in the valley of the **Sungai Bujang**, a kingdom called Kalah developed and flourished. Its ruler was Djaba al Hindi, a prince of the Chola dynasty from south India. For hundreds of years, the wealth of the kingdom attracted merchant ships from east and west, as evidenced by finds of Phoenician glass and Chinese porcelain. The Chinese book of prophecy I Ching, which dates partly to A.D. 671, mentions Kalah, calling its harbor Kietcha.

At about this time, the Hindu kingdom of Srivijaya was beginning to expand. From the 7th to the 11th centuries, its influence spread from southern Sumatra across the Malay peninsula. At the apex of its power Kalah traded with Ligor, a city-state on the east coast of what is today modern Thailand. Ligor itself paid tribute to the King of Siam and later administered the areas of Kelantan, Kedah, Perak and Perlis on his behalf. Kedah's rulers managed to remain more or less independent until the early 19th century. Even after Kedah and Perlis became vassal states of Siam and then, after 1909,

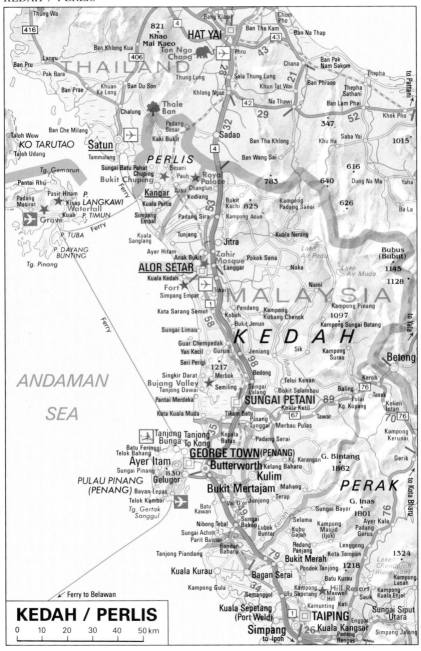

KEDAH / PERLIS

0   10   20   30   40   50 km

came under British colonial rule, the Sultans of Kedah managed to retain more sovereignty than most of the other governments on the peninsula.

As early as 1000 A.D. the Chola ruler Virirajendra I tried to conquer Kalah, which had by that time come under Malay influence. It is not clear if Malay-Hindu Madjapahites, who conquered Java and most of the Malay archipelago, contributed to the downfall of Kalah in the 13th century. In any case, Marco Polo, who sailed through the Straits of Malacca in 1292, makes no mention of Kalah.

Treasures on the Sungai Bujang

Close to the border between Penang and Kedah a road leads from the town of **Tikam Batu** to the coastal village of **Kota Kuala Muda**, ending on the beautiful **Pantai** (beach) **Merdeka**. The largest city in south Kedah is **Sungai Patani**; apart from a few colonial buildings clustered around a clock tower and a colorful vegetable market, however, this place has little to interestvisitors.

From there it is a short distance to **Bedong** or **Gurun**, from which you can explore the excavations at Gunung Jerai. Malaysian archeologists have restored more than 40 temple ruins. Vases, Arabian coins, jewels, statues and gold jewelry have been recovered; the oldest date back to the first century A.D.

To reach the excavations, take the street that leads off to the east between Bedong and **Merbok**. Signs direct you to the **Muzium Arkeologi Lembah Bujang**, the museum near the richest site, **Candi Bukit Batu Pahat**, at the edge of the jungle on the lower slopes of Gunung Jerai. Only the foundations remain of the temple and fortifications, which date from the 7th century. The nearby waterfall, today a popular place for picnics, may have served as a ritual bathing place dedicated, like the temple, to the god Shiva.

Another popular excursion is the ascent to the summit of **Gunung Jerai**. For those who would rather avoid the hike, there are four-wheel-drive vehicles to take visitors from **Guar Chempedak** up the 8 miles (13 km) of curving mountain road. On a clear day, you can see all the way to the north coast. There are a few chalets and a resthouse near the summit.

The coast also provides plenty of rest and relaxation. The fishing village of **Yan** has a lovely beach and is a good starting point for exploring the **Taman Rekreasi Batu Hampar**, a wooded area full of inviting hiking trails. At **Seri Perigi**, reachable from Yan Kecil, the trails lead to romantic waterfalls.

War and Peace on the Kedah Coast

The coastal road passes through **Sungai Limau** – where the mosque **Masjid Sultan Abdul Halim Muadzam Shah** is worth seeing – on the way to the fishing village of **Kuala Kedah**, ferry port for the Langkawi islands. The village has many seafood restaurants serving all manner of delicacies. The fort, now in ruins, was built in the 16th century and fortified in 1770 in anticipation of an attack from Siam. One year later, in the same fort, Sultan Abdullah of Kedah sealed an agreement with Britain ceding ownership of Penang Island to the colonial power. The Siamese waited to attack until 1821; and when they did so, it came completely by surprise. 20 years of Thai rule followed.

The Elegant Capital

Alor Setar, the capital of Kedah, lies 7.5 miles (12 km) inland. In the past few years, it has developed into the economic center of the northwestern part of the peninsula. Most of the interesting sights are in the city center. Prominent among them is **Masjid Zahir**, built in 1912 and considered one of the most beautiful mos-

ques in Malaysia. Especially graceful is the effect of its filigree arches and decorated columns under the sober domes.

Opposite the mosque, the **Balai Besar** (Great Hall), built in 1898, demonstrates the influence of Siamese architecture. It is where the Sultan of Kedah holds audiences on his birthday or on other important occasions. Behind it is the **Old Sultan's Palace** where Tunku Abdul Rahman, the "Father of Malaysia," was born in 1903. The residence of the present Sultan is about 2 miles (3 km) north of the city center at **Anak Bukit**.

Balai Nobat, home of the royal orchestra, also shows the effects of long years of Thai rule. The three-storey tower houses a gong, three drums and a trumpet; these special instruments are used only in coronation ceremonies or on other equally important occasions. Visits to the tower must be approved by the secretary of the *nobat*.

Above: the Zahir Mosque in Alor Setar is a jewel of Islamic religious architecture.

The **Wisma Negari** (House of State) is built in contemporary Islamic style, in contrast to the **Supreme Court**, which is a neoclassical building. The **State Museum**, 1.5 miles (2.5 km) north of the city, was designed to resemble the Balai Besar. It contains valuable artifacts from excavations in Kedah. Wednesday is the day to visit **Pekan Rabu** (Wednesday Market), a colorful and lively local market in Alor Setar.

In the Hinterland of Kedah

The former Sultans of Kedah are interred in an ornate mausoleum in **Langgar**, fewer than 6 miles (10 km) east of the capital city. Two rivers join in rather picturesque fashion some 20 miles (33 km) northeast of Alor Setar in **Kuala Nerang**, a village with many inhabitants of Thai origin.

Anyone interested in *Ma'Yong* (or *Mak Yong*) that traditional Thai-Malayan art form, which combines ballet, opera, drama and comedy, should travel through

Pokok Sena and the rugged mountain landscape to Nami, one of the centers of the art. Apart from Pokok Sena, the only area where *Ma'Yong* is really popular is Kelantan.

PERLIS

Broad rice paddies and strangely-shaped limestone formations characterize the landscape of Perlis. It is the northernmost and smallest state in Malaysia, with only 310 square miles (795 sq. km). Thanks to intensive agricultural development, its 175,000 inhabitants produce high yields of rice and sugar, a great deal of rubber, and the best-tasting mangoes in the country. The coastal villages subsist on fishing, providing Perlis with its other most important product. About 78 percent of the inhabitants are Malays, while 17 percent trace their origin to China.

Originally, Perlis was a part of Kedah, and was therefore also taken over by Siam (modern Thailand) in 1821. When Kedah regained its sovereignty in 1842, Perlis was separated from it and kept as a buffer state governed by Siam. In 1909, it was turned over to the British; in World War II, the Japanese again assigned it to the Thais; and finally, when the British returned in 1945, the tiny state became a member of the Malaysian Federation.

Travelers coming from Kedah can reach Perlis along the coastal road via Simpang Empat, or by rail through the old royal city of Arau. The present Raja still lives in the Istana Arau, the old royal palace. The modern State Mosque is also well worth a look. Another mosque, the Masjid Sayid Alwi, built in 1910, is the main ornament of Kangar, the capital of Perlis with 25,000 inhabitants, just 6 miles (10 km) away from Arau.

Kuala Perlis, at the mouth of the Sungai Perlis, is the departure point for ferries to the Langkawi Islands and to Thailand. The town also has a lively market and plenty of good restaurants in the harbor area serving fresh fish.

The overland route to Thailand passes through Sungai Batu Pahat where, 6 miles (10 km) from the capital, there is a snake farm called Taman Ular. It is the only one of its kind in Malaysia. Rest assured that the snakes are kept in secure enclosures; after all, no one wants to endanger players on the nearby nine-hole golf course.

Chuping, 9 miles (15 km) northwest of Kangar, is an industrial area surrounded by sugar cane plantations. Other notable features of the region's landscape include limestone cliffs up to 490 feet (150 m) in height, and giant anthills, as tall as a man, in the middle of the rice paddies. Historical finds were unearthed at Bukit Chuping: tools of bone dating from the Stone Age.

A subterranean attraction is the cave of Kaki Bukit, a former tin mine 18.5 miles (30 km) north of Kangar. The inoperative mine here is not as interesting as the 1,300-foot (400 m) passage through the Gua Kelam (Dark Cave), where electric lighting illuminates stalactites and stalagmites.

Padang Besar, the northernmost town in Malaysia, is the last stop on the journey through Perlis. There is a lively traffic of peddlers near the border, and many Malaysians go there to shop for goods at bargain prices, as it's the customs depot for international express trains, which have to stop in Padang Besar before crossing the bridge from Malaysia to Thailand.

THE LANGKAWI ARCHIPELAGO

The archipelago at the northern end of the Straits of Malacca is made up of 99 islands. Since the 1980s the main island, Pulau Langkawi, has been known as a tourist mecca mainly in the German-

speaking countries. Geologists and botanists, however, were always fascinated by this island group in the Andaman Sea. The islands, today a part of the state of Kedah, emerged from the sea in the Cambrian period, some 500 million years ago; some of them then sank back into the depths. Independently of one another, the remaining islands proceeded to develop forms of plant life that are found nowhere else in the world. Long before botanists discovered them, the islands, surrounded by dangerous currents, were a favorite haunt of pirates. For hundreds of years, they used them as a strategic hiding place, thanks to their convenient proximity to the Straits of Malacca, for attacks on shipping passing through the busy waterway.

Siamese lords, too, were not above an attack on the archipelago now and again. And of the many German tourists who

Above: Before the Pantai Pasir Hitam, fishing boats are still in action despite heavy tourist traffic.

visit Langkawi today, few are aware that Germany once tried to establish an imperial colony there, but was prevented from doing so at the last minute. The Sultan of Kedah had already pledged the German Consul in Penang use of the islands as a naval station in the tense period preceding World War I; but the British invaded before the papers could be signed. The disappointed Consul was forced to leave without his treaty, which is still on file in the police archives of Alor Setar. In the 20th century, the islands, despite having the best beaches and diving sites in Malaysia, slipped into a sleepy oblivion that only ended with the rise of organized tourism.

The dreamy provincial quality of Langkawi Island, the main island, has in many places given way to the ideals of a tourist paradise. Hotel complexes are replacing the modest thatched huts; bumpy dirt tracks have been replaced by new asphalt roads circumnavigating the island. Souvenir shops and discos have sprung up in fishing villages, and the new airport is being built with jumbo-jet capacity landing strips.

But mass tourism has yet to materialize as expected. In an effort to attract more foreign currency in 1987, the government made Langkawi a duty-free zone for anyone who spends more than 72 hours on the island. In this way, officials hope to encourage visitors who come to stock up on electronic gadgets, alcohol and cigarettes to discover Langkawi's wide range of recreational facilities. Ironically, billboards along the roadsides announce alcohol as the source of all evil!

Around the Island

As the onslaught of tourism has yet to arrive in full force, there are still many parts of the 187-square-mile (480 sq. km) island, which are at a safe distance from the hotel complexes and golf courses and have preserved their traditional leisurely pace of life. Ferries from Kuala Perlis take approximately 90 minutes to reach the port of **Kuah**. On the way from the slip to town, you proceed in style along a street of marble; to build the road, rubble and chips were used from the island's famous quarry. Close by, the exclusive **Langkawi Island Resort** was built in an idyllic setting. Palm trees line the beach and the sea is dotted with the silhouettes of other islands; especially at sunset, this spot fits most peoples' dreams of an island paradise.

Kuah, the administrative capital, is a town of 3,000 inhabitants. It stretches for more than a mile (2 km) along the southeastern coast of the island. Hotels, restaurants and souvenir shops give an indication of the town's ambitions for the future, while the wrecks of fishing boats in the bay and the Moorish-style mosque remind visitors of its past. Equally traditional are the houses on stilts rising out of the lush green foliage. Palms, local plants and imported fruit trees make up the vegetation. Since 1879, rubber has been

LANGKAWI

0   5   10km

cultivated in plantations on these former spice islands.

A reminder of a great miscarriage of justice lies 7.5 miles (12 km) west of Kuah: Princess Mahsuri. The white sarcophagus of **Maham Mahsuri** is the final resting-place of this unfortunate princess from the village of Ulu Melaba, who was sentenced to death for committing adultery. That she was in fact not guilty was shown by the color of her blood at her execution: it was not red, but white, the color of innocence. According to the inscription on her tomb, Princess Mahsuri did have time to place a seven-generation curse on the island before dying.

As if in response, the Thais attacked, an event which is still remembered at the village of **Padang Matsirat**, 4 miles (7 km) from Maham Mahsuri. There, the villagers burned their entire rice crop rather than let it fall into the hands of the enemy. Signs mark the field of **Padang Beras Terbakar** (Field of Burnt Rice), where carbonized grains of rice are still sometimes found under the soil.

The forest park of **Rimba Rekreasi**, which lies inland, makes a good starting point for hikes to the summit of **Gunung Raya**, Langkawi's highest mountain (2,943 feet/900 m). A well-improved road goes from the fishing village of **Kuala Teriang** on the west coast, past the **Pantai Cenang International Airport**, to the village of **Pantai Cenang**. The stretch of coast along here has a number of lovely beaches, all of which face the sunset. The prime address here is the **Pelangi Beach Resort**. Nearby, a large **aquarium** was recently built.

Telaga Tujuh (Seven Fountains), which is fed by a white-water river plunging down into the valley over 288-ft-high (90 m) cascades flowing between sheer cliffs, lies 5 miles (8 km) to the west of Kuala Teriang. It consists of seven natural pools in which you can take refreshing baths. The immediate surrounding jungle can be investigated on foot.

Route 13 begins at **Pantai Kok**, one of Langkawi's most beautiful beaches. **Taman Buaya**, a crocodile farm, comes up a a few miles away. It boasts a large number of attractions, including a display pond featuring fights between man and croc (open daily from 9 am to 5 pm).

Route 13 then continues on to **Pantai Pasir Hitam**, a beach covered in gleaming black sand. Further east, taking Route K 33 at the fork, lies **Tanjung Rhu**, a white sand beach lined with Casuarina trees. *Ikan bilis*, the tiny fish that gives the distinctive flavor to so much of Malaysian cuisine, are often spread out to dry on the beach. The neighboring islands of **Pasir**, **Gasing** and **Dangli** are accessible on foot at low tide.

Gua Cerita (Cave of Legends) is burrowed in a spit of land only reachable by boat. Verses from the Koran have been chiseled into the walls of the cave in the old script. Having come this far, it is best to continue by crossing the mangrove marsh and visiting the nearby bat cave.

A newly-built tourist attraction near **Telaga Air Hangat** (Hot Springs) is located off the main return road recreational complex was put together on a 5-acre tract of land. The water from the hot springs bubbles out of a three-part fountain. The legends of Air Hangat have been chiseled into a 58-ft (18 m) stone panel. A day-long open-air entertainment program includes, among other things, folk dances, traditional sports, games, performances of old Malay customs and demonstrations of traditional handicrafts. Visitors are also invited to participate in village life, e.g., planting rice in a paddy (daily 9 am-6 pm).

The idyllic waterfall of **Durian Perangin** is a mere 2 miles (3.5 km) away. It plunges into a crystal-clear lake, producing a cloud of fine mist.

The Neighboring Islands

The island of **Dayang Bunting** to the south, with its lake of the same name, is an especially interesting place to visit. The story goes that a woman who longed to have her own child for 19 years drank the lake water and miraculously became pregnant; hence the origin of the name "Lake of the Pregnant Woman," and its reputation for fertility. But the attractions of the beautiful island and its picturesque lake are not restricted to childless couples. There is also the 300-foot (91 m) "ghost cave," **Gua Langsir**, filled with bats. Marble from the quarry of **Pulau Dayang Bunting**, in the middle of a thick jungle, is famous all over Malaysia.

The tiny nearby islands of **Pulau Singa Besar** and **Pulau Beras Besah** attract divers and snorkelers. Even more spectacular diving is to be found at the marine sanctuary of **Pulau Paya**. The island, 25 miles (40 km) south of Langkawi, is reputed to have the best coral reef in Malaysia; however, all visits must be approved by the Department of Fisheries in Alor Setar.

STATE OF KEDAH
ALOR SETAR
Getting there / Transportation

BY AIR: **MAS** has regular flights between **Kuala Lumpur, Kota Bharu** and **Alor Setar** (the airport is about 7 miles/11 km outside the city). Small planes run between **Alor** and **Langkawi**.

BUS: **Express busses** leave the bus terminal on the corner of Jl. Langgar and Jl. Stesyen for **K. Kedah, Kota Bharu** via **Gerik**, and to **Ipoh, Kuala Lumpur, Kuala Perlis, Penang, Singapore**. Closer destinations include **K. Kedah, Guar Chempedak, or Gunung Jerai Junction**. Taxis (to share) wait at the bus terminal and train station.

BY TRAIN: The main **railway station** (Tel: 04-7321798) is on Jl. Stesyen / Jl. Langgar. The express train from **Bangkok** to **Butterworth** stops here several times a week. There are daily trains (Railbus) to **Arau** and Butterworth, and local trains to **Guar Chempedak, Gurun, Sungai Patani**.

Accommodations

LUXURY: **Grand Continental**, 134, Jl. Sultan Badlishah, Tel: 04-7335917. **Merlin Inn Kedah**, Lot 134-141, Jl. Sultan Badlishah, Tel: 04-7335917. **Samila Hotel**, 27, Jl. Kanchut, Tel: 04-7322344. **Regent Hotel**, 1536, Jl. Sultan Badlishah, Tel: 04-7311900. *MODERATE:* **Federal Hotel**, 429, Jl. Kanchut, Tel: 04-7330055. **Putra Jaya**, 240 B, Jl. Putra, Tel: 04-7330344. **Mahawangsa**, 449, Jl. Raja, Tel: 04-7321433. *BUDGET:* **Resthouse**, 75, Pumpong, Tel: 04-7322422. **Station Hotel**, 74, Jl. Langgar, Tel: 04-7333855. **Tai Hock**, 1. Limbong Kapal, Tel: 04-7332301. **Mandarin**, 109-111, Pekan China, Tel: 04-7321321.

Restaurants

MALAY: in Leong Huat, Jl. Tungku Ibrahim. *INDIAN:* on Jl. Langgar and at cookshacks behind the bus terminal.

Museums

Muzium Alor Setar, 1.5 miles (2.5 km) north, open daily 9:00 am-5:00 pm, Fri. 9:00 am-12:15 pm.

GUNUNG JERAI
Accommodations / Museum

KEDAK PEAK: *BUDGET:* **Resthouse**, reservations: Tel: 04-462046. **BUJANG VALLEY: Muzium Arkeologi Lembang Bujang**, open daily 9:30 am-5:00 pm, closed Fri from 12:15-2:45 pm.

STATE OF PERLIS
KANGAR
Accommodations

BUDGET: **Pens Hotel**, 135, Jl. Kangar, Tel: 04-9854122. **Federal Hotel**, 104 A&B, Jl. Kangar, Tel: 04-9766288.

Transportation

BUS: Buses leave from the terminal on Jl. Kangar.

KUALA PERLIS
Accommodations / Restaurants

BUDGET: **Pens Hotel**, Jl. Kuala Perlis, Tel: 04-754122. There are also many seafood restaurants.

Transportation

*BY BOAT:*Nearly hourly ferries from **Kuala Perlis** to **Langkawi**, Thai boats also run to **Satun/Thailand**; the trip takes about an hour and a half.

LANGKAWI ISLAND
Getting there / Transportation

BY AIR: **MAS** has daily flights from **Kuala Lumpur** or **Penang** to **Langkawi**. Flights are also available from Bangkok and Singapore.

BY BOAT: Ferries from **Kuala Perlis**, Tel: 04-9854406, and from Kuala Kedah, Tel: 04-7621201. Crossing time about 2 hours depending on weather conditions. **Express boats**, including hovercraft, take from 20 to at most 45 minutes. Ferries also shuttle from Georgetown/Penang.

There are **buses** on Langkawi, but they're not always reliable. It is better to take a taxi if you do not wish to investigate the island by bicycle or moped. **Motorbike** and **bicycle rentals** are very frequent on the island. You can also rent boats to get to the surrounding islands, but only with a driver.

Accommodations

LUXURY: **Sheraton Langkawi Island Resort**, Teluk Nibong, Tel: 04-9551901. **Pelangi Beach Resort**, Pantai Cenang, Tel: 04-9551001. **Langkawi Holiday Villa**, Pantai Tengah, Tel: 04-9551701. **Langkawi Village Resort**, Pantai Tengah, Tel: 04-9551511. **Langkawi Island Resort**, Pantai Syed Omar, Tel: 04-9666209. **Mutiara Beach Resort**, Pantai Tanjong Rhu, Tel: 04-9591091. *MODERATE:* **Sri Legenda Garden Resort**, Tel: 04-9668918. **Burau Bay Resort**, Tel: 04-9551601. **Aseana Seaview Resort**, Tel: 04-9552020. **Hotel Central**, 33 Persiaran Putera, Tel: 04-9668585. **Langkawi Seaview Hotel**, Tel: 04-9660600. *BUDGET:* **Asia Hotel**, 1 Jl. P. Putra, Kuah, Tel: 04-9666216. **Langkasuka Hotel**, Kuah, Tel: 04-9666828. **Beach Garden Resort**, Pantai Cenang. **Langkawi Hotel**, Kuah, Tel: 04-916248. **Sandy Beach**, Pantai Cenang, Tel: 04-9551363. **Inapan Desa Permai**, Kg. Padang Wahid, Mukim Kedawang, Tel: 04-9551086.

Restaurants

Apart from resort and hotel restaurants, there are many cookshacks in **Kuah**: in **Taman Selera** near the mosque and around the fish market. At the market and along the coastal road, restaurants include **Malaysia** (Indian cuisine), **Weng Fu Restaurant** (delicious fish dishes); good Chinese food at **Golden Dragon** and the **Asia Hotel**.

THE ISLAND OF BETEL NUTS

PENANG
GEORGE TOWN
EXCURSIONS ON PENANG

PENANG

Tourist brochures and travel books outdo each other in their attempts to describe the fabled beauty of Penang. It is the "land of the gods," "the emerald isle," an "idyll under the sun," or the "pearl of the Orient." The locals take the praise in stride, and call it simply *Pulau Pinang*, the "island of betel nuts." Whether Penang is the subject of too much praise or too little is open to debate, but one thing is certain. The charm of the 402-square-mile (1,031 sq. km) state, which includes the three neighboring islands of Pulau Tikus, Pulau Rimau, Pulau Jerejak, as well as the region around Butterworth on the mainland, has attracted travelers and businessmen from all over the world for more than 200 years.

More than half (55 percent) of Penang's approximately 1.5 million inhabitants are Chinese. Malays follow with some 35 percent; the rest are Indians or Europeans.

The European who claimed the 112-square-mile (286 sq. km) island for the British East India Company on August 11, 1786, was Captain Francis Light. He believed he had discovered Paradise – or

Left: Kek Lok Si, the Temple of 10,000 Buddhas in the west of George Town.

at the very least, a convenient stopover for ships in the lucrative China trade.

Until then Penang, known as *Pulau Ka Satu* (the solitary island), was the home of a few families of Malay fishermen and the hideout of the much-feared pirates who terrorized the coastal region. It was under the control of Sultan Abdullah of Kedah, who eventually traded Penang to Captain Light and the British East India Company in exchange for protection against the Kingdom of Siam and the Bugis. Francis Light founded George Town and named it in honor of King George III (1738-1820). Sultan Abdullah soon realized he had been cheated when the British refused to send him weapons to help him in the war against Siam. Furious, he demanded the immediate return of Penang and the prompt departure of its British settlers.

That was about the last thing England had in mind. Abdullah attacked Penang in March, 1791, but was unsuccessful against Britain's superior weapons, and was ultimately forced to concede the British possession of the island. The far-sighted Captain Light named the promising territory "Prince of Wales Island" in honor of the British heir to the throne, the future George IV, whose birthday happened to coincide with Light's first landing on the island.

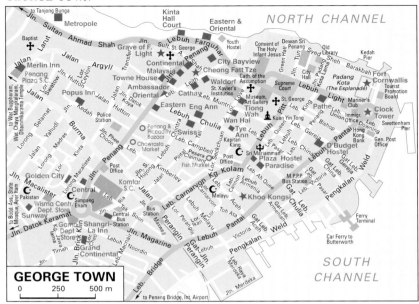

GEORGE TOWN

0   250   500 m

    Later, the East India Company received additional territory on the mainland between the Muda and Kerian rivers and named this area "Wellesley Province" after the Governor General of India.

    At first nearly uninhabited, the island soon attracted new settlers. Francis Light opened the harbor to international shipping traffic. Tax-free status and a general, open invitation to settle in Penang and build up the island's economy helped to create an active business climate and economic prosperity. Chinese, mainly from the province of Fukien, and Indians arrives; Malays from the peninsula and people from Sumatra also settled the island. Fortunes were made in the pepper trade with North Sumatra, as well as by smuggling tin out of Perak and Selangor where the Dutch still held power.

    The British brought Penang into the Straits Settlements and it was not long before it was known far and wide as a fashionable destination for vacationing colonial officials and their families.

    During World War One, Penang's strategic location even drew the attention of the German Kaiser's Navy. A small cruiser called *Emden* attacked Penang in October 1914 and sank one French and one Russian ship.

    When Malaysia became independent, the island and Wellesley Province were united under a Malay name and became Malaysia's 13th state, Penang. Since then, efforts have been made to relocate the island's rapid population growth to the mainland, where new housing and industrial development have been promised. Pulau Penang's reputation as the "pearl of the Orient" is not to be endangered by a population explosion.

GEORGE TOWN

    The best way to reach Penang is to fly directly to **Bayan Lepas Airport**, 10 miles (16 km) south of the city center.

Right: A cannon still stands guard at Fort Cornwallis in George Town.

94

The alternative is to reach it from the industrial – and for tourists uninteresting – port city of **Butterworth** on the mainland. From here, a toll road crosses the 8-mile-long (13.5 km) **Penang Bridge**, the longest bridge in Asia and third-longest in the world. This incredibly expensive bridge was built to last for 400 years and withstand earthquakes registering up to 7.5 on the Richter scale.

The only other way to reach Penang is aboard one of the ferries that shuttle between Butterworth and Pulau Pinang and service the trains arriving from Kuala Lumpur and Thailand at the Butterworth dock.

Most of the 650,000 inhabitants of Penang now live in its cosmopolitan capital city that spreads along the east coast of the island. **George Town** is the clear cultural and historic heart of the province. An impressive attraction, nearly unchanged over the years, is the old British city center, which managed to survive the rebuilding boom of the 1920s and 30s and still stands primly at the heart of the chaotic and sometimes downright filthy downtown area. Here and there English street signs have been rewritten in Malay, but, unlike Kuala Lumpur, George Town has preserved its colonial past without resorting to architectural cosmetic surgery. It is to be hoped that its status as a historic city will justify the continued maintenance and restoration of the colonial buildings, most of which are privately owned. Opponents of a thorough restoration, Singapore-style, maintain that their colonial charm is more attractive to tourists even than the island's beaches.

Fort Cornwallis is on what is now known as **Kedah Pier**, where Captain Francis Light first landed in 1786. It takes its name from the Governor General of India at the time the fort was built; and it was *sepoys*, or Indian prisoners, who built the stone walls between 1804 and 1810 to replace an earlier

fort made of wood. The cannon, cast in Holland and named **Seri Rambai**, still guards the fort. Light had it filled with silver coins and fired into the nearby jungle as motivation and pre-payment for the building of the fort. The *sepoys* combed the jungle looking for the silver; little by little, they cleared the jungle in the process.

In addition to its military function, the cannon is popularly believed to possess magical powers. Its pedestal is often decked with flowers and incense sticks placed there by childless Chinese women who offer them to the mighty gun's barrel in hopes of getting pregnant. The interior of the fort is now used as an open-air theater.

Nearby is the **Padang Kota** park, also known as the **Esplanade**, where Penang residents come in the evenings and on weekends to relax. Fort Cornwallis and Padang Kota park are bordered by Jl. Padang Kota, Tun Syed Sheh Barakbah and Lebuh Light.

Captain Light, the founder of George Town, is buried near the intersection of

Lebuh Farquhar and Jl. Sultan Ahmad Shah; and he's also been immortalized in a statue in front of the **Muzium Pulau Penang** (Penang Museum and Art Gallery) on Lebuh Farquhar. The museum is housed in the building of the "Penang Free School," on Lorong Love; the school, which operated between 1907 and 1965, was the first on the island to teach Malay as well as European children. Tourists would also be well advised to learn the lessons of the area's history in this ornate colonial building before setting out to explore therest of the island.

The museum is in the middle of Penang's past and present administrative center, between Lebuh Farquhar and Lebuh Light, where the surrounding buildings bear silent testimony to the era of British colonial rule. Here stand the **George Town City Council**, the **Dewan Sri Penang** (Old Parliament) the **Supreme Court**, the former **Mariner's Club**, the **Old Penang Library**. Another school, highly regarded since colonial times, is **St. Xavier's Institution**; the Protestant **St. George's Church**, built in 1819, and the Catholic **Cathedral of the Assumption** are also located along Farquhar Street. The 59-foot (18 m) **Clock Tower** near Fort Cornwallis was the gift of Cheah Chin Gok, a Chinese millionaire who had it built in 1897 in commemoration of the 60th anniversary of Queen Victoria's coronation.

The magnificent Victorian edifice of the **Eastern and Oriental Hotel** has been luring visitors to Penang for more than 100 years. Familiarly known as the E & O, the hotel was built on Lebuh Farquhar in 1885 and remains one of the few classic colonial hotels left in East Asia. While not quite as modernized as its "sister" hotels, the Oriental in Bangkok or the Raffles in Singapore, the E & O has retained both its nostalgic flavor and its status as Asia's longest promenade hotel. Rudyard Kipling often drank in its **1889**

Above: A little chat with a street peddler.

Bar. Somerset Maugham preferred the ground-floor suite, where well-heeled guests can stay to this day.

If you'd like to see the graves of some former hotel guests, visit the **English Cemetery** that lies on the road between the city center and the E & O. Here, as well as colonial soldiers and their families, lie sailors, merchants and other emigrés.

The Chinese of Penang

As in every large Malaysian city, the **Shop Houses**, or old stores of the Chinese merchants, are part and parcel of any tourist itinerary. Their stucco-decorated pastel façades have a pleasing, even graceful uniformity. And they always conceal something worth discovering behind them – be it a shop selling Chinese handicrafts, a traditional Chinese pharmacy mixing ancient remedies, or the workshop of a coffin maker. The oldest Chinese house in Penang is the **Cheong Fatt Tze** on Lebuh Leith, about 200 years old.

Impossible to ignore is the 65-story cylinder of the **Komtar** (Komplex Tunku Abdul Rahman) building, which, along with the Penang Bridge, stands as a symbol of the new George Town. Shops take up the lower floors while restaurants and offices have space above. The view from the top is what most people step in for: All of George Town is spread out at your feet, and on a clear day you can see as far as Kedah Peak on the mainland.

The economic clout of Penang's Chinese population is nowhere better visible than in the clan houses or *Kongsi*. The *Kongsi* is the meeting place for the entire clan: all members of a family, that is, people who share a common last name. As clans traditionally live at odds with one another, entering another clan's *Kongsi* is strictly taboo.

A fabulous sight, and unquestionably the most beautiful clan house in Penang, is **Khoo Kongsi** on Cannon Square,

reachable by way of Lebuh Pitt and Lebuh Cannon. The richly-decorated building from 1902 remains a striking monument to the influential Straits Chinese Khoo family who built it. It was, in fact, their second attempt: their first *Kongsi*, built in 1898, burnt down shortly after it was inaugurated. Its splendor was supposed to have made the gods jealous and the Chinese Emperor furious because the house was simply too grand for mere mortals. In fact, the present structure is still astounding and could well awaken both divine and earthly envy. There is nothing in all of Malaysia to compare with the fine, detailed sculptures with their glazed dragons along the roof, nor with the carved and gold-leafed ceiling beams.

Other clan houses dot the city: the **Yeoh Kongsi** in Lebuh Chulia, the **Ong Kongsi** in Jl. Penang or the **Kongsi** of the **Khaw** and **Lee** families on Jl. Burma. A rare glimpse into the daily lives of the clans is possible on **Pengkalan Weld**, or Weld Quay, near the ferry slip. The families of the Lim and Chew clan live there in settlements of pile houses built out over the water. Their main street is the gangplank that leads to a wooden walkway between the houses and shops. Considerate tourists are welcome to walk around, but for members of other clans, access is strictly forbidden.

Temples and Mosques

Penang, the religious capital of Malaysia's Chinese population, offers a rich selection of important temples for Buddhist worshippers; they are also noteworthy for foreign visitors interested in religious architecture because of the strong Thai influence evident in their design and construction. A seven-storey pagoda crowns the temple of the **Penang Buddhist Association**, an organization dedicated to propagating the true faith. The splendid altar is made of Chinese hardwood and

white marble. Statues of Buddha and his followers are also carved in marble.

Very close by is the **Wat Buppharam** on Jl. Perak. This 19th-century temple is characterized by two 98-foot-high (30 m) stone *nagas*, or seven-headed snakes, who guard the entrance. Worshippers pray to the two oversized Buddhas inside the pagoda.

The grandeur of the homes along the coastal road to the northwest have given it the name **Street of Millionaires**. To get there, go to Jl. Sultan Ahmad Shah, which is not far from Jl. Kelawai. The Thai temple complex of **Wat Chaya Mangkalaram** is just beyond the intersection with Jl. Burma. Protected by temple guard figures (*yak*), *naga* and half-bird, half-girl figures (*kinnara*), the huge statue of the reclining Buddha dominates the temple's interior. It is 105

Above: The clan house of the Chinese Khoo family in George Town. Right: Reclining Buddha in the temple complex of Chaya Mangkalaram.

feet (32 m) long, the third-largest statue of its type in the world. The Buddha, a votive offering to the temple from its worshippers, has received a thick coat of gold leaf.

The **Dhammikarama Burmese Temple** is also on Jl. Burma. Itis in face relatively new, having been built in 1965 entirely in the traditional Burmese style, down to the two white stone elephants guarding the entrance. Both temples are in a neighborhood with a number of beautiful villas from the colonial period.

Even more than the splendor of colonial times, Chinese baroque has exerted a great influence on George Town's architecture. The oldest Buddhist temple on Penang is on Lebuh Pitt: **Kuan Yin Tong**, built in 1830 and dedicated to the goddess of mercy Kuan Ying. This 18-armed deity is especially popular with "common" believers: housewives, street peddlers, shoe shiners and rickshaw drivers of the city. Kuan Ying is the only *bodhisattva*, equal to Buddha in the Chinese pantheon: a being who refuses to

enter Nirvana as long as there is injustice in the world. She would rather stand by those who must continue to wait for enlightenment. Even non-Buddhists are impressed by the sight of the humble worshippers in the smoky interior of the temple. Day and night, the huge incense spirals burn while worshippers clap with their fortune sticks to call the goddess of mercy to their aid on their difficult path through life.

Another goddess in the neighborhood holds court in the **Sri Mariamman Temple** on Lebuh Pitt. Built in 1883, the religious center of Penang's Indian population is devoted to Sri Maha Mariamman, the mother of all Hindu gods. The richly-decorated façade over the entrance door depicts the tower-like *gopuram* of myriad Hindu deities, artistically carved in stone.

Inside the temple, the tones of drums and flutes rise into the air, while in the evening women break coconuts on the ground to pray for fertility. At the *Thaipusam* festival, the Lord God Su-

ramaniam has his great day when men slash their bodies with spears and hooks in the frenzy of worship.

The Moslem faith has created the third great house of worship on Lebuh Pitt. The **Captain Kling Mosque** was built in 1800 by the wealthy Indian merchant Cander Mohudeen, who was at the time a "Captain" or community leader. The mosque is inspired by Indian architecture but decorated with Moorish motifs. Its splendor is somewhat misleading in that Moslems remain in the minority in Penang, both socially and politically. Although Moslems were here before the Chinese and Hindus arrived, they were gradually forced out toward the coast; there, they live as fishermen or spice farmers. In George Town, (Moslem) Malays form a large part of the city's unskilled labor force.

Moslems also worship at the **Masjid Melayu** in Lebuh Aceh, built in 1820, as well as in the **National Mosque** in the west of the city. This modern structure on Jl. Mesjid Negeri is fitted out with gold domes over the main hall as well as minarets; it can accommodate more than 5,000 worshippers.

The city bus line that runs past the mosque continues through the suburb of Ayer Itam (Black Water) **to Kek Lok Si**, a temple known as the "Paradise in the West." This temple of 10,000 Buddhas, built in 1890, is the largest and reputedly the most beautiful Buddhist temple in Southeast Asia. It rises up the side of a hill by a series of terraces.

Its architectural and religious high point is the 98-foot (30 m), seven-story **Ban Hood Pagoda** added in 1930, a masterpiece of Asian architecture. The octagonal base of the temple is Chinese in origin; the middle section is typically Thai; and the unusual peak of the pagoda shows distinct Burmese influence. Inside, The Enlightened One is depicted in gold, and there is also a collection of his relics. In their niches are the images of the 10,000 Buddhas, many painted on wall tiles.

The main altar is dedicated to the goddess of mercy, Kuan Yin, shown surrounded by 24 saints and kings of heaven. An important site of pilgrimage for Buddhists, the temple complex also has a library, monastery, prayer rooms and a pond full of sacred turtles; feeding these last is supposed to be an aid to long life.

Souvenir stands and peddlers of devotional items compete for the pilgrim's, and visitor's, business. Few souvenirs, however, can live up to the memory of the climb up the 152 steps of the temple, and the breathtaking view of west George Town seen from the top.

The street at the foot of the temple complex continues to the man-made lake of **Ayer Itam**, the Penang's main water reservoir.

Right: In the Snake Temple of Penang, one of the island's most unique sights.

EXCURSIONS ON PENANG

The Penang Hills were already a popular vacation spot in colonial times. At 2,714 feet (830 m), they are the highest point on the island. But it wasn't until 1923 that the "funicular railway," a cogwheel train, could finally start operations, with a little help from Swiss technology, after the first attempt with a steam turbine engine had failed.

The steep ascent begins at the ground station in **Ayer Itam** and lasts about 30 minutes. A new view of George Town unfolds every few feet. At first, lush tropical vegetation crowds both sides of the track; this gives way to a landscape of giant granite boulders overgrown with ferns and hanging vines. Millionaire's villas appear, alternating with simple farmers' huts, whose inhabitants cultivate bananas and other fruit trees on the slopes.

The funicular ends at 2,550 feet (780 m) above sea level on **Bukit Bendera** (Strawberry Hill, so named because it was here that Francis Light tried to cultivate the fruit), near the summit, where hibiscus bushes bloom in colorful profusion. The temperature is refreshing, remaining constant at some 6° to 8°C lower than temperatures in the city. It is little wonder that hotels have sprung up on the hill. A small Hindu temple and a Moslem mosque cater to spiritual needs. There are playgrounds for children, parks, and lovely trails for nature walks.

You can also climb the Penang hills on foot; there are a number of different routes detailed in a brochure available from the tourist office. The tour up to Strawberry Hill begins at the **Botanical Garden** in the northwest of George Town. The garden, where rhesus monkeys cavort in a variegated the varied flora, can be reached with the city bus from Victoria Street.

About half a mile (1 km) before the Botanical Garden, the Hindu temple of

Nattukotai Cherriar, visible from Jl. Kebun Bunga, occupies the slope above the Ayer Itam reservoir. During the festival of *Thaipusam*, processions of repentant sinners make their way up to this place of worship.

The little town of **Tanjong Bunga** lies on the road to the famous sand beaches of the north. A side street near the town leads to the hill of **Bukit Mutiara**, which commands a lovely view of the coast, the city and the graceful bridge to the mainland.

The heights finally flatten out again at the resort area and former hippie destination of **Batu Ferringhi** (Portuguese Cliffs) on Penang's north coast. Several hotels in different price categories, most booked out for package tours, vie for tourists with promises of lazy days on the beach, friendly service and glorious sunsets. A dip in the ocean is no longer as inviting as it was 20 years ago, but many hotels now have private swimming pools to help out. The restaurants alone lure many guests to come to Batu Ferringhi.

The Malabar fishing village of **Telok Bahang** offers less excitement but better beaches and cheaper lodging. Good snorkeling and diving is found on **Pantai Keracut**, beyond the long fishermen's wharf near the lighthouse of **Muka Head**, as well as on the private beach of **Telok Duyung** (Monkey Beach).

Sri Singamuga Kaliaman Temple, center point of the annual Hindu festival *Masi Maham*, is on the shore. Between Muka Head and the coastal town of **Pantai Aceh**, further south, the woods of the **Pantai Aceh Forest Reserve** extend nearly 5,000 acres (2,000 ha). Its southeastern territory includes the smaller, 250-acre (100 ha) protected area of the **Telok Bahang Forest Reserve**; you can reach this along a street leading from the village of the same name. The park has natural pools for bathing, an orchid farm, the Museum Perhutan (Forest Museum), and an extensive network of marked hiking trails. Further east is **Air Terjun Titi Kerawang**, a romantic waterfall that is worth an additional excursion.

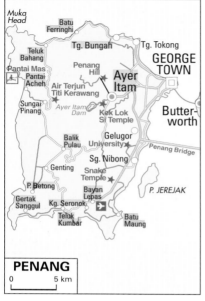

PENANG

0   5 km

The **Penang Butterfly Farm** on the way to Telok Bahang Nature Park is also worth a trip. Brightly colored butterflies in all shapes, sizes and colors flutter beneath the translucent roof; frogs, scorpions and spiders are also a part of this manmade "natural" habitat, which extends over 2 acres (0.8 ha). There is also a gentle lily pond, an artificial waterfall, and a rock garden. Photographs may be taken for an additional charge and a large selection of souvenirs are on sale. But the Butterfly Farm doesn't only serve commercial purposes: zoologists breed endangered insects here and later release them in the wild.

Further west, reachable only by boat, is the exquisite beach of **Pantai Mas** (Gold Beach). A round trip to the neighboring island of **Balik Pulau** is worthwhile for the selection of fresh tropical fruit that is grown there. Depending on the season durian, mangos and other delicious fruit from the surrounding plantations are on sale.

Anyone who has the time should take the opportunity to visit the beautiful beaches at the southwest tip of Penang between **Telok Kumbar** and Gertak Sanggul. Motorboats are available at the fishing village of **Pulau Betong** for the short cruise to **Pasir Panjang**, the best beach in the area.

The footprint of the legendary Cheng Ho is the main attraction at the tiny temple in the fishing village of **Batu Mauung**. The famous Chinese admiral is believed to have gone ashore right here on one of his seven voyages to the Penang. The road splits at **Bayan Lepas** and leads to the village of **Serenok** where a beautifully restored traditional Malay house is open to visitors.

Somewhat north of **Bayan Lepas Airport** stands the **Snake Temple**, which was built in 1850 by a priest who is said to have had magical healing powers. Timid souls are still reluctant to enter the hallowed halls where thousands of snakes once slithered about. Large and small, the green-gold hissing snakes draped themselves over altars and incense burners and decorated the trees and shrubs of the forecourt forming a rather uncanny picture. The poisonous Wagler's Pit Vipers and cobras are believed to be followers of the Hindu god Chor Soo Kong to whom the temple is dedicated. With knowing smiles, acolytes of the temple assure that the snakes, made somewhat drowsy by the incense and smoke of the many candles, leave visitors alone. Truth is, however, that the few remaining snakes have had their fangs removed for the enjoyment of business-minded photographers who snap visitors wearing such an animal for a fee.

Lying off the east coast of Penang is the prison island of **Pulau Jerejak**. Somewhat farther north, the Penang Bridge joins the coast road of Jl. Geludor that comes from the south and leads to George Town. **Universiti Sains Malaysia** (USM), the internationally-recognized university of Penang, is on this road.

PENANG ISLAND

GEORGE TOWN
Getting there / Transportation

BY AIR: **MAS** has daily flights to various domestic destinations (Kuala Lumpur, Ipoh, Langkawi, Kota Bharu, K. Terengganu). There are also regular flights to and from **Singapore, Bangkok, Phuket, Medan**; and direct charters to Europe and Australia.
BY TRAIN: Trains arrive and depart from the **Butterworth Railway Station** at the ferry dock. Tickets are available from the **Railway Booking Office** on Weld Quay, Tel: 04-2610290.
BY BOAT: Regular service to **Belawan/Medan, Langkawi**. 24-hour ferry service between **Butterworth** and **Penang**.
BUS: **The bus terminal** for the M.P.P.P. line is on **Lebuh Victoria**; for blue, yellow, and green buses, it's on **Jl. Maxwell**.

Accommodations

LUXURY: **E & O** (Eastern & Oriental), 10-12, Lebuh Farquhar, Tel: 04-2630630. **Shangri-La Inn**, Jl. Magazine, Tel: 04-2622622. **Sheraton Penang Hotel**, 3, Jl. Larut, Tel: 04-2267888.
MODERATE: **Merlin**, Jl. Larut, Tel: 04-2276166. **The City Bayview**, 25-A Lebuh Farquhar, Tel: 04-2633161. **Continental**, Tel: 04-2636388. **Sunway Hotel**, 33, Lorong Baru, Tel: 04-2299988. **Embassy**, 12, Jl. Burma, Tel: 2267515. **Golden City**, 12, Kinta Lane, Tel: 04-2627881. **Oriental**, Jl. Pinang, Tel: 04-2624211. **Town House**, Jl. Pinang, Tel: 04-2368722. **Ambassador**, 55, Jl. Pinang, Tel: 04-2364101. **Malaysia**, Jl. Pinang, Tel: 04-2363311. **Bellevue Penang Hill**, Tel: 04-2699500.
BUDGET: **Cathay Hotel**, 15, Lebuh Leith, Tel: 04-2626271. **Fortuna**, 406, Jl. Pinang, Tel: 04-2368159. **Peking**, 50A, Jl. Pinang, Tel: 04-2636159. **YMCA**, 211, Jl. Macalister, Tel: 04-2288211. **Swiss Hotel**, 431, Lebuh Chulia, Tel: 04-2620133. There are also a number of inexpensive hotels along Lebuh Leith, Lebuh Chulia and Lorong Love. **Waldorf**, Lebuh Leith, Tel: 04-2626141.

Restaurants

Penang is famous for its cuisine. Even visitors from other Malaysian states who can afford it love to come here for a gourmet weekend. Some local specialties include: *Laksa assam* or *lemak* (noodle soup with fish sauce and herbs, tamarind, and coconut milk for *lemak*), *satay* (marinated kebabs), *Kari Kapitan* (curried chicken) or *Nasi Kandar* (rice with chicken, beef, fish curry, and vegetables), a delicacy of Indian-Moslem cuisine.
CHINESE: Many of the Chinese restaurants of George Town demonstrate the culinary influence of Canton, Szechuan, Hakka or Beijing. Some examples are **See Kong Hooi** and **Goh Swee Kee**, both on Transfer Road, or **Kee Hong**, Jl. Campbell. **Chuan Lok Hooi**, Jl. Macalister, **Dragon Inn**, 27B, Jl. Gottlieb.
INDIAN: **Dawood's**, 63, Queen St. **Hameediya**, 164A, Lebuh Chulia. **Taj Mahal**, corner of Chulia/Jl. Pinang. The cuisine is Malay-Indian at **Kassim Nasi Kandar**, Jl. Brick Klin or **Minah**, Jl. Sg. Glugor.
SEAFOOD: **Oriental Café**, Jl. Macalister, **Penang Seafood Restaurant**, Jl. Tanjong Tokong.
NYONYA CUISINE: **Dragon King**, Lebuh Bishop/Pitt.
WESTERN CUISINE: **Tip Top**, 304, Jl. Burmah, **The Ship**, Jl. Sri Bahari.
FOODSTALLS, COOKSHACKS: in Campbell St., on Gurney Drive and on Jl. Pinang.

Museums

Penang Museum and Art Gallery, Lebuh Farquhar, open daily 9:00 am-5:00 pm, closed Fri. **Koo Kongsi**, Cannon Square, Mon-Fri 9:00 am-5:00 pm, Sat 9:00 am-1:00 pm. **Butterfly Farm**, Mon-Fri 9:00 am-5:00 pm, Sat & Sun 9:00 am-6:00 pm. **Tunku Abdul Rahman-Aquarium**, Bukit Glugor, open daily except Wed. 10:00 am-6:00 pm.

Immigration Authorities

Immigration: Traffic Circle on Lebuh Leith, George Town, Tel: 04-2615122.

Tourist Information

Penang Tourist Association, Jl. Tun Syed Sheh Barakbah, George Town, Tel: 04-2620066, Fax: 04-2623688. Here you can get bus timetables, tourist brochures, and other information. **Information** at the airport: Tel: 04-8931501.

BATU FERRINGHI
Accommodations

LUXURY: **Holiday Inn Penang**, Tel: 04-8811601. **Shangri La Rasa Sayang,** Tel: 04-8811811. **Mutiara Beach Resort**, Jl. Telok Bahang, Tel: 04-8852828.
MODERATE: **Bayview Beach Resort**, Tel: 04-8812123. **Casuarina Beach**, Tel: 04-8811711. **Ferringhi Beach**, Tel: 04-8905999. **Golden Sands**, Tel: 04-8811911. **Palm Beach**, 105A, Batu Ferringhi, Tel: 04-8811621.
BUDGET: **Ali's Guesthouse**, Tel: 04-8811316.

Restaurants

Excellent seafood in the **Eden**; steaks in the **Ship**.

TELOK BAHANG
TANJONG BUNGAH
Accommodations / Restaurants

TELOK BAHANG: Rama's Guesthouse. **TANJONG BUNGAH: Motel Sri Pantai**, 516 Jl. Hashim. You can get seafood at the restaurants **Eden**, **Hollywood**, **Sin Hai** and **Sri Batik**.

FROM MALAYSIA'S BEGINNING TO ITS GOLDEN END

NEGERI SEMBILAN
THE NINE STATES
MELAKA
AROUND MELAKA
JOHOR

West and South of Kuala Lumpur

About 15 miles (24 km) south of Kajang is the border between Selangor and Negeri Sembilan. The "Nine States," located mainly inland, have only 30 miles (48 km) of coastline; the state has a total area of 2,591 square miles (6,645 sq. km). Of the 600,000 inhabitants, 46 percent are Malay, 36 percent Chinese and roughly 18 percent Indian. Most work in agriculture or industry, the leading force in the region's economy. Rice, cocoa, oil palms and rubber are the main agricultural products, but cattle breeding and fishing are also important.

The state's origins lie centuries in the past; the story of its beginnings is not without historic interest. Minangkabau from Sumatra probably crossed the Straits of Malacca in the 15th century, and, drawn by the already flourishing settlement of Malacca, settled in what is today known as Negeri Sembilan. They organized themselves in the nine loose, state-like confederations of Jelebu, Johol, Rembau, Klang, Naning, Jelia, Ulu Pahang, Sungai Ujong and Segamat. In the 19th century, under British influence,

these were unified into Negeri Sembilan, which then consisted of only six states. Their ruler was the *Yang Di Pertuan Besar* ("The Great One Chosen by God"), who at the same time became the first King of Malaysia. For their capital and seventh district, the princes of Negeri Sembilan chose an area 40 miles (65 km) south of Kuala Lumpur, named Seremban, where the British Resident also lived after 1895. The greed for tin led to outbreaks of violence which the British had used as an excuse to move in and gain control of the area.

South of Negeri Sembilan is the state of **Melaka** (Malacca), measuring 643 square miles (1,650 sq. km). Its approximately 500,000 inhabitants are 54 percent Malay, 38 percent Chinese, and 8 percent Indian. The area is also centered around industry and agriculture; and its capital, also named Melaka, is the region's main tourist attraction.

The southernmost state on the peninsula is the 7,794-square-mile (19,984 sq. km) **Johor** (Johore), whose two million inhabitants are split among the three ethnic groups in much the same proportion as in Melaka. Johor remains largely agricultural, Malaysia's leader in the production of rubber, palm oil and pineapples. Attempts are being made to diversify the region's agriculture by introducing shrimp

Preceding pages: A view over Melaka's extensive old town. Left: The flag of Malaysia.

farms and tea plantations. Both industry and tourism profit from Johor's proximity to Singapore.

The state dates its origin from the overthrow of the Sultanate of Malacca; Johor has been seen as a kind of successor to it ever since. In 1819, Stamford Raffles took advantage of the fighting between Malays and Bugis in Johor to seize the island of Tumasek, better known as modern Singapore. That dealt a death blow to the Johor-Riau kingdom. Riau came first under Dutch control and then was taken over by the Indonesians; while Johor remained a British colony until the founding of the Malaysian Federation.

NEGERI SEMBILAN

Seremban, the capital of Negeri Sembilan with some 160,000 inhabitants, lies in a mountainous region. A few of its public buildings reveal the characteristics

Right: Cruising the Sungai Melaka before an ever-changing backdrop.

traits of Minangkabau architecture, recognizable by steep, pointed, curving roof gables, but otherwise it has little in the way of sights to support active tourism.

Descendants of the Minangkabau settlers keep their Islamic cultural heritage alive in more ways than architecture. Traditionally a matrilineal society, they preserve this aspect to this day; property passes from mother to daughter. In families who strictly observe the *adat*, traditional law which survives from pre-Islamic times, a bride doesn't move in with her husband when she marries, but rather brings him into her family's home as a guest.

The architecture of the **Masjid Negeri**, constructed in 1967, is highly symbolic. Its nine columns and nine suspended roofs represent the state's political structure. The mosque is near the **Lake Gardens**, or Taman Bunga, in the city center. The park with its two lakes is often a venue for sports and cultural events. Nearby, the **State Secretariat** is a gleaming, colonial-style building.

A good example of traditional building methods is found somewhat outside the city, west of the city center toward the highway. Built in 1983, the Taman Seni Budaya complex, spreading over 32.5 acres (13 ha), is worth a look; in these relatively new Minangkabau-style houses, local handicrafts are produced and sold. The state museum, **Muzium Negeri Sembilan**, is housed in an authentic Minangkabau palace, the **Istana Ampang Tinggi**. The wooden structure, which originally stood in Ampang Tinggi near Kuala Pilah, was built in the middle of the 19th century by a prince for his daughter. After World War Two, the building was disassembled, brought to Seremban and reconstructed. A few cosmetic errors, such as the use of metal nails in the first reconstruction, were corrected when the palace was moved again to Taman Seni Budaya and restored to its original state in 1984. The museum it houses is devoted to regional history.

EXCURSIONS INTO THE NINE STATES

Nature lovers have plenty of opportunities to enjoy the area surrounding Seremban. East of the capital, approximately 3 miles (5 km) on State Road 86 toward Kuala Klawang, a road to the left leads to **Lenggeng**, a protected forest and nature preserve. Another 10.5 miles (17 km) further down the main road to the northeast, another side road leads off to the right to the 3,901 foot (1,193 m) summit of **Gunung Telapak Burok**. Approximately 10 miles (16 km) east of Seremban, **Gunung Angsi** rises to a height of 2,946 feet (901 m). Further along State Road 51 on the way to Sri Menanti, the nature park and reservation of **Ulu Bendol**, with its waterfall and lake, make an ideal spot to relax.

Minangkabau tradition is on display again in **Sri Menanti**, which nestles in the hills approximately 20 miles (32 km)

east of Seremban, reachable by a spur off the main road between the capital and Kuala Pilah. The provincial town has been the residence of Negeri Sembilan's rulers since 1773; the ancestors of the royal family, who originally came from Sumatra, settled here about 400 years ago.

Two palaces testify to the town's royal past. The wooden palace of **Istana Lama** was constructed in 1908 without a single nail in the Minangkabau style, and served as the official residence of *Yang Di Pertuan Besar* Sultan Tuanku Muhammad until 1931. The lower floor is an enormous open hall with columns up to 65 feet (20 m) high. The building is impressive for its symmetry. Istana Besar is the name of the "new" residence, built in 1930. Both buildings can be visited with official permission from the State Secretariat in Seremban.

Kuala Pilah lies 23 miles (37 km) east of the capital. Old shops and the 100-year old **Chinese Temple** on Jl. Lister are its main attractions. Proudly recorded in the

town's annals is the visit of Chinese politician Sun Yat Sen, who spent some time here collecting money for China in the 1920s.

As well as architecture, the Minangkabau are known for their spicy cuisine. A typical dish is *masak lemak cili api*, consisting of rice cooked in coconut milk and flavored with fiery chilies hot enough to take sear your eyebrows.

Travelers on their way to Melaka have two routes to choose from. One goes through the town of **Tampin**, whose megaliths, like those 12-18 miles (20-30 km) south of Seremban, are worth seeing. The other option is to return to Seremban and pick up the expressway to Melaka. Travelers on the expressway who have a bit of time to spare should take in the town of **Pedas**, 11 miles (18 km) southeast of the capital, and before Alor Gajah,

Above: Oil palm harvest on a plantation near Lukut. Right: The portrait of Admiral Chen Ho in the Po Kong Temple in Melaka.

the exit you take to get to Melaka. Pedas, with its warm springs, restaurants, bath houses, and range of recreational facilities, is a favorite destination for day-trippers in the area. The **Resthouse** in nearby **Rembau** is another good example of Minangkabau architecture, while the **Rumah Undang**, one of the residences of the *undang* (district elder or head man), combines modern and traditional building styles.

If you've got the time, travel along the stretch of road to Port Dickson. Vast plantations of oil and coconut palms line the road, until after some 12.5 miles (20 km) the little town of **Lukut** rises out of the greenery. It is here that the legendary Captain China, Yap Ah Loy, is said to have begun his career – as a cook. A few miles from Lukut, the ruins of a fort built by Raja Juma'at in 1847 are a reminder that the region was long a bone of contention between Bugis and Minangkabau.

In 1885, the Englishman Sir Frederick Dickson turned the charcoal-burners village of Arang Arang, 20 miles (32 km) south of Seremban, into something of greater significance. The little coastal town became **Port Dickson**, a harbor with a railway link. Yet since the 1930s, Port Dickson's economic success can no longer be measured in the gross tonnage of its shipping, but rather by the numbers of vacationers who flock here. The prime attraction is the stretch of beach south of Port Dickson, more than 11 miles (18 km) long. This is the common goal of weekend and long-term visitors to the area who, given the pollution along the west coast, cannot afford to be overly particular. You can find lodging in all categories, from luxury hotels to bungalows and cheap Chinese pensions, standing side by side under the casuarina and banyan trees that line the beach. The seafood restaurants here have a good reputation, and swimming and other water sports are fine, although the pickings underwater are slim. Most popular beaches are **Pantai Bagan Pinang** and the **Blue Lagoon**.

With 35,000 inhabitants, Port Dickson, often dubbed "P.D.," is on the narrowest point of the Straits of Malacca. On a clear day, you can see the coast of Sumatra, or rather the island of Rubat (Riau) just in front of it, 25 miles (40 km) across the water. The best view is from the 589-foot (180 m) lighthouse at **Cape Rachado** or Tanjung Tuan, which was built by the Portuguese in the 16th century.

Another popular excursion on the road to Melaka is the village of **Pengkalan Kempas**, 15.5 miles (25 km) southwest of Port Dickson. Mysterious megaliths here bear ancient inscriptions in an archaic Hindu script – very unusual in southeast Asia. Local inhabitants are unsure of their meaning, but they often gather around the megaliths to pray for a good harvest. Another stone, called the "judgment stone," has a fist-size hole in it; local lore has it that if a liar puts his hand into the hole, the stone will slam shut and hold him fast. The megaliths are

near the grave of Sheik Ahmad Majnun, who died here in an uprising against Sultan Mansur Shah of Malacca.

Gourmets should continue further along the coastal road, because the towns near the border between Melaka and Johor are famous for their giant tiger prawns. These are also available in the holiday resort of **Tanjung Bidara**, where the hotel of the same name on the beach is ideal for a relaxing sojourn.

MELAKA:
WHERE IT ALL BEGAN

The name of this city of 100,000-plus inhabitants, capital of the state of the same name, represents a story that had a decisive influence on the development of the entire region of Southeast Asia. Malaysians generally append to the name of this cradle of their history the epithet "...where it all began." To explain this, they then recount the following legend, which suits Malacca – or Melaka, as it is called in Malaysian – so well.

The Hindu Prince Parameswara, reputed to be a direct descendant of Alexander the Great, had to flee Sumatra, his homeland, in 1396, and sailed southwest to the peninsula across the waterway. One day, exhausted from his journey, he lay down to rest in the pleasant shade of a *melaka* tree. The nap must have done him a lot of good, because when he awoke, he spontaneously decided to found a city on that very spot. A different story is told in Sumatra, where credit for the founding goes to Ratu Melayu, the King of the Malays, who was apparently on a hunting expedition.

Be that as it may, foreign powers were soon showing a keen interest in the newly built city. Early in the 15th century, envoys arrived from China; Admiral Cheng Ho declared Melaka to be a protectorate of the Ming dynasty and, like the legendary Prince Parameswara (actually Sultan Megat Iskandar Shah), converted to the Moslem religion. Under the banner of Islam, the new empire was to increase in size and power.

Its riches attracted the attention of the European powers. First Portugal, then Holland entered the picture. Toward the end of the 16th century two German merchant families, the Fuggers and the Welsers, were also reaching their spice- and gold-hungry feelers out toward Melaka. The Sultan of Melaka, driven into exile in Johor by the Portuguese, tried 20 times to win his kingdom back. Holland managed to conquer the land in 1641 and were conquered in turn by the British 156 years later. Melaka was made part of the Straits Settlements and remained under British administration, with the exception of the three-year-long occupation by the Japanese during World War Two, until 1957.

Palpable History

Melaka's turbulent history has left traces in stone and steel. Some are better preserved than others, but all belong among the most important tourist sights in Malaysia. And there is no shortage of lodging. Melaka offers a broad choice of luxury hotels, Chinese inns and small hotels full of colonial charm.

A good place to begin exploring the city's past is on **St. Paul's Hill**. To the northwest, by the bridge over the Sungai Melaka, is the **Tourist Office**; the **Tourist Police** is nearby.

Directly across the street on **Dutch Square**, formerly the Marketplace, is the salmon-red **Stadthuys**, representing the Dutch aspect of Melaka's past. Built in 1650, once the residence of the Dutch governor, the building is the oldest Dutch stone house in Southeast Asia. Its extraordinary color stems from an ordinance passed in 1930 that all buildings from the Dutch colonial period had to be painted the same glowing red as the Christ Church. In 1982 the Stadhuys was turned into the **Malacca Historical Museum**. In it are reminders of the colonial period, as well as traditional clothes and tools of the Straits Chinese and Malays. The past comes alive until you could almost believe yourself back in the days when Melaka was one of the greatest port cities in Asia. In one of its rooms you can still see the original ceiling from the 17th century.

Next door is **Christ Church**, built by the Dutch in 1753. It is the oldest Protestant church still in use in the country. Its red bricks were brought from Holland as ballast in Dutch ships. Take note of the 17 ceiling beams, each carved from the whole trunk of a single tree. The pews, pulpit and baptismal font are also original; and the brass-covered bible likewise dates from 1753. Above the altar, the Last Supper is depicted on glazed tiles. It may come as a surprise to some visitors to note that some of the tombstones set into the floor bear Portuguese inscriptions; for the Dutch took great pains to destroy all signs of their colonial predecessors. The church also contains an Armenian tomb from 1774.

The third important building on Dutch Square is the **Tan Beng Swee Clock Tower**, named after the Chinese patron who had his son build this clock tower – virtually an obligatory feature of all Malaysian cities – in 1886. It too is red, but not for its Dutch colonial connection; rather because red is the color of good luck to the Chinese. The original clock was imported from England; it has since been replaced by one from Japan, despite protests from older citizens who remember the atrocities committed on this very spot during the Japanese occupation of the city during World War Two. The **Kuo Ming Tang Cenotaph** at the corner of Jl. Munshi Abdullah and Jl. Laksamana Cheng Ho commemorates the many thousands of Melaka Chinese killed during the occupation.

In the middle of the historic square is the **Victoria Fountain**, which the inhabitants dedicated to the Queen in 1904. Somewhat farther northeast on Jl. Laksamana, the church of **St. Francis Xavier** was built in a neo-Gothic style in 1849.

As well as the old lighthouse, the ruins of **St. Paul's Church** survive on St. Paul's Hill, once the site of the Portuguese fort *A Famosa*. The Portuguese built a chapel on the spot in 1521, the first Catholic church in the Far East. Their countryman Francisco Xavier, who was later canonized, was a frequent visitor. He had already commissioned his tomb in the chapel before his death in 1522. His body, however, was exhumed a year later and sent to the Portuguese colony of Goa. The church, whose outer walls still stand, was built between 1560 and 1580. The tower was used, first by the Portuguese and later by the British, to store gunpowder. Once they had completed Christ Church and built St. Peter's Church in 1710, the Dutch no longer needed the Portuguese house of worship. They used the hill as a cemetery for their aristocrats and colonial administrators; the tomb stones can still be seen there.

Below the summit of St. Paul's Hill, the wooden building of the **Malacca Sul-**

tanate Palace tells a still older tale, even though it is itself of more recent date. The original palace, residence of Sultan Mansur Shah, was consumed by flames in the early 15th century. The present structure, a reconstruction also built of wood without the use of nails, houses the **Muzium Budaya**, dedicated to Melaka's culture. Here, life-sized, beautifully dressed mannequins are posed in scenes from Malay life at court or famous popular legends. One tableau tells the story of **Hang Tuah**, one of the Sultan's four bodyguards, who killed Hang Jebat for conspiring against his ruler. His grave can still be seen in the Lorong Hang Jebat. Hang Kasturi, another of the Sultan's swordsmen, is also buried in Melaka near the northwestern end of Jl. Hang Jebat.

The **Porta Santiago**, rising up at the southern end of St. Paul's Hill, is the only

Above: The Victoria Fountain on Dutch Square in Melaka. Right: The Chinese Cheng Hoon Teng temple, built in 1645.

gate of *A Famosa* that is still extant. Built in 1511, the fort fell to the Dutch in 1641 and was almost completely destroyed. Thanks to Sir Stamford Raffles, the Porta Santiago, at least, has survived. The inscriptions of VOC (*Vereenigde Oostindie Companie*) and the Dutch coat-of-arms are still clearly visible over the arched door.

Across from the weathered gateway is the **Padang Pahlawan**, one of the most historically important places in all of Malaysia. Although England officially lowered its flag in Kuala Lumpur in 1957, Malaysia had already declared its independence on February 20, 1956 at this site between Jl. Taman and Jl. Parameswara. The declaration was an act of political self-confidence that hastened the end of the colonial era in Malaysia. It is on display along with other memorabilia at the museum inside the impressive **Independence Memorial Hall** on Padang Pahlawan. The beautifully restored old building was, until 1958, home of the Malacca Club, built in 1812 as a meeting place for the area's wealthy white planters.

A Dutch cemetery honors those who died for their country far from home. Across from Porta Santiago and the Memorial hall the Light & Sound Show commemorates the centuries of struggle of Southeast Asian countries against foreign powers, as well as the wars they fought among themselves. With a lot of smoke, thundering cannon and loud war cries, Melaka returns every night – thanks to the Techno Theater – to the days when it lay in the crosshairs of the sights of European colonial conquerors.

Holland's continued fear of losing the power it had struggled to gain is still evident in **St. John's Fort**, built at the end of the 18th century on the hill of the same name about 2 miles (3 km) east of the city center. You can still see the cannons they put there, which face inland, as Melaka's sea flank was far better protected than its

landward side. For the Portuguese, the hill was religious terrain; they built a chapel to St. John the Baptist on its summit.

Their descendants, Catholic Eurasians, still actively honor the saint: his feast day, June 24th, is a huge festival for Melaka's Portuguese-Malay community. This minority has retained a strong communal identity; in fact, some 1,500 Eurasians of Portuguese descent live in **Perkampungan Portugis**, about 3 miles (5 km) east of the city center. The inhabitants, most of whom make their living by fishing, have retained many of their old customs; they even still speak *Christão*, a 16th-century Portuguese dialect that has survived in Malaysia. Since 1930, when two Jesuits established Perkampungan Portugis with the help of the British Commissioner, the tiny "colony" has been an attraction in its own right. Often, you can see local men and women in colorful folk costumes singing *cantigas* (Portuguese *Christão* songs). The best time to see them is Saturday evening on the *Medan Portugis*, the settlement's main square, which is surrounded by several Portuguese restaurants.

June is the time of celebrations in Perkampungan Portugis. In addition to the feast of St. John the Baptist, there is a celebration for St. Petrus at the end of the month. The villagers decorate their boats and stage all manner of cultural events to entertain visitors and, even more, themselves.

Melaka's Temples and Mosques

The city that saw the beginning of Malaysia's recent history also possesses the oldest Islamic, Hindu and Chinese temples in the land. They are all concentrated on the right bank of the Melaka River. The **Kampong Keling Mosque**, dating from 1748, is on Jl. Tukang Emas. Its striking architecture incorporates Sumatran elements, as does that of Melaka's two other old mosques. A three-storey pyramid-shaped roof and pagoda-like minaret are characteristic of the style. The Stadthuys square was once occupied by the original **Kampong Hulu Mosque**. After it was destroyed by the Portuguese in 1728, Dato Shamsuddin rebuilt it on Jl. Kampong Hulu. The **Tranquerah Mosque** is on Jl. Tengkera, about 2 miles (3 km) from the city center. The original building, also dating from 1728, was destroyed in the war between Holland and the Bugis; the present structure was built in 1850 to replace it. The cemetery around the mosque contains the mausoleum of Sultan Hussain Shah, the ruler of Johor who died in 1835.

Poyyatha Vinayagar Moorthi Temple, the first Hindu house of worship in Malaysia, was built in 1781 on Jl. Tukan Emas (Street of Goldsmiths). Inside, the Hindu god Vinayagar, who has the body of a man with the head of an elephant, is depicted in a statue carved out of black Indian granite.

Malaysia's oldest Chinese temple still in use for worship is also in Melaka: the **Cheng Hoon Teng Temple**, dating from 1645. The venerable building on Jl. Tokong was built by Captain China Lee Wei King, and was finally completed in its present form in 1804. Its interior manages to demonstrate in a lovely way the harmony of Taoism, Confucianism and Chinese Buddhism which the Chinese call *san e chiao* (the system of three doctrines). All of the building materials for the temple came from China. Valuable woodcarvings, some of them gilded; gold-leaf images on enamel; and paintings depicting scenes from Chinese mythology are among the treasures of the "Temple of the Green Clouds."

Bukit China (Hill of the Chinese), said to be the oldest cemetery outside of China, lies in the eastern part of the city. Its oldest tombstones go back to the 17th century, but its name and importance stem from the 15th century, the very beginning of Melaka. Admiral Cheng Ho, the Ming envoy, lived here in 1409 and established what was to be a long and resilient relationship between China and the early Malays.

Half a century later, the historic wedding of Sultan Mansur Shah and Princess Hang Li Poh, daughter of the Chinese Ming Emperor Yung Lo, was celebrated here. The hill became the residence of the legion aristocrats and their retainers, including 500 ladies-in-waiting, who took part in the wedding.

Portuguese Franciscans later erected a monastery and chapel dedicated to the *Madre de Deus* on Bukit China; but it was all completely destroyed by the attackers from Aceh in 1629. Captain China bought the symbolic hill from the Dutch and turned it over to the administrators of the Cheng Hoon Teng Temple he had founded. Since the mid-17th century, the 107-acre (43-ha) has been used for the dead. One of the largest cemeteries outside of China, it contains more than 12,500 graves.

The legendary **Sultan's Well** is on the southern part of the hill. According to the legend, whoever throws a coin into it is assured of his return to Melaka. It was originally dug for the Princess Hang Li Poh and her entourage. Later it served as the principle water source for the city because, even in periods of draught it never failed to yield water. Foreign conquerors frequently used to try to poison it.

Nearby, the Poh San Teng or **Sam Po Kong Temple**, at the corner of Jl. Munshi Abdullah and Jl. Puteri Hang Li Poh, is dedicated to the famous admiral Cheng Ho. Unfortunately, his statue was stolen some time ago; today, there's only a photograph in its place.

No less interesting is the abovementioned **Church of St. Peter**, built in 1710. Portuguese Eurasians who elected to remain in Melaka despite the Dutch occupation built the church on Jl. Tun Sri Lanang, northwest of Bukit China. A

Right: Modern Melaka also has its poor side – on the way home from doing the laundry.

major focal point here for Malaysia's Catholics is its larger-than-life-sized alabaster statue of Christ. Each year on Good Friday, believers carry the statue in a procession through the city.

Babas and Nyonyas

One source of Melaka's special attraction is the juxtaposition of buildings of various historical periods, cultures and religions. Chinese influence predominates, especially in secular architecture and especially along **Jl. Hang Jebat**, where many Chinese restaurants and good antique shops are crowded into the rows of old shop houses.

In addition to the vases, fabrics and masks on sale in curio shops, some merchants also sell a rather odd souvenir: reproductions of the tiny shoes made to fit the bound, crippled feet which were a hallmark of fine Chinese ladies in days gone by.

A new ethnic group called *Baba-Nyonya* has grown up from the descendants of Malaysian woman (*nyonyas*) and Chinese men who began settling in the Straits Settlements in the 18th century. Their children call themselves Straits-born Chinese or *Peranakan* (born here). The Chinese immigrants, predominantly male, married native women and adopted Malay culture, also picking up some European influences along the way. The male children of these families were called *Baba*.

The **Baba Nyonya Heritage Museum** gives further information about this ethnic group. It was founded by a *baba* in two beautiful old Baba-Nyonya houses on Jl. Tun Tang Cheng Lock. The street was known to the English residents of Melaka as "Millionaires' Row" and to the Dutch as "Herrenstraat" (Street of Gentlemen), an indication of the comfortable living standards of the Baba-Nyonyas. Generally, their income derived from the wealthy plantation economy.

Nyonya cuisine, justly famous for its tasteful use of spices, is served at the **Per-**

117

anakan Restaurant in another lovely Baba-Nyonya house at the northern edge of the city.

AROUND MELAKA

Local guides are happy to offer trips to visit the palm oil and rubber plantations around Melaka, excursions which provide a nice contrast to city sightseeing. Another interesting excursion is to the **Mini Malaysia Cultural Village**, 9 miles (15 km) outside the city. Thirteen traditional houses, representing the states of the Malaysian Federation, are on display, and on weekends there are cultural shows and exhibits of Malaysian crafts.

The **Mini Asean Cultural Village** in thesamearea demonstrates architecture typical in other ASEAN countries. Mini Malaysia is part of the **Ayer Keroh Rec-**

reational Park, a facility that includes butterfly and crocodile farms.

The inhabitants of the **Orang Asli Village**, not far away, are also seen as a sightseeing attraction. Visitors can admire their simple way of life and try their hand at the art of using a blow-gun. The 18-hole **Ayer Keroh Golf Course**, which is set between the rain forest and **Ayer Keroh Recreational Lake**, is a challenging venue for golfers. The **Melaka Zoo** extends for 55 acres (22 ha) along the shore of the lake; it offers the visitor a rare chance to see a live Sumatra rhinoceros.

The 332-acre (133 ha) island of **Pulau Besar** lies directly off the coast. Old sea charts mark it as an excellent anchorage. A few settlers lived on the island, notably Almarhum Sultan Ariffin Sheikh Ismail, an Indian missionary and merchant said to have lived for 308 years. If that was the case, he certainly deserved his *keramat* or holy grave on the island.

Since 1991, the solitude of the island has been disturbed, or dissolved, by its

Above: A visit to Mini Malaysia's Cultural Village. Right: The canopy over this oxcart quotes from Minangkabau architecture.

new recreational center, which includes a yacht club, restaurants, sport facilities, a motel and chalets to attract vacationers, in addition to the natural lure of clear water for swimming and diving. Boats bound for the island leave from **Pengkalan Pernu** on the mainland.

There are several other small islands off Melaka's coast. Less interesting as a tourist attraction than for its legends and history is **Pulau Haynut**. It is said to be one of the "rebellious" islands, according to myth, and supposedly once lay at the mouth of the Perak River. **Pulau Upeh** was called *Ilha das Pedras* (Island of Stones) by the Portuguese, as it was where they gathered the stones to build the fort of *A Famosa*.

On **Pulau Undan**, where there's a lighthouse built in 1879, rusted railroad wheels have been found which would seem to indicate that a mysterious train must once have gotten very lost indeed. **Pulau Jawa**, close to the coast, was formerly called *Ilha dos Naus* and served Holland as a base for its repeated, and ultimately successful, attacks on Melaka.

JOHOR: THE GOLDEN END

The state of Johor stretches over the entire southern point of the peninsula. Formerly known as the "Golden End," the region is surrounded on three sides by water: the Straits of Melaka are to the west; to the south is the Strait of Johor, which circles the island state of Singapore; and the South China Sea lies to the east.

The son of the last Sultan of Melaka founded the kingdom of Johor when he fled south from the Portuguese in 1564. But the new sultanate, with its exposed location, was ill-fated from the start. Bugis, Minangkabau, Portuguese and invaders from Aceh left Johor little chance for peace until Abu Bakar entered its history. He grew up in the middle of the nineteenth century in Singapore, a

protege of the British. They officially recognized him as Sultan of Johor in 1885, long after he had promoted the fishing village of Johor Bahru to capital in 1866, naming himself Maharaja of the territory two years later. The old dynasty, by that time little more than a puppet state of the Bugis, was finally disempowered.

Abu Bakar's advent ushered in better times for Johor, which the British subsequently controlled, through their General Advisor, after 1914. This was the last of Malaysia's Sultanates to slip under European rule.

On the Way to Johor Bahru

A short way past Kesang the coastal road crosses the Melakan border; 9 miles (15 km) later, it comes to **Muar**, the first town of any significant size in Johor. Apart from a number of food stalls and *satay* stands, the quiet town offers several neo-Classical government buildings and the Friday Mosque. 11 miles (18 km)

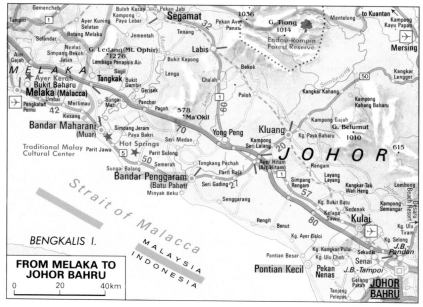

south of town, visitors can stop to admire the only preserved **Bugis House** in Malaysia. Muar, along with the more northerly city of **Segamat**, is a departure point for climbers of the 4,173 foot (1,276 m) **Gunung Ledang**. The mountain, also known as Mount Ophir, is the highest point in Johor. The real climb starts at the town of **Sagil**, but climbers should be warned: Princess Gunung Ledang waits at the summit, like Lorelei on the Rhine, to lure men into temptation.

For those who prefer to ignore such mythical warnings there is an easier ascent from Tangkak in the south along the path to the Telecom station, about 650 feet (200 m) below the summit. Still another option is to begin the ascent further west in Melaka, where the trail from **Lembaga Penapis Air** goes through dense jungle and climbs gradually to the summit.

At **Ayer Hitam**, several roads come together. State road number 1 from Segamat meets the highway and coastal road number 50. Anyone traveling to Kuala Lumpur or Johor Bahru has to pass through the town, which is known for its ceramic industry. Slightly more interesting is the textile manufacturing center of **Batu Pahat** in the southwestern part of the state.

JOHOR BAHRU – SINGAPORE'S NEIGHBOR

Johor Bahru (J.B.) is no longer just a bedroom suburb of Singapore. The proximity of the economic giant has also prompted development of the capital city of Johor. With 300,000 inhabitants, Johor Bahru is the third-largest city in Malaysia. Since 1924, the 3,600-foot (1,100 m) **Causeway** has connected the two unequal neighbors, a kind of umbilical cord of road, rail, telecommunications and water lines.

Johor Bahru's attractions include the **Istana Besar**, the palace Abu Bakar built in 1866. The north wing contains the throne room and museum where jewels, clothing and weapons once used by the

Sultan are on display. Even today, ceremonies and state receptions are held at this old palace, while the Sultan resides in **Istana Bukit Serene**, the new residence built on the outskirts of the city in 1933. This new palace is protected from view by its beautiful, park-like grounds; both palace and grounds are unfortunately closed to the public.

The famous founder of Johor Bahru also built the mosque that bears his name. **Masjid Sultan Abu Bakar**, finished in 1892, overlooks the sea and can accommodate 2,000 worshippers. The interior is decorated with traditional wood carving.

The furnishings of the **Dewan**, Johor Bahru's 1857-vintage City Hall, are also worth noting. Although the building was extensively renovated and reconstructed in 1957, the carved ceilings, columns and furniture were already there in 1885, when Johor's first constitution was presented to the people.

The Dewan and Istana Besar are surrounded by the public park of **Istana Garden**, which contains playgrounds, gardens, and a zoo.

A landmark of the city is the **State Secretariat** or Bangunan Sultan Ibrahim on Bukit Timbalan, with its four-sided tower. The building was constructed in 1940; its most interesting interior feature are the mosaics decorating its Great Hall.

Traveling in Johor

The region around the capital has also profited from its economic boom. The former fishing village of **Pasir Gudang Port**, east of Johor Bahru, has developed industries and a deep-sea harbor. It is a free trade zone, connected by expressway to the capital.

The next town has more of a Malaysian ambiance: **Kampong Pasir Putih** has nice restaurants where visitors can taste local dishes while enjoying a lovely view of Singapore.

Delicacies from the sea are also served in the coastal village of **Kukup**, before the southwestern end of the peninsula, **Tanjung Piai**. To get there, however, you have to return several miles northwest along the expressway and take the road via Kangar Pulai and Pontian Kechil to Kukup.

Kota Tinggi, 25 miles (40 km) northeast of Johor Bahru, is an old Sultan's city known for its famous tombs. About a mile (1.5 km) to the south at **Kampong Kelantan**, 15 members of the Sultan's family are interred; to the north, just before the turnoff to Desaru, is the mausoleum of Sultan Mahmud, the last ruler of the Melaka dynasty. His son Alauddin Shah built his residence in Kota Tinggi in 1530. Waterfalls 100 feet (30 m) high are the main attraction of the park of **Air Terjun Lumbong**, 9 miles (15 km) north of the city.

A trip by rented boat up from Kota Tinggi along the **Johor River** to **Johor Lama**, some 18 miles (30 km) to the south, is exciting. The village was the capital of the Sultanate from 1547 until 1587. The ruins of **Kota Batu**, the fortress that held the Portuguese at bay for three years until it finally capitulated in 1587, still stand on the bank of the Johor river.

Construction on the beach resort of **Desaru** on the southeastern tip of the island has been completed. The hotel's design fits well into the landscape. Golf, riding, tennis, surfing are just some of the sports on tap at the resort. The latest favorite of investors is the yacht harbor **Sebana Cove Marina**, with a golf course, hotel, restaurant, and so on. The car ferry harbor to Singapore contributes its own fair share to the popularity of Desaru.

Mersing, the city in the northeast of Johor, is principally known as a ferry port for the island of **Tioman**. The town and the island are described more thoroughly in the chapter about the east coast (see p. 146).

NEGERI SEMBILAN
Getting there / Transportation
SEREMBAN: *BUS:* Daily express buses to **Kuala Lumpur, Port Dickson, Johor Baru, Kota Baru, K. Terengganu.** Buses also service surrounding areas. **Bus terminal:** Jl. Sungai Ujong. *TRAIN:* from the **central station**, traffic circle of Jl. D. Bandar Tunggal/Jl. Tuanku Antah, to **Singapore** and **Kuala Lumpur**.
PORT DICKSON: *BUS:* There are several express buses daily to **Seremban, P. Klang** (lovely coastal route!), **Kuala Lumpur**, **Melaka.** A bus to **Pengkalan Kempas** leaves hourly.

Accommodations
SEREMBAN: *MODERATE:* **Tasik Hotel,** Jl. Tetamu, Tel: 06-7630994. *BUDGET:* **Carlton**, 47, Jl. Tuan Shek Seremban, Tel: 06-7625336. **Century**, 25-29, Jl. Tuanku Munawir, Tel: 06-7636261.
KUALA PILAH: **Government Guesthouses,** Jl. Seremban; K. Klawang, Jl. Simpang Pertang; **TAMPIN: Government Guesthouse**, Jl. Seremban.
REMBAU: Government Guesthouse, Jl. Kg. Mulia.
PORT DICKSON: *MODERATE:* **Ming Court Beach Hotel**, Coast Rd., Tel: 06-6475244. **Pantai Dickson Resort**, Jl. Pantai, Tel: 06-6475473. **Seri Malaysia Port Dickson**, Jl. Pantai, Tel: 06-6476070. *BUDGET:* **Happy City Hotel**, 26. Jl. Raja Aman Shah, Tel: 06-6473103. **Youth Hostel**, 4 miles (6 km) outside of town. **Seaview Hotel**, 841, Batu 1, Tel: 06-6471818. Along the beach there are some other simple hotels and bungalows.

Restaurants
SEREMBAN: *MALAY:* **Jempol**, Kompleks Negeri. **Fatimah**, Jl. Tuanku Munawir. There are other restaurants, including *CHINESE*, on Jl. Dato Bandar Tunggal, the main shopping street.
INDIAN: **Samy**, 120, Jl. Yam Tuan.
PORT DICKSON: there are many seafood restaurants in town and along the beach.

MELAKA
Getting there / Transportation
BY AIR: From the **Batu Berendam** airport, **Pelangi Air** flies once a week to **Pekan Baru**/Sumatra. Air connections to Malaysia's most important cities also exist or are being planned. **MAS**, Tel: 06-2835722.
BUS: Bus terminal: Jl. Kilang/Jl. Hang Tuah. Daily express buses to: **Kuala Lumpur, Seremban, Port Dickson, Ipoh/Butterworth, K. Bahru, K. Terengganu, Kuantan, Temerloh, Johor Baru, Singapore, Tampin, Muar.**

BY BOAT: Weekly service between Melaka and **Dumai/Sumatra**. Information: Madai Shipping, 320, Jl. Kilang, Tel: 06-240671.

Accommodations
LUXURY: **The Emperor Hotel,** 123, Jl. Munshi Abdullah, Tel: 06-2840777. **Malacca Renaissance**, Jl. Bendahara, Tel: 06-2848888. **The City Bayview**, Jl. Bendahara, Tel: 06-239888. **Plaza Inn**, Jl. Munshi Abdullah, Tel: 06-2840881.
MODERATE: **Palace Hotel**, 201, Jl. Munshi Abdullah, Tel: 06-2825115. **Wisma Hotel**, 114A, Jl. Bendahara, Tel: 06-2839800. **Malacca Hotel Sentosa**, 91, Jl. Tun Perak, Tel: 06-358288.
BUDGET: **Cathay Hotel**, 100-106, Jl. Munshi Abdullah, Tel: 06-2823337. **Central Hotel**, 31-41, Jl. Bendahara, Tel: 06-2822984. **Eastern Lodging Hotel**, 85, Jl. Bendahara, Tel: 06-2831541. **Majestic** (old house with colonial flair), 188, Jl. Bunga Raja, Tel: 06-2822367.
There are a number of budget accommodations along Jl. Bunga Raja.
BEACH and HOLIDAY RESORTS: **Malacca Village Park Plaza Resort**, Ayer Keroh, Tel: 06-323600. **Ayer Keroh Country Club**, Ayer Keroh, Tel: 06-325211 (both of these are close to an 18-hole golf course). **Shah's Beach Resort**, 6.5 miles from Batu, Tanjung Kling, Tel: 06-511120. **Tanjung Bidara Beach Resort**, Tanjung Bidara, Tel: 06-542990.

Restaurants
MALAY: **Restoran Anda**, 8B, Jl. Hang Tuah, Tel: 06-2831984. **Melati Lounge**, Plaza Inn, Tel: 06-2827959. **Restoran Kesidang**, Ayer Keroh Country Resort, Tel: 06-325211.
CHINESE: **Hiking Restaurant**, 112, Taman Malacca Jaya, Tel: 06-2833293. **Lim Tian Puan**, 251, Jl. Tun Sri Lanang, Tel: 06-2822727. **Village Court Chinese Restaurant**, Malacca Village Park Plaza Resort, Ayer Keroh.
PORTUGUESE: (all in the Portuguese quarter) **Restoran De Lisboa**, Tel: 06-2848067. **Restoran De Portugis**, Tel: 06-2843156. **San Pedro Restaurant**.
TAMIL: **Restoran Banana Leaf**, 36, Jl. Munshi Abdullah, Tel: 06-2837252.
INDIAN: **Sri Lakshmi Villas**, 2, Jl. Bendahara, Tel: 06-2824926.
BABA & NYONYA: **Ole Sayang**, 198-199, Taman Malacca Jaya, Tel: 06-2831966. **Nyonya Makko**, 123, T. Malacca Jaya, Tel: 06-2840737. **Peranakan**, 317 C, Kleang Besar, Tel: 06-354436.
THAI: **My Place**, 537, Taman Malacca Jaya, Tel: 06-2843848.
The Night Market is located in Jl. Bunga Raya.

Shopping

There are a large number of **antique stores** along Jl. Hang Jebat (formerly Jonker Street). Salespeople can inform you about the applicable export regulations. There are larger **shopping centers** with fixed prices on Jl. Bunga Raya, Jl. Hang Tuah, Jln Tun Ali. In smaller shops and markets, bargaining is generally called for. **Souvenirs and crafts** are sold at various stores along the waterfront, on Jl. Parameswara and in Mini Malaysia.

Tourist information

Malacca Tourist Information Center, Jl. Kota (closes at 5:00 pm), Tel: 06-2836538. **Tourist Police**, Tel: 06-222222, ext. 148.

JOHOR BAHRU
Getting there / Transportation

BY AIR: **MAS** operates daily flights to **K. L.** , the islands and all state capitals including **Kuching, K. Kinabalu.**
BUS: Daily express buses **to K. L., Kota Bharu, K. Terengganu, Ipoh, Taiping, Butterworth, Alor Setar, Mersing, Kuantan, Singapore.** Bus terminals for various lines: Jl. Trus. **Express Nasional**, Tel: 07-2245182; **Hosni Express**, Tel: 07-2223404; **Express Ekoba** (to Kuala Lumpur), Tel: 07-2236076.
TRAIN: Station on Jl. Tun Abdul Razak, information: Tel: 07-2233040.
TAXI: Central office for several taxi firms: Banguman Letak Kereta MPJB, Jl. Wong Ah Fook. **Comfort Radiotaxi:** Tel: 07-2322852.
CAR RENTAL: **Avis Rent a Car**, Tropical Inn, Jl. Gereja, Tel: 07-2228357. **Hertz Rent a Car**, 1, Jl. Trus, Tel: 07-2237520. **Budget Rent a Car** 216, Jl. Wong Ah Fook, Orchid Plaza, Tel: 07-2243951.

Accommodations

LUXURY: **Puteri Pan Pacific Hotel**, Jl. Salim, Tel: 07-2233333.
MODERATE: **Holiday Inn Crown Plaza**, Jl. Dato' Sulaiman, Taman Century, Tel: 07-3323800. **Tropical Inn**, 15, Jl. Gereja, Tel: 07-2247888. **Rasa Sayang Baru Hotel**, 10, Jl. Dato' Dalam, Tel: 07-2248600. **Merlin Inn**, Lot 5435, Jl. Bukit Meldrum, Tel: 07-2227400. **Straits View Hotel**, 1D, Jl. Skudai, Tel: 07-2241402. **Causeway Inn**, 6A-6E, Jl. Meldrum, Tel: 07-2248811.
BUDGET: **First Hotel**, Jl. Station, Tel: 07-2222888. **Hawaii Hotel**, 21, Jl. Meldrum, Tel: 07-2240633. **JB Hotel**, 80A, Jl. Wong Ah Fook, Tel: 07-2234788. **Malaya Hotel**, 20, Jl. Bukit Meldrum, Tel: 07-221691. **Regent Elite Hotel**, 1, Jl. Siew Nam, Tel: 07-2243812. **Mareera Hotel**, 42A, Taman Maju Jaya, Tel: 07-3332492.

Restaurants

MALAY: **Sata Ria**, Holiday Plaza, Jl. Dato' Suleiman, Tel: 07-3311136. **Banafe Baru**, 62/34, Jl. Segget, Tel: 07-2240702.
CHINESE: **Straits Cruise Seafood Restaurant**, Batu 41, Jl. Skudai, Tel: 07-3375788. **Moon Palace**, Johor Tower, Jl. Gereja, Tel: 07-2321888. **Prawn House**, Jl. Harimau, Century Garden. **Blue Star Rest.**, 52, Jl. Jaya, Taman Maju Jaya.
INDIAN: **Granee's Banana Leaf**, Jl. Segget. **Kerala Rest.**, 33, Jl. Ibrahim, Tel: 07-2324283.
WESTERN: **Coffee House**, Merlin Inn, Johor Bahru. **Boulevard Coffee House**, Jl. Dato' Sulaiman, Tel: 07-2323800.
City specialties are *sea cucumber, Laksa Johor* (rice noodles) and *Lontong* (rice cubes).

Shopping

Textiles: Plaza Kota Raya, Jl. Trus. **Kerry's Kompleks**, Taman Pelangi, Holiday Plaza, Jl. Dato' Sulaiman. You can find other souvenirs, such as **Johor** crafts at: **KOMTAR**, ground floor, Jl. Wong Ah Fook. **Crafttown**, 36, Jl. Skudai, Tel: 07-3367346. Sri Ayu **Batik Industries & Promotion**, 77, Jl. Storey, Off Bukit Changar, Tel: 07-2241978.

Museums, Zoo

Royal Abu Bakar Muzium, daily (except Fri) 9:00 am-4:00 pm. **Zoo Negeri Johor Derul Takzim**, Jl. Gertak Merah, open daily 8:00 am-6:00 pm.

Hospital

Hospital Sultanah Aminah, Jl. Tun Dr. Ismail, Tel: 07-2231666.

Immigration Authorities

Immigration, Block B, 1st Floor, Jl. Ayer Molek, Tel: 07-2244255.

Tourist Information / Police

Malaysia Tourism Promotion Board (MTPB), KOMTAR, Jl. Wong Ah Fook, Tel: 07-2223590. **Tourism Development Corp. Info Center**, 52, Tun A. Razak Complex, Jl. Wong Ah Fook, Tel: 07-2223590. **Johor State Secretary (Local Government Branch – Tourism)**, Sultan Ibrahim Building, Tel: 07-2241957 ext. 30. **Police**, Jl. Meldrum, Tel: 07-2245522.

DESARU
Accommodations

MODERATE: **Desaru Golf**, Kota Tinggi, Tel: 07-8221101. **Desaru Beach View**, Kota Tinggi, Tel: 07-8221101. **Desaru Garden**, Kota Tinggi, Tel: 07-8221211.

IN THE WORLD'S OLDEST RAIN FOREST

PAHANG DARUL MAKMUR
TAMAN NEGARA
ORANG ASLI
FROM COAST TO COAST

PAHANG DARUL MAKMUR

Pahang Darul Makmur, at about 9 million acres (36,000 sq. km) the country's largest state, encompasses the center of the peninsula. Two-thirds of its 800,000 inhabitants are Malay, about 26 percent Chinese and 7 percent Indian. Dense rain forests still cover extensive parts of this state. However, here, as well as in Borneo, deforestation is rampant; Malaysia has in fact "sawed" its way into the ranks of the world's leaders in destruction of its natural forests. About 18 million cubic feet (one half million cubic meters) of lumber is cut in Pahang for export each year.

In addition to lumber, the other major trading commodities are rubber, palm oil, coconuts, coffee, cocoa, tea, fruit and rice.

Like the neighboring state of Kelantan, Pahang was under control of the Hindu Empire of Srivijaya before it became a vassal state of Malacca and, later, Johor-Rihau. In 1888, British sovereignty began, though it was rocked by insurrections in 1891 and 1896.

The east coast and the off-shore island of Tioman are important tourist attrac-

Left: Giant of the jungle in the Malaysian rain forest.

tions; in the interior of the country, it's the tropical lake region around Lake Chini that attracts visitors. For those who are not content merely to bask on the beach, the Endau-Rompin Forest Reserve in the southeast is well worth seeing: it contains nearly virgin lowland rain forests.

TAMAN NEGARA

For nature lovers, the biggest attraction on the Malaysian peninsula is Taman Negara. This huge national park, 11,677 sq. miles (4,343 sq. km) in area and taking in parts of Pahang, Kelantan and Terengganu, consists of a rain forest which is still intact.

Malaysia's primeval forests are a paradise for botanists. They date back more than 130 million years, which makes them older than the jungles of Africa and South America. They were never subjected to climatic fluctuations, such as the Ice Ages which affected other parts of the world, and the negative influence of man didn't make itself felt until this century. As lumbering for international export began to increase, the region of today's preserve was officially turned into the "King George V National Park" in 1925, in order to preserve the flora and fauna of at least a part of these ancient forests.

125

Sandstone, calcium deposits and granite form the geological basis of Taman Negara. And quartzite is found atop Gunung Tahan, the peninsula's highest mountain at 7,003 ft (2,187 m).

The flora of the national park is fascinating and, to a certain extent, endemic, i.e. unique to this region. Many plants along the paths are labelled. In the park's lowland jungles, the giant Tualang trees are noteworthy. The vegetation on the slopes is mainly oaks and laurel bushes. Just below the summit, where the rain forest is often enveloped in clouds of fog, expanses of moss and lichen can be found. Many kinds of ferns thrive here, such as the nest fern (*asplenium nichus*), known to the Orang Asli as *paku langsuir*. A multitude of different tree species tower above the earth, including the tutok (*hibiscus macroplyllus*) from which the natives carve their blowpipe arrows. The natives also use wood from other in-

Above: Huge ferns are typical of the rain forest vegetation.

digenous trees, such as the *kekatong* (*cynomeira malaccensis*), the *sepetir licin* (*sindora coriacea*) or the *marbau* (*instia palembanica*), to build their dwellings. From the *merawan* (*hopea*) tree, the Orang Asli harvest the resin for their torches. Liana and parasite plants are abundant, protected by the dense canopy of the rain forest, under which the ancient cycle of this incredibly varied forest flora can continue undisturbed.

A huge number of animals make their home in Taman Negara. Many of Malaysia's approximately 1,000 wild elephants live in the park. Tigers and rhinoceroses wander about, though they are rarely seen by humans. From one of the observation posts, however, it is possible to catch a glimpse of deer, tapir or wild boar. Hornbills, eagles and parrots, as well as about 250 other species of birds, can be seen soaring through the skies. Several species of monkeys (macaques, gibbons) swing playfully through the trees.

The Taman Negara is open to tourists from mid-January to mid-November, i.e. before and after the monsoon season. Starting point for hikes (allow several days) is the **Park Headquarters** in **Kuala Tahan**, which can be reached by boat from **Kuala Tembeling** in about four hours. There's also access by both road and rail. All permits, accommodations and guided tours must be booked before entering the park at the **Taman Negara Booking Office** in the Wildlife & National Park Department in Kuala Lumpur.

The trails around the headquarters are safe, and visitors come away from short boat trips on the rivers with memorable impressions. One of the special treks is the new **Canopy Walk** near the park's headquarters. These knotted bridges using neither nails nor screws, are hung between the trees at a height of up to 65 ft (20 m). Over 1,300 ft (400 m) have already been installed, and an extension is being worked on. Some sections are over 260 ft (80 m) long and can carry up to 20

tons. The panoramic view over the jungle and the river is spectacular, and with a little luck you will spot wild animals.

A high point of any visit to Taman Negara, literally and figuratively, is a hike up **Gunung Tahan**, which leads through a variety of vegetation zones. The 81-mile (130 km) round trip takes about nine days, and should only be attempted with a reliable guide. Tents and supplies must be carried in from the starting point, **Kampong Kuala Tahan Headquarters**. On the second day, which is extremely strenuous due to the ups and downs of the path, one usually reaches **Kuala Puteh**, where a river offers refreshment and sometimes even fresh fish. More rivers await on the following day and, perhaps, the odd jungle animal. Then the climb begins. In camp **Padang**, at about 4,900 ft (1,500 m), the temperatures can drop to a nippy 40°F (4°C). However, knowing that you'll reach the summit and look out over all of Taman Negara within a matter of three hours is generally enough to warm the soul.

ORANG ASLI

It's a real advantage to have a member of the Orang Asli along as a guide through the park. Their home is the jungle; they have lived here for thousands of years. Orang Asli (aboriginal people) is the collective term for a large number of different ethnic groups which move around the peninsula as semi-nomads. These include the Negrito group called Semang, the oldest of the Orang Aslis. Only about 2,000 of this group still live in Malaysia. Europeans term them Negrito because of their Negroid characteristics (kinky hair, dark skin, short stature). The Semang tribe is composed of seven loosely-defined tribes or dialect groups (including Kensiu, Jahai, Batek). They are democratically organized, with elected leaders – usually the oldest members of the tribe – who can, at any time, be relieved of their position. Within their groups, which consist of extended families but never exceed 30 individuals, the Orang Asli share booty from the hunt

and other food. Their only property are fruit trees (mainly durians, the harvest of which is divided up among the group) and blowpipes. These extremely dangerous weapons, about 6.5 ft (2 m) long, are made of two bamboo shoots stuck inside one another. The Orang Asli coat their arrows with poisonous sap from trees and with wasp and snake venom, and use them to hunt birds, monkeys, wildcats and wild boar. Over time, they've developed a long-distance system of trading with the settled Malays. They deposit forest products (honey, resin, fruits, roots) near settlements; and, several days later, go back to these same spots to collect the goods offered in exchange (knives, salt, tobacco, beads).

The **Senoi**, numbering about 36,000, is the largest group of the Orang Asli. These light-skinned natives, which include especially the **Semai** and **Temiar**, probably immigrated here after the Se-

mang but before the proto-Malays. They are non-migratory and live in settlements of houses on stilts, usually at the edge of the jungles in the center of the country.

The proto-Malays, the natives who settled on the peninsula before the Malays, also belong to the Orang Asli. They number about 25,000 and are a sedentary people mainly settled along the banks of the tributary rivers. Like the Senoi, the proto-Malays, the majority of whom are Jakuns, plant fruit trees; in addition to cultivating their plantations, they also fish. Their houses are built in the stilt style of the Malays; they no longer use blowpipes.

The Orang Asli, still basically a native people in a natural environment which is now disappearing, traditionally believe in spirits. They live according to certain laws and taboos, all of which are designed to regulate the harmony between man and nature. Thus incest, as well as cruelty to animals, is forbidden.

As is true in many other countries, the native inhabitants of Malaysia are an

Above: The Orang Asli still use blowpipes for hunting.

exotic people in their own land. It was not too long ago that Malays were still captured and kept as slaves. Countless Orang Asli lost their lives this way. Even today they are still treated as *sakai*, as a primitive and provincial people.

Under the pretext of progress and because of the destruction of the forest, the Orang Asli are increasingly being forced to settle down; efforts are being made to convert them to civilized Malaysians. The government proudly points to the programs of medical care and education which it has officially made available to the native inhabitants.

FROM COAST TO COAST

It doesn't take long to cross from the east coast to the west, whether by flying or on the federal highway, Route 2, which links K.L. and Kuantan. To the south, you can quickly traverse the peninsula on Federal Route 50; while in the north, the East-West highway between Penang and Kota Bharu has linked Lake Andamanen with the South China Sea since 1982. This highway through the peninsula's remaining jungle begins in the town of **Gerik**. It can be reached from the west coast via one of two routes; preferable is the one passing through Bukit Mertajem and **Kulim**. An old Chinese temple stands nearby, the **Hal Tah Ma**. (For a further description of this route, see the chapter on Perak, page 79.) By the state of Kelantan, near the truck stop **Batu Melintang**, you can see the spectacular limestone formations of the **Gunung Reng** towering overhead.

From **Jeli**, the end of the most difficult stretch of the highway, the road follows the border with Thailand for a few miles before leading off into the lowlands of the Kelantan River. **Tanah Merah** is located on the east coast train line, in a fertile agricultural region. From here, it is only 33 miles (53 km) to Kota Bharu, the metropolis on the east coast.

NATIONAL PARK TAMAN NEGARA
Getting there / Transportation

BY AIR: **Pelangi Air**, Tel: 03-7463000, has flights several times a week from **K. L. to Sungai Tiang**. From there, Kuala Tahan is about 45 min.

TRAIN: Night train from **K. L. or Singapore** via Gemas to **Tembeling** (train stops only on request!) From there, it's about a 3-hour boat ride. Information in K. L.: Tel: 03-2747435. From the east coast, a train runs from **Kota Bharu** to **Jerantut**; from there, after an overnight stay, take a bus or taxi to the dock for **Kuala Tembeling**.

BUS/TAXI: From the bus and taxi terminal **Perhentian Bas Pudu Raya** to **Temerloh** or **Jerantut**. Buses and taxis (usually to be shared) run between both places.

CAR RENTAL: Reserve at agencies (see K. L. chapter), or at **Asian Overland Services**, Kuala Lumpur, Tel: 03-2925622. Route: From either **Kuala Lumpur** or **Kota Bharu** to **Jerantut**. Continue from there to the dock at **K. Tembeling**.

Accommodations

It's advisable to book lodgings and the boatride from K. Tembeling 10 to 14 days ahead of time. By telephone: **Wildlife and National Parks Department**, km 10, Jl. Cheras, Kuala Lumpur, Tel: 03-9052872. Bottlenecks are usually during vacation time, first half of March, mid-May to mid-June, November.

LUXURY to BUDGET: The park only has the state-run **Taman Negara Resort** for accommodations, but it offers every category from bungalow suite to chalet, dormitory and camping site. For reservations: 03-2455585 or 09-2662200.

BUDGET: **Byoing's Hostel**, outside the park itself on the "private" bank of the river; from there, a little upstream, is the **Nusa Camp**

Restaurants

Besides a large restaurant serving Malay and Western food at the park headquarters, there are also cantines for the visitors. The private sector offerings on the other bank of the river are better and more varied, however. Ferry service free of charge.

Hospital

State Clinic, Tel: 09-2661122.

JERANTUT
Accommodations

Overnight accommodations on the way to Taman Negara National Park: **Government Resthouse**, Tel: 09-2662214. **Jerantut Hotel**, Jl. Besar.

GERIK (GRIK)
Accommodations

BUDGET: You can stay in simple Chinese hotels along **Jln. Takong Datoh** or **Jln. Tan Saban.** These generally also have restaurants or coffee shops; and there are markets & shops in the town.

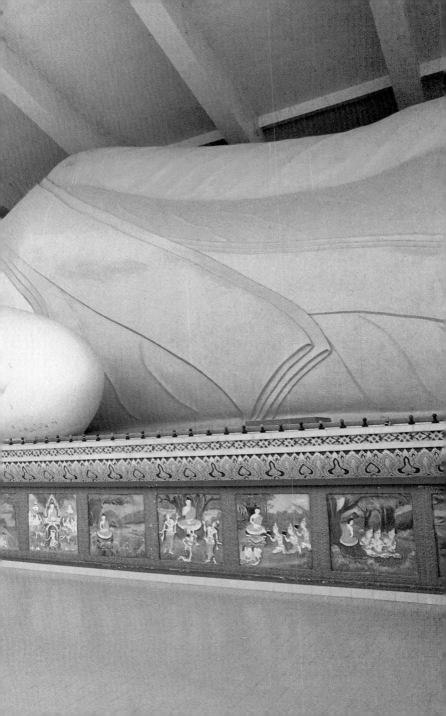

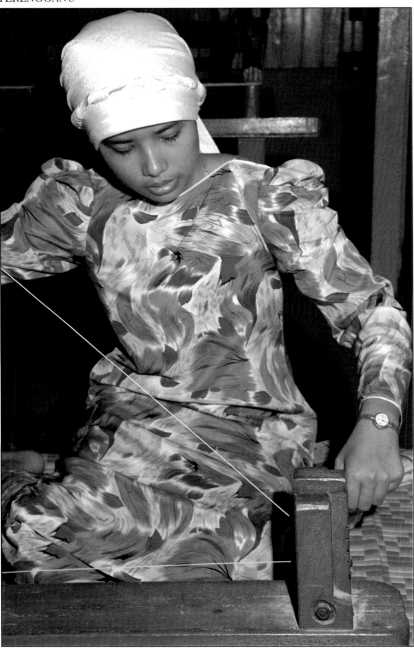

ORIENTAL
PROVINCE

KELANTAN
KOTA BHARU
EXCURSIONS FROM KOTA
BHARU
TERENGGANU

KELANTAN

Often described as the original Malaya, the east coast of the peninsula does indeed differ greatly from the west. There are few cities, and tall buildings are rare; rural roads wind through secluded fields. Besides the oil fields, the major industries are rural handicrafts and fishing. What plantations exist are of relatively modest size.

The attraction of the coast lies mainly in its long, palm-lined beaches; another draw are its lovely islands, which offer good opportunities for diving. The inhabitants of the kampongs (villages) seem to have preserved their traditional, peaceful pace of life. Comprised of almost 90 percent Malays, the population on the east coast tends to follow a conservative Islamic lifestyle. This, of course, puts something of a damper on the kind of liberal tourism we know in the west; still, the economic benefits of tourism have not gone unnoticed here. The rustic type of accommodations which once predominated can still be found, but luxury hotels have also been built, placing some towns on the international tourist circuit.

Preceding pages: Reclining Buddha in the Wat Photivihan Monastery near Kota Bharu. Left: Woman spinning in Terengganu.

The state of Kelantan, with its 3.7 million acres (15,000 sq. km), borders to the north on the South China Sea. The Islamic religion arrived here from Malacca, which was formerly part of the empire of Srivijaya. Kelantan enjoyed a lengthy period of independence before the Thais and the British began passing control of the area back and forth. This lasted until 1948, when Kelantan joined the Malaysian Federation of States.

With 93 percent of the approximately one million inhabitants Malays, it is no wonder that the opposition party, the Partai Islam Sa Malaysia (PAS), is in the majority here. Visitors to this state will become cognizant of this fact at the very latest when they discover that no alcohol is served in the state-owned hotels.

KOTA BHARU

The name of the capital translates literally as "new town," although it is actually about 200 years old. Boasting almost 400,000 inhabitants, it is located close to the Thai border. The fact that it can be easily reached from K.L. and Penang has bolstered the city's economy, which has also profited for quite some time from the border traffic with **Rantau Panjang/Sungai Golok** (also Ko-Lok). With about 30 hotels, guesthouses and

133

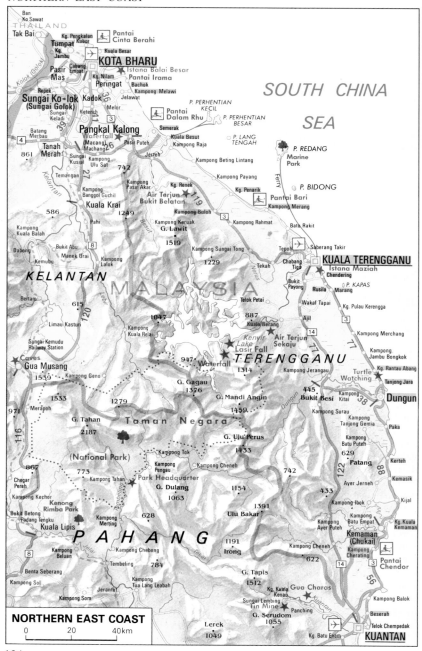

NORTHERN EAST COAST

0   20   40km

beach resorts, Kota Bharu is well prepared for visitors.

It also offers several interesting attractions. The **Central Market** on Jl. Tengku
Chik is a colorful sight with a variety of
fruits, spices and vegetables on display.
Women draped in gold stand amidst their
wares, dominating the market scene.
Housed in a round building, the Pasar can
be seen as a kind of giant stage if viewed
from the vantage point of one of its storeys. Stands for batik and crafts located
throughout the floors supplement the offerings of the market.

Fabrics typical of the region can also
be found, at very reasonable prices, in the
shopping center on the northern stretch of
Jl. Sultanah Zanaib. The renowned sil-
versmiths of Kelantan can be seen at
work in the southern part of the street.
For other craft shops, try Jl. Temenggon.
The **Kelantan Cultural Center** or Gelanggang Seni offers more culture and
art. Between March and October, *wau* is
demonstrated here. This is the local word
for kite-flying, a traditional competition
with colorful, artistically-constructed
kites made of (rice) paper and bamboo.
The tradition of *wau*, including the construction and festive flight demonstra-
tion, dates back thousands of years and is
handed down in families from generation
to generation. In Malaysia, moon kites
and cat kites are the most well-known
varieties of these delicate creations. In
the north of the city, along the route to the
Cinta Berahi beach, you can watch kite-
makers at work.

Other popular sports and cultural
events are held throughout the state as
part of the opulent festivals held between
February and October. These can also be
seen in the Cultural Center: they include
the martial art of *silat*; the drum competition *rebana ubi*; the art of spinning tops
known as *gasing*; dances and games such
as *menora*, *puteri*, *inai*; the dance drama
Mak Yong; the shadow puppets of the
Wayang Kulit; and a poetry competition

known as *Berdikir Barat*. In addition, the
inhabitants of Kelantan love their bird-
call competitions. Every year in August
in Kota Bharu hundreds of *Merbuk*, "pi-
geons," are given a chance to demonstrate their loveliest cooing and warbling
talents.

The state museum in the **Istana Jahar**,
near Jl. Pintu Pong, is a good place to im-
merse yourself in tradition. In this small
palace, built in 1889, exhibits include archeological finds, drums, gongs, jewelry,
furniture and old kites. Diagonally across
from this museum is the **Istana Balai
Besar**, which dates from 1844. The large
audience hall with its lovely wooden
carvings is still used for festive occasions. In front of the palace, stands offer
profane yet delicious snacks that are a
welcome treat, whether your appetite is
large or small.

In the center of town, somewhat east of
the Kelantan River, is the **Padang Merdeka**. On Independence Square, the Malaysians pay tribute to the soldiers who
gave their lives during World War I, as
well as to the freedom fighter Tok Jang-
gut, who was hanged here by the British.
To the north is the **Masjid Muhamadi**,
the city mosque, built from 1916 to 1926.
One of the oldest stone houses in the city
is found on the corner of Jl. Masjid and
Jl. Sultan; today, it houses an art gallery
and craft center.

In addition to the craft shops within the
city, several towns near Kota Bharu also
offer traditional handicrafts. Silver
jewelry and vessels are crafted by residents of **Kampong** (Kg.) **Morak**, 5.5
miles (9 km) away, as well as in the local
Handicraft Center in **Kg. Badang**, about
6 miles (10 km) north of Kota Bharu. **Se-
masa Batik**, in **Kg. Puteh** (almost 2
miles/3 km) and in **Kg. Penambang** (2
miles/3.2 km along the route to the northern beach), produces an excellent selection of batik and songket fabrics.

The Tourist Office arranges boat and
trekking tours, in conjunction with the

Perdana Hotel, as well as a 3-day stay with a local family. The program *Be a Villager or a Dancer*, while not cheap (about 180 M$ per person, children under 12 stay for free), offers courses in traditional handicrafts and dancing. A minimum of two people is required for this program.

EXCURSIONS FROM KOTA BHARU

Kota Bharu's dream beach is the **Pantai Cinta Berahi**, the beach of passionate love. It may be that hot romances have been played out here, but the attractions of this tree-lined strip of coast to the north of the city are not immediately overwhelming. A new hotel on the beach at least offers a certain degree of luxury, and the abovementioned craft centers

Above: The broad selection at the Central Market in Kota Bharu. Right: Snorkelling is a pleasure along Kota Bharu's beaches and bays.

make a visit to the area well worthwhile. The village of **Kuala Besar**, at the mouth of the Sungai Kelantan, is a good departure point for snorkeling expeditions.

Following the route to the airport from Kota Bharu, it is about a 6 mile (10 km) journey to **Pantai Dasar Sabak**. This is a historic spot: it was here, on December 8th, 1941, that the Japanese landed. Within six weeks they had conquered all of Malaya and Singapore. Today, it's only colorfully-decorated fishing boats, as seen in the tourist brochures, which sometimes land on this popular beach.

Traveling to the north through a landscape dotted with rice and tobacco fields, you arrive at the beaches of **Pantai Sri Tujuh** on the largest lagoon in Malaysia. Ferries leave from nearby **Kg. Pengkalan Kubor** for the trip across the border river of Kolok (Golok) to Thailand.

7.5 miles (12 km) to the southeast, you can see one of Asia's largest stone Buddhas in the village of **Cabang Empat Tok Mengah**. This reclining Buddha, 130 ft (40 m) long and 36 ft (11

m) high, is in the **Wat Photivihan Monastery**, which has become an important pilgrimage site since it was built in 1980. About 200 members of the Thai minority live in nearby **Kampong Jambu**. A boat trip up the Sungai Kelantan can be an adventure; you can rent boats in **Tumpat**, the last stop on the train line. Residents of **Pulau Jong** in the delta build traditional boats, which can be seen in action at the annual March regatta, held to honor the sultan. **Wat Uttamaram** is another impressive Thai temple near **Repek**.

About 6 miles (10 km) south of Kota Bharu is the Muslim holy site and national monument of **Masjid Kampong Laut**. Dating back 300 years, it is probably the oldest mosque in Malaysia. Javanese missionaries constructed it entirely from wood. Because its original location on the river was threatened by floods, it was moved to **Kg. Nilam Puri**.

The beaches near **Bachok**, 9 miles (15 km) further, are among the most beautiful on the east coast. Just north of the village, **Pantai Irama** (Melody Beach) is alluring for its name alone; the beach is ideal for picnics or camping. South of Bachok, roaring breakers make **Kg. Melawi** a surfer's paradise, while **Pantai Dalam Rhu** (Beach of the Whispering Breeze), 16 miles (25 km) further southeast, attracts those looking for more peaceful waters. The nearby fishing village of **Semarak** is renowned, like the towns around it, for quality woodcarving.

TERENGGANU

Like Kelantan, the state of Terengganu (also Trengganu), measuring 3.2 million acres (13,000 sq. km), bears the strong stamp of the Islamic lifestyle. Even before the founding of the Malacca Sultanate, Islam had already gained a foothold here. Trengganu, like Kelantan, became a vassal state of Malacca and Johor and later came under the rule of Thailand. Along with its neighbor to the north,

Trengganu had to accept British sovereignty in 1909 before it joined the Malayan Federation.

The state is one of the least developed regions of Malaysia. The discovery of offshore natural gas and oil have sparked hopes of an economic surge, hopes which have already manifested themselves in the modern structures in the capital of Kuala Terengganu, the power plants, refinery and harbor terminals. These industrial complexes are still only individual islands of activity dotting the 150 miles (240 km) of sandy coast.

Passing through rice paddies, the trip continues to the popular beach town of **Kuala Besut**. Noteworthy here is the traditional wooden palace **Istana Tengku Indera Sejera**, on Jl. Tengku. The main reason for a stopover, however, is to visit the islands of **Perhentian Besar** and **Perhentian Kecil**. Leaving from the Fisheries Complex in Besuit, one can travel the 13 miles (21 km) to the islands by boat in just under two hours. One of Malaysia's best beaches is found here, and the ocean around the islands has been declared a protected area. The reefs are ideal for diving. Reef sharks and turtles sometimes pass through the coral gardens, and dolphins jump playfully in the clear waters. Wooded paths wind through the interior of the islands. The Pulau Perhentian Besar, formerly uninhabited, has now been converted to the Perhentian Island Resort. A chalet village resort is located on another of the island's beaches. If only the trash problem could be brought under control, then Perhentian might truly be able to fulfill the promise made on a sign welcoming tourists to the island: "Where reality becomes a dream."

After passing Kuala Besut, the paved road winds into the interior of the country. Rice paddies once again dominate the scenery. Near **Kg. Renek** is the recreational area of **Air Terjun Bukit Belatan** with its refreshing waterfall. At **Kg. Buloh**, a small street connects the highway to the coast, and leads along the ocean. **Kg. Penarik** has lovely beaches, such as **Pantai Bari** to the south.

The departure point for the next island detour is **Kg. Merang**, where ferry boats shuttle passengers to **Pulau Redang**, 25 miles (40 km) away; there's also a ferry to the island from the capital, Kuala Terengganu. The island is part of a wildlife preserve and the inhabitants, although dependent on fishing, appear to be obeying the regulations – except for collecting turtle eggs illegally. Coral, which can be found growing even between the pile dwellings, is an impetus to venture out for a dive on the reefs. Swimming is wonderful in the bay of **Telok Dalam**, and in the island's jungles you can see birds, monkeys and flying squirrels. At certain times of the year, the turtles lay their eggs on the beach of Pulau Redang. This little island also has a large resort

Right: This small terrestrial turtle is a distant relative of the huge leatherback turtles of Rantau Abang.

and a golf course by now. Up to 72,000 Vietnamese boat people found refuge on **Pulau Bidong**, to the southwest, between 1978 and 1989.

Oil, the New Fortune of the East Coast

Kuala Terengganu is no longer merely a provincial fishing village. The economic miracle, in the form of oil and natural gas production, administrative buildings and shopping centers, has spread over this city of nearly 300,000 inhabitants. This progress has also led to the construction of classy hotels in prime beachfront locations. A visit to the **Central Market** gives insight into the goods typical of this region: bamboo, wooden and rattan crafts, fruits and vegetables of every variety, dried fish, rice cakes and turtle eggs, popular as an aphrodisiac.

Nearby, on the ocean side, is the small French-influenced **Istana Maziah**, built as the Sultan's residence in 1884 and still used today by the royal family for festive occasions. The modern palace, **Istana Badariah**, outside the city on the route to Dungun, has its own golf course.

Adjacent to the old royal residence are the **Masjid Abidin**, built in 1893 and similar to the national mosque of K.L., and the royal **Mausoleum**, containing the remains of Sultan Ismail, who died in 1979. To the east is the **Kg. Dalam Kota** (Village Within the City) with its old Malay houses. Most of Terengganu's relatively small Chinese population live in this bustling neighborhood along the river on **Jl. Bandar**. From the harbor, you can travel to **Pulau Duyong**, where boat builders are busy constructing traditional fishing boats as well as yachts for international customers.

History buffs can brush up on their knowledge of the region's past in the **State Museum** on Bukit Kecil, in the southern section of the city. One exhibit displays one of the bicycles which the

Japanese used to conquer the peninsula during World War II.

The crafts centers are located a bit outside of the city. The **Suterasemai Center**, about 4 miles (6 km) to the south, in Chendering, specializes in the manufacture of silk. Songket fabric, batik, mats and baskets made in the Handicraft Center are sold at the city market as well as in **Rusila**, 6 miles (10 km) away on the road to Marang.

From Route 14, which leads into the country's interior, a road to **Kuala Berang** branches off in Ajil. This village is important historically as the site of the discovery of the so-called Trengganu Stone, with Malay-Arabic inscriptions dating from 1326, the oldest evidence of Islam in Malaysia. Nearby, the **Air Terjun Sekayu Park** is a refreshing oasis. Just to the west is the huge reservoir of **Tasek Kenyir**, which has flooded the jungle since 1985. The newly-constructed **Primula Lenyir Lake Resort** on the island of Pulau Ipoh attracts anglers and water sports enthusiasts.

The coastal route soon reaches the picturesque fishing village of **Marang**. Just off the coast is **Pulau Kapas**, an island long considered an insider tip by diving enthusiasts. Nowadays, there are accommodations available both in Marang and on the island; the latter, while certainly not in the luxury category, has the distinct advantage of being a nature preserve.

Where the Turtles Come Ashore

They come from afar, these survivors of a prehistoric species which has existed for about 100 million years.

The leatherback turtles (*dermochelys coriacea*), measuring over 6.5 ft (2 m) in length, weighing over 1,300 pounds (600 kg) and living to a ripe old age of several hundred years, are endangered today. Only about 30,000 to 40,000 still live in the tropical oceans between North America, Chile, Australia and Southeast Asia. They feed on molluscs and water plants. The females come on land only to lay their eggs. Of the total of eleven nest-

139

ing sites throughout the world, two of the turtles' favorite are the coast of Surinam and the stretch of beach between Dungun and Rantau Abang.

The threat to their existence is caused solely by man. Although the meat of the leatherbacks, the largest turtles in the world, is inedible, as it contains a lethal poison which attacks the nervous system, locals believe the eggs increase male potency. Thus, Malaysian fishermen collected this delicacy as soon as the reptiles had completed the strenuous procedure of laying and burying their eggs in the sand. In 1960, the Ministry of Fishing of Terengganu and the World Wildlife Fund (WWF) of Malaysia developed a program designed to protect the interests of the fishermen and the turtles, as well as, more recently, to satisfy the curiosity of the tourists. Now, when a leatherback female has completed laying her more than 80 eggs in the season – generally be-

Above: A Malaysian peasant family in front of its house on stilts.

140

tween February and October, but mainly from June to August – the eggs are immediately retrieved. More than half are brought by state rangers to a breeding station. The rest are then allowed to be sold at the markets.

Turtle watching, only possible at night, has become a major tourist attraction. Fortunately, there are strict regulations about this, which are strictly enforced. Flash photos are forbidden, as is riding on the turtles, a sport once very popular among the Malaysians.

Oil Boom and Luxury Resorts

A stay in the hotel complex at **Tanjung Jara**, south of Rantau Abang, is not unlike being a guest in a sultan's palace. This pilot project of the country's Tourist Office has been decorated in the traditional Istana style. The gigantic **Intan Zarah Mosque** in Jl. Masjid in **Dungun** is also reminiscent of bygone days. Until the 1960s, Dungun was an important harbor for the export of iron ore from the mines of Bukit Besi. Today, the inhabitants' main livelihood is fishing.

Kerteh and **Paka**, until recently two sleepy fishing villages, have evolved in the opposite direction. Since the discovery of oil, power plants and refineries have become the village landmarks. **Kemasik** has retained its ancient charm. **Kg. Kuala Kemaman**, near Chukai, is a truly lovely fishing village. Between May and October, the green turtles lay their eggs at **Pantai Chendor**, a popular beach resort. The area around **Kampong Cherating**, location of Asia's first Club Mediteranée, is very touristy; but the swimming and surfing are excellent. **Beserah**, 6 miles (10 km) away from Kuantan, is a picturesque village. Water buffalo pull gaily painted boats ashore. The catch is processed into the popular salt fish. With kite flying, carving and spinning top games, this town maintains its traditions, for itself as well as for the tourists.

KOTA BHARU
Getting there / Transportation
BY AIR: **MAS** has daily flights from Kota Bharu to other major cities.

BY TRAIN: **Wakaf Bharu** Station, Tumpat. **To Kuala Lipis** via Gua Musang, **to Mentakab**, Gemas, Segamat **to Johor Bharu**.

BUS: Long-distance terminal (south, southeast und west): **Langgar Bus Station**, Jl. Pasir Puteh. Southwest from **Jl. Hamzah**. Local trips: **Jl. Pendek**.

Accommodations
LUXURY: **Perdana Resort**, Jl. Kuala Pa'Amat, Pantai Cinta Berahi (Beach of Passionate Love), Tel: 09-7733000. **Perdana Hotel**, Jl. Mahmood, Tel: 09-7485000.

MODERATE: **Temenggong**, Jl. Tok Hakim, Tel: 09-7483844. **Kencana Inn**, Jl. Padang Garong, Tel: 09-7447944. **Murni Hotel**, Jl. Dato' Padi, Tel: 09-7482399. **Pantai Cinta Berahi Resort**, Tel: 09-7481307.

BUDGET: **Milton Hotel**, 5471-A, B, C, Jl. Pengkalan Chepa, Tel: 09-7482744. **Suria Hotel**, Jl. Padang Garong, Tel: 09-7446567. **Long House Beach Motel**, Pantai Cinta Berahi, Tel: 09-7440090. **Tokyo Baru**, 3945, Jl. Tok Hakim (near the bus terminal; there are other cheap hotels in this area), Tel: 09-7449488.

Restaurants
MALAY: **Malaysia Restaurant**, Jl. Kebun Sultan. Cookshacks every evening on **Merdeka Square**, between the bus terminal and the market.

CHINESE: **Golden Jade Restaurant**, Hotel Perdana. **Lok Kau Hook**, 2959, Jl. Kebun Sultan. **Mee Chin Hotel**, near the Tokyo Baru Hotel.

THAI: **Sham Restaurant**, Berek 12.

WESTERN: **Rebana Coffee House**, Hotel Perdana. **Senangin Restaurant**, Perdana Resort.

SEAFOOD: on Cinta Berahi beach.

Museums / Palace
Istana Jahar with the **Kelantan State Museum**, open daily except Wed. 10:30 am-5:00 pm. **Istana Balai Besar,** by appointment.

Cultural Events
Kelantan Cultural Center (Gelanggang Seni), between March and October (except Ramadan) performances Wed. and Sat 3:30-5:30 pm, dancing Wed 9:00 pm-midnight. **Folklore** and traditional dancing also in **Senangin Restaurant**, Perdana Resort, daily from 7:30 pm.

Shopping
The best place to buy fabric and clothing is **Hangku Jaya**, Jl. Tok Hak; or in Jl. Pintu Pong, Jl. Parit Salam (**Bersaru Shopping Center**). Souvenirs and local crafts can be purchased in **Che Minah Songket**, Jl. Pantai Cinta Berala, Tel: 09-7441616.

Good silverwork: **Mohd Salleh**, Jl. Kg. Sireh, and at the **Pantai Cinta Berahi**.

Tourist Information
Tourist Information Center, Tel: 09-7485534. **TDC**, Tel: 09-6221433. Both in Jl. Sultan Ibrahim.

Immigration Authorities
Immigration Office, Jl. Sultan Ibrahim, Tel: 09-7482644.

KUALA TERENGGANU TO CHERATING
Getting there / Transportation
MAS has daily flights between Kuala Terengganu and other major cities, Tel: 09-6221415.

Bus terminal: Jl. Masjid/Jl. Banggol.

Accommodations
KUALA TERENGGANU: *LUXURY:* **Primula Beach Resort,** Jl. Persinggahan, Tel: 09-6222100. *MODERATE:* **Permai Park Inn**, Tel: 09-6222122. **Motel Desa**, Bukit Pak Apil, Tel: 09-6223488. *BUDGET:* **Sri Terengganu**, 120A, Jl. S. Ismail, Tel: 09-6236622. **Seri Hoover**, 49, Jl. Sultan Ismail, Tel: 09-6233823. **K.T.Mutiara Hotel**, 67, Jl. Sultan Ismail, Tel: 09-6222655.

DUNGUN: *LUXURY:* **Tanjung Jara Beach Hotel**, 8 miles (12.5 km) from Jalan Dungun, Tel: 09-8441801. *MODERATE:* **Merantau Inn**, between Rantau Abang and Tanjong Jara, Tel: 09-8441131. **Sri Dungun**, K. Dungun, 135, Jl. Tambun, Tel: 09-8441881. *BUDGET:* **Rantau Abang Visitor Center**, 12.5 mi (20 km) from Dungun, Tel: 09-8441533.

CHERATING: *LUXURY:* **Club Mediterranée**, Chendor Beach, Cherating, Tel: 09-439131. *MODERATE:* **Cherating Holiday Villa**, Mukim Sungai, Karang, Tel: 09-2431066.

PULAU REDANG: *MODERATE:* **Redang Lagoon Chalet**, Tel: 09-8272116. **Redang Pelangi Resort**, Tel: 09-6223158. **Redang Beach Resort**, Tel: 09-6222599.

Accommodations with bed and full board can also be booked on Pulau Redang.

PULAU PERHENTIAN: *LUXURY:* **Coral View Island Resort**, Tel: 011-9870943. *MODERATE:* **Perhentian Island Resort**, P. Perhentian Besar, Tel: 011-345562.

PULAU KAPAS: *MODERATE:* **Primula Kapas Island Village**, Tel: 09-6236110. *BUDGET:* **Zaki Beach Chalet**, Tel: 09-6120258.

KEMAMAN: *MODERATE:* **Muni Hotel**, K-312, Jl. Che Teng, Kemaman, Tel: 09-8682322.

Tourist Information
You can get information about cultural events and restaurants from **TDC**, 2243, Tingkat Bawah Wisma MCIS, Jl. Sultan Zainal Abidin, Tel: 09-6221433, Fax:09-6221791.

SOUTHERN EAST COAST

0   20   40km

BEACHES AND DIVERS' PARADISES

KUANTAN
AROUND KUANTAN
TEMERLOH
PEKAN
SOUTHERN EAST COAST

From Kuantan to Tioman

The southern region of the east coast, most of which is in the state of Pahang, is similar to the coast of Kelantan and Terengganu: miles of beaches dotted with fishing villages where a traditional lifestyle predominates. Old customs and handicrafts play an important role here. The inhabitants of Pahang are proud of their traditional *songket*, the Malaysian version of brocade weaving.

Aside from the peninsula's beaches and the Tioman Archipelago, tourist attractions include destinations in the interior of the state: the national parks around Lake Chini, an adventure on the Pahang River, or mountain climbing. The roads are generally good, making it easier for visitors to travel around the area.

KUANTAN

Kuantan, capital of the state of Pahang, is located where the Kuantan River flows into the South China Sea. This city of about 150,000 is the commercial metropolis of the east coast. Its airport, access to the harbor in Tanjung Gelang 16 miles (26 km) to the north, and the conjunction of several major highways combine to make it a regional hub. The downtown area is clean, modern, yet peaceful.

Its relatively inexpensive hotels make Kuantan a popular departure point for excursions into the surrounding countryside. **Wisma Sri Pahang**, the seat of the local government, and the **Teruntum Shopping Center Complex** are the most noticeable modern structures at the city center.

The **Court House**, on Jl. Mahkota near the river, is a good example of colonial architecture, surrounded by gardens and paths. A variety of craft shops, snack stands and restaurants contribute to the boardwalk atmosphere. A visit to the Buddhist temples in Jl. Bukit Setongkol and in Jl. Bukit, as well as the Hindu temple in Jl. Tanah Puteh is a must.

About 3 miles (5 km) east of downtown, the strip of land dividing the southern **Telok Sisek Beach** from the eastern **Telok Chempedak Beach** is the site of several luxury hotels as well as **a Tourist Information Counter** (in the Karyaneka Shop), restaurants, nightclubs and a **Botanic Garden**.

Every year during the last week of January, excitement runs high as the international windsurfing regatta is staged at **Balok Beach**. The strong monsoon winds ensure plenty of action at sea; on dry land, the accompanying celebrations include the traditional East Coast sports of kite flying and top spinning.

143

AROUND KUANTAN

About 15 miles (25 km) northwest of Kuantan is **Panching**. This town is famous for its limestone cliffs and the nearby caves, one of which houses the **Gua Chara**, a Buddhist temple. The 33 ft (10 m) long reclining Buddha here was created by a Thai hermit.

From here it is 5.5 miles (9 km) to the mines of **Sungai Lembing**. The country's largest tin mine, and the world's deepest at 3,280 ft (1,000 m), has been inactive since 1987. For tours register at the Tourist Information Center, located near the Post Office in Kuantan.

Tasek Chini: Lake of Legends

What Loch Ness is to Scotland, **Tasek Chini** is to Malaysia. This lake is said to

Above: Bizarre rocks on the coast near Kuantan. Right: Lotus blossoms cover the lakes in the natural paradise of Tasek Chini.

be home to a mythical serpentine monster called *naga sri gumum*. At least, this is the legend related by the Jakun, who once inhabited the entire hinterlands of Kuantan. Tales are also told of the lost city of the Khmer, now lying on the floor of the lake, submerged beneath its deep waters, but which once lay directly on the seacoast and was as magnificent as the renowned temple city of Angkor Wat in Kampuchea. Once a year, the natives await the appearance of the miraculous stone *batu sri gumum* on the lake's surface. Archeologists, using aerial photographs, and linguists, comparing Thai languages with those of the local Orang Asli, claim to have found evidence pointing to the actual existence of this city.

In Thai, the word *cini* means "gibbons," and swarms of these monkeys still swing through the surrounding rain forest. The lake's waters are filled with carp, tilapia and other fish; in addition, crocodiles are also right at home here.

Tasek Chini becomes truly enchanting between June and September, when it's

enveloped in a tender pink cloud of flowering lotus blossoms.

This natural paradise, twelve separate lakes linked with one another, lies about 60 miles (100 km) southwest of Kuantan. You can either take the fork off to the west about 12 miles (18 km) south of Batu Balik, which allows you to drive right up to the lake, or rather the resort; or you can enjoy a boat ride on the Pahang and Chini rivers. For the latter, take the road to **Kg. Belimbing** that branches off the Kuantan-Temerloh route after about 35 miles (56 km). From there, a motorized longboat takes visitors up the Pahang River to the Sungai Chini, which flows to the lake. **Lake Chini Resort**, one of several possibilities for accommodations in the lake region, offers modest chalets or camping facilities; it's a favorite haunt of sport fishermen.

More variety is offered on jungle excursions, during which one often encounters small bush elephants, or visits to the scattered settlements of the Orang Asli.

TEMERLOH

Temerloh is 78 miles (125 km) from Kuantan, in the middle of central Malaysia. It is located at the junction of several roads as well as two rivers, making it an attractive base for visits around Taman Negara. Travellers with a little more time can take a marvellous raft tour up the Pahang, the longest river in the Malaysian part of the peninsula, returning to Pekan on the east coast. The tour, organized by the Kuantan Tourist Office, begins in **Kg. Guai**, where the **Mosque** with its golden dome and the old warehouses on the river banks are worth a look. The large **market** held here every Saturday attracts local inhabitants from the surrounding riverside towns.

The train station of the line running from Johor via Kuala Lipis to Kota Bharu is 6 miles (10 km) to the west, in **Mentakab**. There is also a road leading to Kuala Lipis, the sometime capital of the former Malaya; from there, the road continues on to Kota Bharu.

145

PEKAN

One of the loveliest towns, and most interesting from a cultural-historical standpoint, is located 27 miles (44 km) south of Kuantan: the old royal city of **Pekan** near the mouth of the Pahang. Pekan existed as early as 1470, during the era of Sultan Mansur Shah of Malacca. In the last week of October, the city celebrates, along with Kuantan, the birthday of DYMM, the Sultan of Pahang. Although Pekan is normally rather provincial, during these festivities it becomes the ideal setting in which to observe the formal life of Malaysia. The celebrations include a wide variety of cultural, artistic, craft, sport and culinary events.

In addition to the new palace of **Istana Abu Bakar**, with its own expansive polo grounds, King Abu Bakar (1932-1974) also had the **Masjid Abu Bakar** built on the banks of the river. This is, in addition, the site of the **Sultan Abu Bakar Muzium**, housed in a colonial structure which was formerly the seat of the British Resident before becoming the Sultan's quarters. Exhibited here are finds from the Stone Age, weapons, regalia and ceramics, items from a Chinese junk which sank off the coast; textiles; and a *Wayang Kulit* stage.

Under Sultan Abdullah, who ruled from 1917-32, the art-deco **Abdullah Mosque** was constructed, also on the banks of the river. Most magnificent of this historic complex of buildings is the restored wooden palace of **Istana Lebang Tunggal** on Jl. Rompin Lama.

SOUTHERN EAST COAST

Route 3 follows the coastline right along the sea. The road passes numerous typical fishing villages, and crosses a number of rivers flowing into the South China Sea. Excursions by boat as well as ferries to the islands lying off the coast leave from Mersing. A hovercraft has started operations in Tioman. This section of coast also has nice beaches, however, notably **Pantai Batu Sembilan** and **Pantai Tanjung Batu**.

Two other rivers have lent their names to an internationally renowned nature reserve which – nature lovers hope – may well become a national park: **Endau Rompin**. In this zone of dense lowland rain forest in the states of Pahang and Johor, an estimated 25 Sumatra rhinoceroses (*dicerorhinus sumatrensis*) make their home. Bengal tigers and elephants are also found here. When the government of Pahang began to issue permits for forest use in 1977, the Malaysian Society for the Protection of Nature vehemently protested any further encroachment on the habitat of these rare animals. The result was that all logging activity was – supposedly – stopped.

The beach near **Kuala Rompin** is lovely. Boat trips up the Endau depart from **Padang Endau**. You can get more information about these trips, or about a visit to the Endau Rompin Park, from the tourist offices in either Mersing or Johor Bharu. One adventurous excursion is a raft trip combined with a climb up the 3,327- foot-high (1,014 m) **Gunung Besar** (a.k.a. Gunung Tiong). For those with less time, the mountaintop can be reached more quickly from **Labis**, the town southeast of Segamat. The Department of Wildlife in **Segamat** issues permits and information.

Penyabong, located on the coast 11 miles (18 km) south of Padang Endau, is an attractive beach resort. From here, rented boats carry passengers to the uninhabited islands of **Pulau Sembilan** and **Pulau Seribuat.**

Mersing, mainly renowned as a departure point for trips into the Tioman archipelago, is a lively fishing village. If you decide to stay here, you can take in the mosque or hang out on the beaches near **Kg. Kayu Papan** and on the island of **Pulau Sentindan**.

Boat excursions to the off-shore islands are basically available, but sojourns there are limited owing to the tides. The resorts on the islands are well-equipped for longer stays.

TIOMAN – QUEEN OF THE ISLANDS

Two mountain peaks measuring over 3,280 ft (1,000 m) are the conspicuous landmark of Tioman Island. The legend of the island's creation describes them as horns of a dragon which, in its battle for a lovely maiden, was defeated by a heroic adversary. Mortally wounded, the dragon fell into the sea, creating a terrible storm. Since then, according to the inhabitants of Tioman, the people on the mainland can see the "dragon's horns" rising out of the sea. Another variation of the myth has it that Tioman was created when a dragon princess, on her way from China to Singapore, stopped for a rest in the ocean, and transformed herself into the island.

In any case, mariners have used the mountain peaks for millennia as points of orientation, and have often landed on the island. When the Srivijayan Empire was founded in the 7th century under Indian influence, traders and sailors from India used this important route through today's Straits of Singapore to Tioman. It was also a point on the main trading route between Oman and China.

Winds and currents also brought European ships to Tioman. Just as the English Commodore Byron wrote of his trip around the world in the 18th century, so, too, did a certain Dr. Hawkesworth in his *Stories of an Ocean Voyage to the South Seas*, published in the 1770s. This book makes clear that the Tioman Islanders were by no means living at the end of the world, and understood the value of cash very well indeed: "They viewed our axes, knives and hatchets with scorn, and demanded rupees instead. We had none, and I eventually remembered that we had handkerchiefs on board. They selected a number of these..."

147

"These people are small," Dr. Hawkesworth continued, "but very well built and dark skinned. Their abodes are built quite artistically of hollow split poles, and rest on stilts about eight feet high... The island is mountainous, covered with woods; it has a great many palm and coconut trees. They did not want us to take anything from these. The bay is full of fish, and the people looked at us askance when we pulled in our nets with a good catch... We bought an animal which had the body of a hare and the feet of a deer, the meat of which tasted superb..."

Tourist managers and brochures today bill this as the Queen of Islands, "one of the 10 most beautiful islands in the world." Hollywood movies such as the musical *South Pacific*, based on the novel by James A. Michener, have been filmed here. Experienced island-hoppers might view this praise for Tioman as somewhat

Above: A fisherman from Kemasik. Right: Coastal fishermen.

148

exaggerated, but it cannot be denied that the island has a truly lovely landscape. Tioman, with its 47,880 acres (193 sq. km), has a population of just slightly over 1,800. During peak season, the number of tourists on the island far exceeds the number of natives.

Small planes bring visitors to land on the smallish target of the island, which measures 24 miles in length and 12 in width (39 x 19 km). Tioman can also be reached by boat: modern ferry boats make the crossing from Mersing in about three and a half hours, docking directly at the chalet-style **Tioman Island Resort** on the west coast. This resort boasts restaurants, a swimming pool and a variety of sports facilities. The island also offers less expensive accommodations, for instance at **Kg. Tekek**, where the normal boats dock.

Despite the large numbers of tourists, most of the beaches are still attractive, their sands ranging from snow-white to yellow-gold in color. The only paved road leads from the Island Resort to the village of Tekek, 1.9 miles (3 km) away. From here, a cement path leads to **Kg. Ayer Batang,** where, on a less than prepossessing bay, stand a number of chalets ranging from modest to luxurious. The more conventional embodiment of one's dreams of an island paradise come true materializes at the end of a two-hour hike – alternatively, a boat ride – via **Kg. Penuba, Monkey Bay** to **Kg. Teluk Salang**. The coral reefs lining the coast here are a popular destination for divers; if you haven't brought your equipment, it can be rented on the spot.

A three-hour hike from the dock at Kg. Tekek leads through primeval forest, across the island to **Kg. Juara** on the east coast, where you can rent chalets. Kg. Juara can also be reached by ferry from Kg. Tekek. The ferry also services other villages which cannot be accessed via jungle paths: **Kg. Genting, Teluk Nipah** and **Kg. Mukut**.

Tioman's fishermen, who now work almost solely for the tourist industry, transport guests to the 64 mostly uninhabited islands surrounding Tioman. The underwater views you can get when diving from these islands are truly spectacular. Two of these diving grounds are at **Pulau Tulai** in the north and **Pulau Rengis** near the Island Resort.

Near the coast, swimming is safe. Neither dangerous currents nor sharks disturb vacationers. The millions of sandflies, however, are a different story. Scratching their bites can result in serious infection. If you'd rather be challenged on dry land, you can tackle the 3,406 ft (1,038 m) high **Gunung Kajang**. The trekking tour on the mountain takes about eight hours. The best starting point is in **Kg. Paya**, southwest of the Island Resort.

Although it's impossible to overlook the influence tourism has had on Tioman, the island still offers interested and sensitive travelers good opportunities to experience Malaysian village life. On a hike across the island, the visitor does not have to wander far from one of the eight kampongs to the next. *Kampong*, incidentally, isn't only a term for the village, the actual hamlet with its stilt houses and palm-leaf roofs; it also denotes the gardens and fields around the village.

Fishing is traditionally the main occupation of these islanders, who may be descendants of the Javanese. They are *orang laut*, people of the sea, as opposed to the *orang darat*, the people of the mainland and rice farmers. Their boats are indispensable, even today, now that their main livelihood has become catching tourists rather than fish. Tioman fishermen use at least a dozen different types of boat, mainly large ones.

They still follow all the old rules of their trade, including those which regulate the distribution of the catch. After the expenses for the boat and the participation in the catch are deducted, each member of the boat crew is paid a portion of the market value of the catch. This pay

varies from crew member to crew member; the *juruselam* receives the biggest share. This is the diver, whose talent is the ability to scout schools of fish underwater by ear. Some of the divers even claim to be able to hear the type of fish.

Other figures of respect in the village, aside from the *juruselam*, are the *ketua kampong*, the village elder, and the *pawang*, the omnipotent witch doctor.

Other Small "Paradises"

Overshadowed by the "island queen," but no longer an insider tip for all that, is **Pulau Rawa**, about 6 miles (10 km) from Mersing. Measuring only 124 acres (half a square kilometer), the island lies amidst magnificent coral reefs and offers comfortable accommodations, restaurants and a diving station.

South of Rawa, a bit closer to the coast, **Pulau Babi Besar** attracts visitors with

Above: Pile houses under palms – a typical Malaysian scene.

its white beaches, lush jungle and tidy cottages adjacent to a kampong.

From the coastal village of **Tanjung Leman**, you can reach the island of **Sibu** in half an hour. Here, tourist cottages are also available.

To the northwest, **Pulau Tinggi** ("the tall island") rises out of the ocean. Beautiful beaches and accommodations enable visitors to this island to enjoy a solitary, therefore serene vacation.

Far removed, a 6-hour boat trip from Mersing, are the islands of **Pulau Pemangill** and **Pulau Aur**. Divers and anglers are particularly attracted to these two islands, since they don't mind roughing it in the islands' simple huts.

All of the islands near Mersing, including **Pulau Babi Hujung** and **Pulau Babi Tengah** close at hand, have the status of protected ocean parks. The underwater world is therefore still relatively undisturbed, that around the smaller islands even less so than that around Tioman – which is, after all, a tourist mecca, for all its fabled beauty.

KUANTAN AND ENVIRONS

Getting there / Transportation

BY AIR: **MAS** has flights between **Kuantan** and **Kuala Lumpur, Singapore, J. B., K. Terengganu, Penang. Pelangi Air** has flights to **Kuantan, Kuala Lumpur, Singapore – Tioman**.

BY BOAT: Cruises once a week: Kuantan – Kuching – Kota Kinabalu – Kuantan. Kuantan – Singapore – Kuantan. **Information: Feri Malaysia**, Wisma Bolasepak, Jl. Gambut, Tel: 526800.

CAR: The existing east-west connection is currently being improved to highway status from K.L.

BUS: **Terminal Kuantan**: Jl. Besar (long-distance trips); Jl. Bukit Ubi (city buses). **Terminal Mersing**: by the boat dock.

Accommodations

KUANTAN: *LUXURY:* **Hyatt**, Telok Chempedak, Tel: 09-5131234. **Coral Beach Resort**, 152, Sungai Karang, Beserah, Tel: 09-587544.

MODERATE: **Merlin Inn Resort**, T. Chempedak, Tel: 09-511388. **Ramada Beach Resort**, Balok Beach, Kuantan, Tel: 09-587544. **The Legend Resort**, Tel: 09-439439. *BUDGET:* **Min Heng**, 22, Jl. Mahkota, Tel: 09-5134885. **Samudra River View Hotel**, Jl. Besar, Kuantan, Tel: 09-555333. **Pacific Hotel**, 60, Jl. Bukit Ubi, Kuantan, Tel: 09-5141980. **Classic Hotel**, Tel: 09-554599.

PEKAN: Resthouse, Padang, Tel: 09-421240. **Pekan Hotel**, 60, Jl. Tengku Ariff, Tel: 09-421378. **TEMERLOH: Hotel Isis**, Jl. Jl. Tenku Bakar, Tel: 2963136. **The Centrepoint Inn**, Jl. Kuantan, Tel: 09-2965588.

SOUTH OF KUANTAN

Accommodations

MERSING: *MODERATE:* **Merlin Inn**, 2 km north, toward Endau, Tel: 07-7991312. **Country Hotel**, Tel: 07-7991799. **Embassy Hotel**, 2, Jl. Ismail, Tel: 07-7993545.

BUDGET: **Mersing**, 1, Jl. Dato' Timor, Tel: 07-7991004. **Golden City**, 23, Jl. Abu Bakar. **Resthouse**, 490, Jl. Ismail, Tel: 07-7991101. **Khalid Guest House**, Tel: 07-7993613.

K. ROMPIN: Resthouse, Tel: 09-455234.

SEGAMAT: *BUDGET:* **Resthouse**, 750, Jl. Buluh Kasap, Tel: 914566.

LAKE CHINI: Lake Chini Resort, Tel: 03-2414095.

PULAU RAWA: *MODERATE:* **Island Resort**, can only be booked through Rawa Safaris, whose office is in the Tourist Center in Mersing, Tel: 07-791204. The restaurant on th island offers Western, Chinese and local sepcialties.

Restaurants

In and around **Kuantan**, all the better hotels, resorts and rest houses offter a good selection of Malayan, Chinese, Indian and Western food. In addition, there are several Chinese restaurants on the corner of Jl. Haji A. Aziz/ Jl. Bank. In T. Chempedak, the **Seafood Restaurant** opposite the Handicraft Center is worth a visit. In **Mersing**, the restaurants in the hotels **Merlin Inn**, **Mersing** und **Embassy** offer good food, as does the **Chinese restaurant** next to the Chinese temple at the corner of Jl. Abu Bakat and Jl. Ismail.

Tourist Information

LKNP Tourist Information Center: Komplex Teruntum, Jl. Mahkota, Kuantan, Tel: 09-505566. **TDC**: See TDC K. Terengganu. Information (also from the Tourist Information Center, Mersing) and permits for the **Endau-Rompin-Park**: State Security Coucil, Bangunan Sultan Ibrahim, Bukit Timbalan, Johor Baru.

TIOMAN ISLAND

Getting there / Transportation

BY AIR: **MAS** has daily flights from **Kuala Lumpur** and **Singapore** to Tioman. **Pelangi Air** offers both regular and charter flights from **Kuantan, Kuala Lumpur** and Singapore to **Tioman,**. Charter flights are also available to and from Mersing.

BY BOAT: Speedboats from Mersing (about 1 hour). Regular ferry service lasts a little longer. Only 2 miles (3 km) of roads. The only other means of transportation is the *Seabus*.

Accommodations

LUXURY: **Berjaya Imperial Beach Resort**, Tel: 09-4145445.

MODERATE: **Tioman Island Resort**, Tel: 09-445445/03-2305266. **Persona Island Resort**, Tel: 09-4146213.

BUDGET: In **Tekek, Salang, Genting, Lalang** and in **Juara** there are a number of simple bungalows and chalets; recommended are: **Samudra Swiss Cottage**, Kg. Tekek. **Nazri's**, Kg. Tekek. **Zahara**, Kg. Tekek. **Manap Chalet**, Kg. Tekek. **Jumat Guest House**, Kg. Tekek. **ABC**, located at the end of the bay. **Zaid's**, Kg. Salang. **Sunny Hussein Chalet**, Kg. Juara. **Au Awang Chalet**, Kg. Juara.

Restaurants

On Tioman, besides the restaurants in the hotels and resorts, you'll find many small eateries directly on the beach. Women wearing only a bikini and a wrap-around towel might not be served!

LAND OF ADVENTURE

EAST MALAYSIA
SARAWAK
BAKO NATIONAL PARK
TRAVELING IN SARAWAK
CAVES OF NIAH
GUNUNG MULU PARK

EAST MALAYSIA

Impenetrable rain forest, monkeys, crocodiles and snakes. People who live in longhouses and who as recently as a few decades ago still went head-hunting. That's how one imagines East Malaysia.

We think of Borneo, the world's third-largest island at 291,311 sq. miles (746,951 sq. km), as a land of adventure. The stories about the "White Rajahs" who steered Sarawak's fortunes for 100 years make it seem all the more exotic. This is the stuff of history which has inspired filmmakers and great writers. Sarawak prompted Joseph Conrad to write *Lord Jim*, while Somerset Maugham got a great many short stories out of the time he spent in Borneo.

The province of Kalimantan, which takes up most of the island, is part of Indonesia. The island's two Malaysian states in the northwest, Sarawak and Sabah, together cover an area of about 78,000 square miles (just under 200,000 sq. km). Squeezed in between them is the Sultanate of Brunei, whose riches so impressed Europeans centuries ago that they gave its name to the whole island.

Preceding pages: jungle landscape in Sarawak. Left: Iban man adorned with traditional tattoos.

These outlying states are separated from West Malaysia by more than just 400 miles (650 km) of water. Even today, socio-cultural differences and histories which have hardly anything in common, except for the British colonial period, have meant that the two halves of the country have developed in very different ways. It is true that east and west, sharing an antipathy to their white overlords, united politically into the Federation of Malaysia. Nevertheless, today, almost 40 years after independence, Sarawak and particularly Sabah, both led by Governors, hardly miss a chance to demonstrate their independence to the central government in Kuala Lumpur.

Sarawak, the largest and richest state in Malaysia, is, for one thing, the land where pepper grows. Every year around 25,000 tons are harvested and exported for the world market. Other main sources of revenue are for the two states are rubber, oil, natural gas and tropical timber.

Islam has relatively little influence in Malaysian Borneo, in contrast to peninsular Malaysia, where it is spreading vigorously. In the cities the imposing state mosques do attract immigrant Malays, but in the interior of the land it is the Catholic and Anglican churches that have more influence, even if their missionary success with the traditionally animistic

native peoples can often only be detected in the statistics. Sarawak's Malays make up no more than 20% of the population, matched by the same number of Christians; the remaining 60% are adherents of traditional tribal religions. Even the Chinese, at 30% of the population, outnumber the Malays. In Sabah, around 40% of the people pray to Allah, 20% are baptized Christians, and the rest follow the customs of their forefathers.

Even traveling here in East Malaysia takes a different form than getting around on the more modern western peninsula. Roads are the exception, rather than the rule. In Sabah there is one small railway. It is actually the airplane which rules over wide expanses of Borneo – provided it can operate reliably. Otherwise, the main transportation arteries are the rivers. Boat trips, which are undertaken in West Malaysia more in a spirit of amusement and

Above: The plumplori, a prosimian in the Borneo rain forest. Right: Logging - the biggest business in Sarawak.

adventure, are a completely normal way of traveling in the east – for tourists, too, if they want to get to know the country.

The disappearing rain forest

Whether the rain forest of Borneo, like that of the peninsula one of the most ancient forests in the world, can survive is uncertain. Its trees are being felled at a frightening pace. Within the last 30 years Sarawak has advanced to being the largest export of tropical timber in the world. In 1980 there were already 275,000 acres (110,000 ha) of cleared jungle in Sarawak, and by 1990 this had increased to 675,000 acres (270,000 ha). The figure for all Malaysia was 1,675,000 acres/670,000 ha. Since 1984, 60 percent of Sarawak's jungles have been released to logging. More than 60 percent of the wood is shipped to Japan. In 1983, Sarawak alone made up 39 percent of worldwide timber exports (and in the same year Malaysia accounted for 58 percent of all tropical timber shipments). In this way each year billions of dollars flow into government coffers.

Economic advantage is bought with ecological consequences. Environmental activists have been warning for a long time now that this overlogging of Sarawak's forests has gone to such a point that 1,530 sq. ft (140 sq. m) of a unique ecosystem are being destroyed every second. One-third of this 130-million-year-old rain forest has already been lost forever. In a matter of years, a habitat boasting a huge variety of flora and fauna is being steadily transformed into a karstic wasteland. Reforestation is restricted to eucalyptus and acacia, which are fast-growing but delicate.

International disapproval of Malaysia's irresponsibility toward the environment was boosted when the Penan, nomads of the Sarawak jungle, launched protest actions against the logging camps and the tracks leading to them. The Penan

are also supported by Bruno Manser, a Swiss national who lived with them for six years and who was only just able to escape from the police. This "enemy of the state" drew attention to the hopeless plight of the original inhabitants of Borneo by means of a hunger strike in his home country in 1993.

Again and again, nature conservationists end up behind bars. Even western travelers who are overly interested in protecting the rain forest or the orang utan (the "old man of the woods") risk arrest or at the least expulsion.

It may appear contradictory, but it's still a fact that even the generously-proportioned national parks restrict the living space of the forest peoples. The traditional fishing and hunting grounds are made into nature reserves, opened up to lucrative tourism, and finally, in melancholy remembrance of the vanished rain forest, declared national monuments.

It remains to be seen whether the decision of Western governments to ban the importation of Malaysian hardwood has been a success. Even the import restrictions decreed by the European Parliament in 1988 had no great effect, especially as a major proportion of the forests is being felled to create farmland for oil palms, rubber and soya. Officially, members of the European Community – and of them Germany is the largest importer of highgrade Malaysian timber – only account for 13 percent of total consumption.

Government representatives in Malaysia, who have got rich themselves on logging concessions, maintain, just as their colleagues in Indonesia do, that they have the right to their own resources. They accuse the industrial countries – and rightly so – of destroying the environment themselves by pouring most of the carbon dioxide into the atmosphere and exporting poisonous waste to the developing nations.

The *Orang ulu* of Borneo are fighting against powerful enemies. International currency and sales markets will decide whether they and the rain forests have a future.

Forest Peoples and Seafarers

Orang ulu is how most of the 60 or so national minorities of Sarawak refer to themselves. For the most part, they are descendants of the proto-Malays who started arriving from the Malayan peninsula, the Philippines and Sumatra in the fourth millennium B.C. A statistical survey carried out in 1985 distinguishes the following major ethnic groups: the Iban or Sea Dayaks (439,000), the Kendayan, Ngaju, Bidayuh or Land Dayaks (123,000), the Kenyah (25,000), the Kayan (19,000), the Murut (13,000), the Punan (7000) and others (14,000). With the Malays (1985: 20.3 percent) and Melanu (5.8 percent) and the Chinese (30 percent), there are around 1.75 million people living in Sarawak, and each year the population grows by 2.7 percent.

Finds of skeletons in the caves of Niah point to human settlement going back at

Above: The Layar river meanders through Sarawak.

least 50,000 years. It is fairly certain that the Punan (subdivided into the Ukit, Punan Ba, Baketan, Oloh Ot, Bukat and Penan) are among the oldest inhabitants. They are probably the remnants of a people who were already living on Borneo before the island separated from the Asian mainland around 10,000 years ago after the last great Ice Age. Completely adapted to living in the jungle, they survive on fruits and roots, and hunt monkeys, deer, wild pig and smaller animals with the blowpipe. The Punan, who are organized into family groups, live in caves or primitive huts. When they have exhausted the food resources in one place, they continue their wanderings. Otherwise they live in economic symbiosis with the Dayak, exchanging feathers and animal skins for rice and tools.

The collective name of Dayak refers to those groups who live predominantly inland. They include the Iban (Sea Dayaks), the Kayan, Kenyah, Murut and the Ngaju, Kendayan and Bidayuh (Land

Dayaks). It was the Dutch who introduced the name Dayak, deriving it from the Malayan word for inland, *daya.* The peoples themselves name themselves after the rivers where they are settled. Probably much later than the Punan, tribes of Mongolian origin landed in Borneo from South China. These include the Kayan. They must have been followed by the Murut, who today live in Sabah; this ethnic group may well have originated in Assam. The Iban, the last group of immigrants who arrived from Sumatra in the 16th century, were referred to by the Kayan as Ivan, or wanderers. A seafaring people, they were often involved in piracy. The English, who controlled Sarawak at that time, introduced the distinction between Sea Dayaks and Land Dayaks.

Head-hunting and Life in the Longhouse

All Dayak peoples engaged in head-hunting as part of the rituals of initiation to manhood and a condition of marriageability. Taking an enemy's head was for the Dayak an attempt to acquire the good characteristics, the strength, bravery and standing, of the dead man – at least, this is the prevalent view of Western anthropologists. What really was behind this ritualistic custom is hard to make out. Sometimes, a head – which could also be that of a child or a woman – was acquired through pure cunning. The heads were subsequently dried in the course of a festive ritual ceremony and the skulls kept in bundles in the *barok,* the round head-house. Most of the skulls still existing today are around 70 to 80 years old. The English made great efforts to stamp out what they considered to be a barbaric custom, and only achieved this goal after the end of the World War Two.

The form of village which is still preferred by the Dayak is the longhouse built on stilts. This style of building owes its origins to their warlike traditions, providing as it does excellent protection from attack. Multiple families of a single clan live under one roof, with the space apportioned more or less according to social position. The most inferior family members live, therefore, in the *bilek,* which is situated towards the entrance.

The chief of the longhouse is the senior head of the families. He holds the power to administer justice in accordance with the *adat* or customary law. The notion of hereditary succession of chiefs is foreign to the Iban. Their leader, the *tuai rumah,* is chosen by the most important men of the longhouse. Kayan chiefs, on the other hand, can appoint their successors themselves, and as a rule the new chief in the longhouse is a son, or, indeed, a daughter, of the previous incumbent.

The next most important man after the chief is the *manag* or medicine man. He is in contact with the world of the spirits which exert an influence on the living. Here dreams also play a major part, and illnesses are never attributed to organic, but always to spiritual causes.

Still important today for the attainment of manhood is the *bejalai* or the "time of wandering." In those months when the young men are not needed for heavy work in the fields they go off wandering, gathering experiences and collecting objects of value for their longhouse community. Only after repeated *bejalai* has a man earned the right to wear tattoos. Hardly practiced today, this tradition, which included women as well as men, involved artistic patterns on the arms, legs, torso, face and back. The patterns indicate one's social position, and are at the same time supposed to protect against illnesses and enemies.

Even though most of the Dayak today are Christians, and many of them are well acquainted with the "blessings" of civilization in their daily lives, traditions and *adat* have not entirely lost their meaning. Particularly in their struggle for living

space, the peoples of Borneo wield their cultural heritage as a weapon against their modern adversaries: greed and despoliation of the forest.

The "White Rajahs"

From early in the 7th century, Chinese junks appeared regularly off the coasts of Borneo to trade porcelain for wood, camphor, and the coveted aphrodisiac, swallow's nests. The Chinese also began settling at that time; today, they make up roughly a quarter of the population of Sarawak.

Muslim missionaries began arriving at the beginning of the 15th century, and the dominion of the Sultanate of Brunei over Sarawak was to last a good 400 years. It was not a very stable rule and was repeatedly challenged by rebellious Dayak. Not until 1993 was the 352-year-old

Above: Head-hunting was one of the Dayak rituals of manhood.

grave of the only Malay ruler of Sarawak, Sultan Tengah, discovered at Santubong, 18.5 miles (30 km) from Kuching. Tengah was the second son of the ninth king of Brunei, Sultan Muhamad Hasan. In order to settle a dispute over the succession, Abdul Jalilul Akbar entrusted Sarawak to his brother Tengah. In 1641 Tengah was murdered by a bodyguard.

The first European to visit Borneo was the famous Franciscan from Friuli, Odorich of Pordenone, in 1320. 200 years later the remnants of Magellan's crew, including the Italian chronicler Antonio Pigafetta, landed on the northwest coast of the island after their admiral had been killed in the Philippines. At this time, Sarawak was already part of the Sultanate of Brunei, and, according to the first Western reports, an impassable region of thick rain forest and swamps. Borneo was still a "green hell" in 1839 when James Brooke, later to be known as the "White Rajah," arrived on his schooner *Royalist* and penetrated the interior of the jungle island.

In that year, the Dayak, Chinese and Malays openly revolted against Rajah Omar Ali Saifuddin, the Sultan of Brunei. His uncle, Rajah Muda Hassim, asked the adventurer Brooke to use his ship's cannons to suppress the rebellion in return for being given northwest Borneo to rule. In 1841, after succeeding in pacifying the area more by diplomatic skills than by gunpowder, the Englishman was granted this piece of real estate. At this time, the Sultan allegedly used the words "Serah kapada awak" – "I turn it over to you" – whence derives the name Sarawak. James Brooke had asked the Sultan to grant amnesty to the rebels; he thus won even the Dayak as his friends. The dynasty of the White Rajahs was to endure until 1946.

With increasing confidence, James Brooke now himself challenged the Sultan of Brunei. In 1846, his ships took up position off Bandar Seri Begawan, the Sultan's capital; Brooke demanded for the crown the coal-rich island of Labuan, which lay off the coast. In the course of many bloody expeditions he took action against the Dayak pirates, Malays and Chinese. Other groups of Dayak and members of the Royal Navy fought under his command. While the natives busied themselves with collecting as many heads as possible, the Europeans paid a kingly sum of head money for every pirate killed.

James Brooke (1803-1868) was succeeded on his death by his nephew Charles (1829-1917). During his strict paternalistic rule, which he did not wish to entrust to bureaucratic civil servants, Charles always kept up close contacts with the chiefs. He achieved control through reform. True to the British colonial concept of "indirect rule," he introduced a modern legal system which worked with the traditional hierarchical structures and supplemented, rather than replaced, the *adat*. In this way the tribes of Sarawak were able to save, if not their

political independence, at least some of their cultural autonomy. In 1888, Charles made his realm over to the British crown, which thenceforth administered Sarawak as a protectorate, like Sabah and Brunei.

The calculating and ascetic administrator Charles Brooke was succeeded by his son Sir Charles Vyner Brooke (1874-1963), who enjoyed his life as rajah (1917-1946) in idleness and the company of numerous mistresses. In the meantime Sarawak had become extremely prosperous due to deposits of oil and to rubber plantations. The third "White Rajah," together with his brother Bertram, had just modernized the constitution when, in December, 1941, Sarawak was invaded by the Japanese, just before the centenary of the Brooke dynasty's rule.

After the war, the reign of the "White Rajahs" on Sarawak was ended; both London and the people's representatives in Sarawak were against it. This almost fairy-tale dynasty of white rulers was no longer in harmony with the spirit of the age. Charles Vyner returned once more to Kuching in 1946, but only in order that he might formally abdicate. In the same year, the Council Negri declared the protectorate a crown colony, and in 1963 Sarawak was received as a member state into the Malaysian Federation.

SARAWAK: UNDER THE SIGN OF THE HORNBILL

On its state coat-of-arms, Sarawak bears the hornbill, whose 13 feathers symbolize the states of Malaysia. The national flower, the hibiscus, has its place there too, and between the claws of the bird is the inscription *Hidup Selalu Berkhdimat,* which is Sarawak's motto, and translates as: "Live to serve."

Sarawak may be divided into three topographical regions: the coastal zone, dominated by mangrove swamps; the rain forest which abuts onto it; and finally the chain of mountains covered with primeval jungle which runs along the border with Indonesia. In its northern section rises the 7,972 feet (2,438 m) of Sarawak's highest mountain, **Mount Murud**. The numerous rivers which flow into the South China Sea have in the course of time created extensive floodlands, which every year advance some 80 feet (25 m) further into the sea. Places once on the coast are now inland.

The longest river in Sarawak is the 350 mile (564 km) **Batang Rajang** in the south, which is navigable by ocean-going ships for 150 miles (242 km) upstream. In the north the 249 miles (402 km) of the **Sungai Baram** reaches the sea at the border with Brunei. The **Batang Lupar** is 141 miles (228 km) long, and, after traversing the great wetlands flows into the sea east of Suching. Finally the 135 mile (217 km) **Sungai Sarawak** should be mentioned; situated on its banks is the capital city, Kuching.

The only hardtop overland road stretches 558 miles (900 km) across Sarawak from Kuching to Miri, after which it continues onwards to Brunei.

KUCHING

The capital supposedly owes its name to a misunderstanding. When James Brooke was approaching the coast in his schooner for the first time, he inquired of his Malay pilot the name of the place, which at that time was no more than handful of simple palm huts. The pilot, thinking the captain was pointing to an animal, replied "Kuching!" – which in Malay means simply "cat."

Today, **Kuching** is a lively town with over 300,000 inhabitants; though it didn't receive its town charter until 1988. This trading metropolis, divided by the **Sungai Sarawak,** lies about 20 miles (32 km) from the coast. The town is port of entry for most visitors to Sarawak, as the international airport is located there. On the drive into the town center along Jl. Tun

Abang Haji Openg, you see the emblem of Kuching: a white cat made of cement.

The same street is home to the internationally-known **Sarawak Museum**, which is a good place to begin a city tour. Charles Brooke had the museum – today the oldest in Malaysia – built in 1891, inspired and supported by his friend Alfred Russell Wallace, the famous naturalist, who was a frequent visitor to Sarawak. In addition to housing the valuable ethnographic, archeological, historical and natural history collections, the two buildings are also still used for scientific research. The older building, later enlarged, is for the most part taken up by natural history exhibits. Preserved snails, shells, insects of all kinds, snakes, lizards and mammals provide an impression of the diverse fauna found on Sarawak.

In 1984, the new complex, the **Dewan Tun Abdul Razak**, was opened across the street from the old museum. Here an excellent ethnographic exhibition can be viewed. There are wax figures of members of the ethnic groups, dressed in their traditional costumes. In a small pool in the entrance hall rises a pile dwelling of the *Orang ulu*. On display are prehistoric finds from the cave of Niah, among them a skull approximately 40,000 years old; you can also see tools, carvings and grave offerings of the original inhabitants, as well as Dayak wall-paintings and Iban symbolic representations of animals. However, there is also information on the Sarawak of today, its agricultural products and the oil industry.

Hard by the museum is a casting of one of the mysterious stone sculptures found in the mangrove swamps of the Sarawak delta, near the historical site of Santubong, where the originals still stand.

Colorfully painted taxi-boats, once they have more or less filled up with passengers, ply back and forth over the Sarawak. They constitute the sole connection between the two halves of Kuching. The boats depart from Jl. Gambier, close

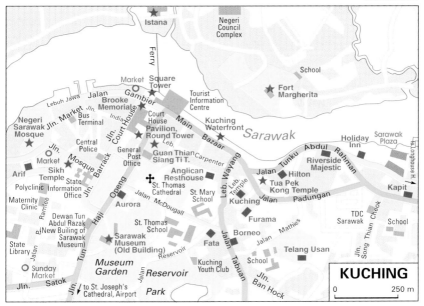

to the Court House. It is an easy matter to arrange a boat trip on the river, whether in order to see the sights or simply as a pleasant way to pass the time.

On the right bank, **Fort Margherita** embodies the bygone power of the White Rajahs. This trim fortress, which resembles an English castle, takes its name from Rana Margaret, the wife of Charles Brooke. He had the fort built in 1879 to protect the town from intruders. It has never been damaged, despite having such a turbulent history. Today its walls and well-kept lawns house a police museum bristling with weapons. On display here is the only cannon to have been cast in Sarawak, which taught the meaning of fear to the Iban leader, Rentap. Heroic deeds from Malaysia's more recent history – such as the struggle against the Communists – are also commemorated. Visitors can even trace on maps those parts of Sarawak's rivers that are particularly favored by the crocodiles.

Also dating from the days when Charles Brooke ruled Sarawak is the **Is-tana.** This palace, built in 1870 in the form of three very grand bungalows, is today the Governor's residence. It is closed to the public except when the Governor holds an open house on the occasion of the feast-day of *Hari Raya Puasa* ("the breaking of the fast").

Another edifice from the time of the second ruler of the Brooke dynasty is the **Court House** (the Supreme Court) which was erected in 1874 and to which the bell tower was a later addition. Out front stands the **Brooke Memorial** in honor of Charles Brooke, which was unveiled in 1924. Bronze reliefs depict the four major ethnic groups of Sarawak: Dayak, Malays, Chinese, and Kayan. The Court House served as the seat of office of the rajah and later of the governor; the Council Negeri continued to meet in the building until 1973. The present parliament sits in the **Negeri Council Complex**, a 20-storey high-rise north of Fort Margherita.

Kuching's oldest stone building from the era of James Brooke is the **Pavilion**

163

opposite the Central Post Office. The somewhat younger **Square Tower** by the main bazaar was converted during the White Rajah period from a prison into a fortress, functioning at the same time as a dance-hall. The **Round Tower**, hard by the Pavilion, dates back to 1886. It is not clear what its intended purpose may have been, but the Brookes may have used the tower as an additional fort.

Two temples in Kuching merit a mention. At the intersection of Jl. Reservoir Temple and Jl. Padungan stands the richly decorated **Tua Pek Kong**, Sarawak's oldest temple, dating from 1876. It is dedicated to the god of fortune. A stone lion guards the **Gan Thian Siang Ti Temple** in Lebuh Carpenter, and every evening he extends his protection over the eating stalls set up in the square opposite.

The gleaming golden dome is the **Masjid Negeri Sarawak**, completed in 1968. Christianity, which has spread widely in Sarawak, is represented in Kuching by **St. Thomas Cathedral** on the square on Jl. Tun Haji Openg, which was built in 1951 to replace the diminutive wooden Anglican church which stood on the site a hundred years earlier. Catholics have their church in **St. Joseph's Cathedral**, on the same street, about 1,000 feet (300 m) south of the museum.

Indicative of the attraction exerted on tourists by Kuching are the two luxury hotels, the Holiday Inn and the Hilton, on the left bank of the muddy brown river. Their guests, and other visitors to the city, can stroll down Jl. Satok any Sunday morning to enjoy the public **market** where, as well as foodstuffs and groceries, all kinds of craft products are on sale. In addition to its antiques and artwork, Kuching is also known for its pottery. Traders and the Chinese brought the technique to Sarawak around the turn of the century. By bringing in elements of Dayak ornamentation to combine with this, the region has since then created its own style. Shops in Kuching and potteries on the outskirts of the town may well be rewarding places to shop.

Every year a number of festivals are celebrated in Kuching. In the middle of March teams of powerfully-built oarsmen race each other on the Sarawak in 20-man longboats in the Baram Regatta. The entire country celebrates the King's Birthday on June 6th and also Independence Day on August 31st. Parades, cultural shows and regattas are held from September 13th to 19th in honor of the Governor of Sarawak.

AROUND KUCHING

With the motorboat which departs from the landing-stage on Jl. Gambier, you can reach the village of **Santubong**, on the coast to the north, in less than an hour. Or you can travel the 20 miles (32 km) to the peninsula by bus or car. A fishing village and today a popular bathing resort, Santubong does not lack historical importance. The Hindu and Buddhist engravings on the stone figures in the mangrove swamps, mentioned above, indicate that over 2,000 years ago Borneo must have been ruled by a powerful Indian kingdom. More of these sculptures were, incidentally, discovered in Sarawak in 1948, as well as some 310 miles (500 km) to the south in the Kelapit Uplands at a height of around 6,540 feet (2,000 m). From finds of coins and porcelain it is clear that Santubong must have been an important trading post for the Chinese Tang and Sung dynasties, from the 7th to the 13th centuries.

A few miles to the north is the exclusive **Damai Beach Hotel**, which is a member of the Holiday Inn chain. Anyone who has come to Santubong to swim may use the beach here only upon payment of an entrance fee.

Right: Fort Margherita in Kuching recalls the days of the White Rajahs.

Certainly instructive is the **Kampong Budaya Sarawak** Cultural Village, opened as recently as 1990, located right beside the luxury hotel and in front of the impressive, jungle-covered hill of Santubong. Referred to as a "living museum," the village uses authentic houses, tools and household utensils, replicas of skull trophies and of instruments to present the seven main groups of Sarawak's inhabitants. Every day there are theater and dance performances; while a range of special seminars, courses and workshops aim at deepening interest in tradition and culture. In each of the museum's houses, members of the various ethnic groups demonstrate activities from their daily life, including the production of *tuak*, the rice wine of the Iban.

The Damai Hotel organizes day excursions to **Pulau Satang Besar**, the turtle island to the west, which you can also visit on your own after registering with the "Turtle Board" at the Sarawak Museum in Kuching. Boats from Santubong make the crossing in about an hour.

Buses also depart from Kuching for beaches to the west, which, while impressive, are a considerable distance away. It is 62 miles (100 km) to the coastal village of **Lundu**, while **Sematan**, almost on the Indonesian border, is 80 miles (130 km) away.

There is a range of accommodation available in both places. Lundu lies to the north of the **Gunung Gading National Park**, at the center of which is the 2,891-foot (884 m) mountain of the same name. On the way there, you can stop off for a visit to **Bau**, an old mining village 22 miles (35 km) southwest of Kuching where Hakka Chinese mined for gold from the 18th to the late-19th century. They also discovered valuable antimony in the year 1824.

Unlike their compatriots in Kuching, the Chinese of Bau and thereabouts had no interest in amicable intercourse with James Brooke. When he started meddling in the opium trade and in the business of the Chinese secret societies, the gold miners rebelled. They poured into Kuch-

ing, set the Malay quarter on fire and killed many of Brooke's employees. The White Rajah himself only just escaped the bloodbath. In the punitive expedition which followed, led by his nephew Charles, many Chinese were slaughtered, and 4,000 fled into what was then the Dutch part of Borneo. The mine was later flooded, and the lake that this created is today a great draw for day-trippers from Kuching.

BAKO NATIONAL PARK

Bako National Park lies 23 miles (37 km) north of Kuching on a peninsula 10.5 square miles (27 sq. km) in area. A ferryboat departs each morning and afternoon from Jl. Gambier on the approximately 2-hour trip to **Kampong Bako**. The journey by bus, from the terminal in Jl. Masjid, takes an hour longer but is

Above: In the mangrove belt of Bako National Park. Right: Murut children.

considerably more rewarding due to the spectacular backdrop of the landscape en route. Once in Kampong Bako, you transfer to a smaller rented boat which brings you to **Telok Assam**, the park headquarters, in about half an hour. Here on the coast you have the choice of chalets, hostels or campsites (tents can be rented).

This park, which dates from 1957, is Malaysia's oldest and Sarawak's smallest, but due to its compactness most interesting, nature reserve. Tropical primary forest grows here, bordered on each side of the peninsula by attractive coastlines with small sandy coves and steep cliffs. You can wander along any of the 16 paths of different lengths to experience the park's fascinating animal and plant world. Many of these paths lead to lonely beaches.

The park presents five different types of vegetation: grasses and bushes on the beach; the mangrove belt, where with some luck you can spot sea eagles and otters; swampland forest; lowland jungle;

and the low woodland of the high plateau where carnivorous pitcher plants (*Nepenthes*) find plenty of insect nourishment. The attentive visitor will encounter – acoustically, at least – many of the 550 bird species of Sarawak. Between September and November, numbers rise with the arrival of the migratory species from Siberia.

Bako Park is also home to a notably large number of apes. These are the cheeky Java apes and the proboscis monkeys which live only on Borneo; the latter reminded the Malays so strongly of their former colonial masters that they dubbed them *orang belanda* (Dutchmen). They are best sought out early in the morning or late in the afternoon in the mangroves of **Telok Delima.**

Other park inhabitants are deer, among them the rabbit-sized mouse deer (*Tragulus nigricans*), wild pig, honey bear, wild cat, gibbon, and varana a yard long.

A safer place for viewing the crocodile is **Jong's Crocodile Farm**, 18.5 miles (30 km) or so east of Kuching. More than a thousand are kept there, together with apes, flying squirrels, binturong (a kind of civet), turtles, snakes and falcons.

A Visit to the Longhouse

Sarawak's tourist industry relies not only on the natural world but also on the ethnic environment. A visit to a Dayak longhouse has become an essential part of any organized trip to East Malaysia. **Kampong Benuk** and **Kampong Gayu** are two day-trip destinations close to Kuching where at least two dozen Land Dayak families live under one roof. The 31-mile (50 km) car or bus journey takes you through rice fields, pepper and rubber plantations to these Bidayuh villages. They have however been pretty much kitted out for tourism. More impressive, and affording more insight into the day-to-day life of the people, is a longer visit, arranged ahead of time, including overnight stays in the **bilek**, the Dayak living quarters. A trip like this to the Skrang river begins with the 124 mile (200 km) bus journey from Kuching to Bandar Sri Aman, where visitors transfer to narrow boats to reach the Iban longhouses further inland.

As with all encounters with tourists, contacts such as these involve both advantages and disadvantages for the local people. Dayak who live in the vicinity of towns have been particularly affected by modern life. Young people leave their villages seeking long-term work, often in vain, and wind up finding diversion in alcohol and other dubious urban entertainments.

Until recently, the directors of tourism in Sarawak and also in Sabah believed that social and economic action could be combined. They allowed tourists, equipped with the permits and guides appropriate to the region they were visiting, to push into the jungle to the longhouses. Part of the income, as a rule the smaller part, was to go to the hosts and encourage

them to remain living in their longhouses, and there to present their dances and handicrafts. Money was supposed to act as a stimulus for them to preserve their culture, and even to induce the semi-nomads to settle down in one place. For the sake of putting on a certain kind of face for the tourists, shacks of corrugated tin were even built to look older than they were, and "sold" as authentic to unsuspecting visitors.

Be that as it may, visiting a longhouse will bring the visitor closer to the situation of people in Sarawak than any information he could glean from a book or museum. A local guide, who may even be related to the host family group, will make the experience even more effective. He will also show visitors the traditional customs and everyday manners which need to be observed, and may deliver a more personal view as a whole.

Above: Daily life in a Dayak longhouse.
Right: Traditions are revived at festivals and for tourists.

The house itself, which may be as long as 850 feet (260 m), may only be entered barefoot and provided, of course, one has been invited in. In addition to payment for food and lodging, the *tuai rumah*, or headman of a longhouse community, naturally expects presents, such as lighters, sweets, tobacco and salt. Food or drink should not be refused, but accepted appreciatively with both hands. Consent should be obtained before taking photographs, and a potential subject's refusal graciously accepted.

At certain times, a longhouse is strictly off-limits to visitors – for example, when there has been a death in the community. Today only very few longhouses, and most of those in remote places, still have roofs of palm leaves. For the Dayak, tin roofs, generators and even televisions have become part of their familiar, everyday standard of living. All the same, they have preserved many of their old traditions. They still keep pigs, which roam around the village in the daytime but are penned up beneath the longhouse at

night. Villagers bathe in the river close by, which is also the source of drinking water.

Depending on the soil in the locality, on which they grow pepper, green vegetables, sweet potatoes and rice, the Dayak move their residence almost every year, continuing their traditional agricultural pattern of shifting cultivation, which is rather little to the liking of the government. In the remoter areas, they still hunt with blowpipes, but the Dayak on the Skrang river have in the meantime become very well acquainted with firearms. They still value the traditional knowledge of their *manang*, the shaman and healer, even if they do avail themselves from time to time of what modern medicine can offer.

Life in the longhouse is community life, the private sphere is reduced to a minimum. Work in the house and in the fields begins early in the morning, while after sundown and dinner the evening is spent on the *ruai*, or verandah, in front of the *bilek*. The men bring out *tuak*, and, depending on the occasion (or tourist arrangement), the men and women perform dances, accompanied by sonorous gongs.

TRAVELING IN SARAWAK

A good starting point for trips into the interior of the country is, as mentioned above, the town of **Bandar Sri Aman**, with its 70,000 inhabitants. It lies about 124 miles (200 km) from Kuching, where the Skrang flows into the Lupar. It can be reached by road from the capital, and also by air. Until 1978, when around 500 Communist rebels surrendered here, the town was called Simanggang; its new name is intended to commemorate the victory. The only noteworthy sight in the town is **Fort Alice**, which was built in Charles Brooke's time in 1864. The fort housed the law court, government offices and the police station, and served primarily towards bringing the belligerent Skrang Dayak of that time under control. After spending some weeks in Simanggang, Somerset Maugham recorded his impressions of the area in novellas such as *The Yellow Streak*.

Two-thirds of the inhabitants are Dayak. Close at hand are several longhouses that merit a visit, some of which have running water, electricity and glass windows. The town itself can offer a number of comfortable hotels.

A further 43.5 miles (70 km) inland is **Lubok Antu,** a town on the Indonesian border. Northeast of it, the main stream of the Sungai Ai has been dammed despite the energetic protests of conservationists. The 92-megawatt power station of **Batang Ai**, built in the mid-1980s with substantial assistance from the German Institute for Technical Cooperation, also supplies Kuching with water. Before it could be built, the government resettled almost 3,000 Iban with the prospect of free housing and power. Compensation was paid for land and fields, but all of the other promises have been kept either halfheartedly or not at all. The consequence was a massive disintegration of social structures, and a general disillusionment with and loss of trust in the state authorities. Since then, a national park of 67.5 acres (27 ha) has been marked out in the region, where the Iban have supposedly rediscovered to a certain extent their identity as hunters and farmers.

The small town of **Sarikei** lies 112 miles (180 km) to the northeast of Bandar Sri Aman. This where the Kuching-Sibu road once ended. Even though the highway has now been completed, it is still possible to continue the journey with an interesting 2-3 hour ride along the **Batang Rajang** in an express boat.

Sibu, with 150,000 inhabitants, is the second-largest town in Sarawak. Like Kuching, it lies inland, 80.5 miles (130 km) from the coast behind the belt of coastal swamplands crisscrossed by rivers. All the same, smaller ocean-going ships can easily navigate the deep Rajang as far as Sibu, where they take on cargoes

of pepper, rubber and timber. With the exception of the **Night Market** between Cross Road and Cannel Road, there is little of interest to detain tourists, who generally use the town as a departure point for trips into the jungle. Remote places can be reached by boat or plane; here, again, it's possible to arrange longhouse visits.

Threatened wilderness

Kapit is an outpost with no direct road connection. The logging industry has lent this little town some prosperity. In 1880 Charles Brooke had Fort Sylvia built here to check the war parties of the Iban. Even today Kapit is rich in contrasts: *Orang*

SARAWAK

0   50   100 km

ulu meet Malay and Chinese, forest-dwellers encounter forest-fellers. For the tourist the town is a springboard for adventures on the **Sungai Rajang** upstream, where the rain forest is still intact. Any tourist intending to travel outside Kapit must obtain a permit from the Government State Complex.

River level permitting, boats depart at regular intervals each day for **Belaga**, a town on the upper Rajang which can be reached in 12 hours during the rainy season between October to May. The journey takes you through most impressive jungle, with longhouses coming into view from time to time, and leads to the settlement of **Merit**, from which you can also make side trips into the hinterland.

But before this comes one guaranteed high point of your journey – the **Pelagus Rapids**. A laden boat fighting its way upstream can only successfully traverse these miles of white water during the rainy season. At other times, passengers have to disembark for a two-hour journey on foot.

Until the end of the 1980s, Pelagus stood for a very controversial dam project, ultimately abandoned, which would have to a large extent annihilated the living space of native inhabitants. The threat to the *Orang ulu* has not, however, been entirely averted, as plans are being pursued to mine the coal seams at Pelagus and bring out the coal with the help of a new railway line.

A much larger area has been threatened by the Bakun dam project on the Balui, a tributary of the Rajang. It was to have been the star turn of the seven power stations of the Sarawak Masterplan (SAMA), delivering 2400 megawatts of electricity to industry in Sabah and Sarawak and even feeding the surplus to the peninsula via two submarine cables. In a study of the Institute for Technical Cooperation (GtZ), which also wanted to take over the necessary costs, it was estimated that 5,000 people would have to be resettled for its construction alone. Their hunting grounds would have been inundated and the graves of their ancestors destroyed forever. An area of 7,800 square miles (20,000 sq. km), almost as large as Wales, would have been affected. The Kayan and Kenyah refused offers of compensation. "We do not need money. You can always print new money, but you can't print land," said one of their spokesmen wisely.

In 1990, the Malaysian government decided to halt the gigantic project, due partially to critical assessments on the part of the GtZ and the World Bank. Whether it will be kept on ice or abandoned completely remains to be seen. Certain Scandinavian institutes have in the meantime suggested that numerous smaller power stations be built along the Rajang. But it would be a risky business in any case, local security authorities earlier warned, to make the economy of West Malaysia dependent on underwater power cables. Terrorists would only need to sever the cables to put the lights out in K.L. as well.

What was once a truly adventurous trek from Belaga – which now, like Kapit, has an airfield – to the northern coastal town of Bintulu has lost its interest due to vast areas of the jungle having

been cleared by logging, and the roads which have been built to open up the region to the timber trucks, as well. The feasibility of tours in the highlands of Sarawak, such as in the triangle formed by **Long Seridan, Bareo** and **Gunung Murud** (the highest mountain in Sarawak), will depend on the political situation, specifically with regard to ecological issues. As a rule, the Resident in Miri, at the District Office of the 4th Division, must grant his permission.

Riches on the Coast

Bintulu, 124 miles (200 km) from Sibu, has transformed itself from a fishing village into a small city of over 70,000 inhabitants. Off its coast are the largest natural gas fields in Malaysia. Aluminium smelting, petrochemicals, a liquefaction plant and deep-sea harbor have contributed to its economic growth. At **Tanjong Batu** the beach is quite reasonable. The most popular destination for trippers from Bintulu is the **Similajau National Park** located 10 miles (16 km) east of the town. Sea turtles come now and then to lay their eggs in the (one hopes) reasonable safety of the sand.

For about 80 years, **Miri,** on the northern tip of Sarawak, has been a real boom town. Today, more than 100,000 people live here, 139 miles (224 km) by road from Bintulu. It is not far to the border with Brunei and there are regular bus connections with this neighbor country. It was in 1910, on **Canada Hill**, that oil spurted for the first time. The original bore-hole can still be seen, but since then oil has been pumped up off the coast. Workers on the offshore rigs and seamen have made their contribution to the bustle of the town, and certainly don't have to forego extracurricular entertainments. Beaches outside Miri, such as **Brighton Beach, Luak Bay** and **Kampong Beray**, are extremely popular and thus not very attractive.

Right: In many places, such as here at Bandar Seri Aman, the jungle has had to give way to rubber and oil palm plantations.

Like Bintulu, Miri serves tourists as a point of departure for the famous Niah caves in the middle of the national park of the same name. The other natural sight in the north of Sarawak is the Gunung Mulu National Park.

THE CAVES OF NIAH

Niah National Park covers an area of approximately 7,750 acres (3,100 ha) around **Gunung Mulis**. This 1,300-foot (400 m) mountain conceals one of the most important natural treasures of Sarawak: an enormous system of caves where, in the 1950s, a human skull was found that turned out to be more than 40,000 years old. The discovery stirred up some agitation in the international scientific community, as until then it had been assumed that the cradle of mankind was in Mesopotamia in the Middle East and that people spread out eastwards from there only at a much later date. In 1958, the caves of Niah were declared a national monument, administered by the Sarawak Museum in Kuching. Since 1974, the caves in the 20-million-year-old limestone cliffs and mountain have been a national park.

Skeletal remains of orang utan, buffalo and rhinoceros have also been found. In addition, scientists have come across tools from the paleolithic and mesolithic eras, which give grounds for believing that men could have lived here even as long as 100,000 years ago.

The caves were discovered accidentally in 1948 by Punan collecting bird's nests, the raw material for the bird's-nest soup which is so prized in Southeast Asia. Millions of salanganes, a swallow-like swiftlet which has the scientific name of *Collocalia*, live in the subterranean labyrinths, together with innumerable bats. Their droppings, or guano, are also collected by the Punan for fertilizer.

The salanganes are among the fastest and most interesting avian species. They cannot settle on branches but hold tight with their claws to cliff-faces, no matter how steep. What makes them so desirable

173

for gourmets and particularly for Asians troubled with impotence is the albumen-rich saliva they secrete from glands in the throat, which they use to glue together their nests. They build them at heights of 160-200 feet (50-60 m), and if a bird loses its nest it immediately builds another. This means that the locals can "harvest" the nests up to four times a year. Clambering up long bamboo ladders and scrabbling over naked rock 160 feet (50 m) up is an extremely perilous activity which has already cost many men their lives and crippled even more. Often, too, the nestlings are all destroyed. For this reason, nest-collecting is now only permitted twice a year, in January and August, by a small number of licensed "nest robbers." The larger part of the haul is snapped up by Chinese buyers. The Punan have already been risking their lives in the Niah caves for

Above: Pinnacles, the famous limestone formations in Gunung Mulu National Park. Right: Caves in the Mulu underworld.

1,500 years – something documented in ancient Chinese reports – to exchange bird's nests for goods and money.

Once you have got the 3 miles (5 km) or so of the lengthy and often slippery path from the **Pengkalan Lubang** headquarters to the cave safely behind you, and have gone in at the entrance – called West Mouth – you'll find yourself in the **Great Cave,** 245 feet (75 m) high and 817 feet (250 m) wide. A good 10 soccer fields would fit into the cave's 27.5 acres (11 ha); a giant tropical tree could stretch out its branches here in comfort. Although you can visit the Great Cave on your own, equipped with a powerful torch and sturdy shoes, for the **Painted Cave** or *Kain Hitam* you have to obtain permission from the museum in Kuching and to take on a guide at the caves. Prehistoric hunters left pictures of people and animals on these painted walls; these images, together with the miniature boats which have been found here (which were probably used for burial rituals), point to the caves' having been used until the 14th century. After this the Niah people seem to have disappeared. They may have been the ancestors of the present-day Punan, who maintain they remember once worshipping the grave boats. Accommodation may be found in the park hostel, chalets, or the Park View Hotel in the village of Batu Niah, 45 minutes on foot from park headquarters.

GUNUNG MULU NATIONAL PARK

Covering over 207 square miles (530 sq. km), the limestone and sandstone massif around the Gunung Api (5,722 feet/1,750 m) and the **Gunung Mulu**, the second-highest mountain (7,770 feet/ 2,376 m) of Sarawak, has been, since 1974, the largest nature reserve in East Malaysia. Only at the beginning of the 1980s did explorers from the Royal Geographical Society discover the **Sarawak**

Chamber among the many systems of subterranean chambers. It is 1,960 feet (600 m) long, 1,470 feet (450 m) wide and 330 feet (100 m) high, making it the largest known cavern in the world today; it could accommodate 40 jumbo jets. So far only 25 caves, estimated to be a mere 30 % of the total Mulu underworld, have been explored. Three of the caves have been earmarked for tourism and are to a partially illuminated.

In the **Clearwater Cave** a system of passages approximately 37 miles (60 km) long, which reaches down to depths of 1,160 feet (355 m), has been surveyed. **Deer Cave**, more than 1.5 miles (2.5 km) in length, is located behind an entrance 390 feet (120 m) high and 555 feet (170 m) wide, where innumerable hoofprints in the floor explain the origins of the cave's name. You then come to a steep wall down which practiced climbers will have no trouble proceeding, in part with the aid of a ladder. After wading through a subterranean stream, you will have completed your journey through the longest cave passage in the world (7,063 feet/2,160 m). From the opposite entrance there is a view down into the idyllic valley, enclosed by limestone cliffs, which is called the **Garden of Eden**. In the late afternoon, myriad bats stage a spectacle of their own as they stream out of the caves in a seemingly endless black cloud.

The Gunung Mulu National Park is home to virtually all of the animal and plant species of Sarawak. No fewer than 1,500 flowering plants have been counted, including 170 species of orchid, as well as thousands of mushrooms and ferns. Here, too, live hundreds of different ant and butterfly species, eight species of hornbill and 67 varieties of mammal.

You should allow at least 3 days for climbing Gunung Mulu and enjoying the glorious jungle landscapes. Even the two-day excursion to the famous **Pinnacles**, the picturesque limestone needle formations on Mount Api, takes you through all vegetation stages from the hot

and steamy lowland jungle up to the coolness of the moss-draped higher forest.

A visit to this national park should be well prepared beforehand; devote special care to selecting proper equipment, including shoes, flashlights, and warm clothing to protect against the weather for the climbs. Guides can be hired for visits to the caves.

The MAS flight from Miri to the park has considerably shortened what used to be a two-day bus and boat trip there via Kuala Baram and Marudi. Independent travelers must still, however, obtain their visiting permits in Miri beforehand; they're issued by the Park Booking Officer in the **National Park Office**. Often, you have to submit to a police interview first – anyone who seems to show more interest in environmental protection than tourism will rapidly be declared *persona non grata*.

Above: Luminous tree fungi thrive in the jungles of Borneo.

STATE OF SARAWAK

KUCHING
Getting there / Transportation
BY AIR: **MAS** has daily flights between Kuching, Miri and K. L., Johor Bahru, K. Kinabalu, Singapore, as well as connections to Brunei. **Royal Brunei** links Kuching with Bandar Seri Begawan. **Charter flights** within Sarawak: **Boskym Udara**, Miri, Tel: 085-34242, **Hornbill Skyways**, Kuching, Tel: 082-411737, Miri, Tel: 085-37355.
BUS: **Terminals** (Kuching and environs): Chin Lian Long-Line and Bau Transport Co. on **Jl. Masjid**. Matang Transport Co. on **Power Street**. Sarawak Transport Co. on **Leboh Jawa.**
BY BOAT: **Express boats** to Sibu, Sarikei daily, or at least several times a week, from Kuching's harbor in **Bintawa**. Timetables and information: Sarawak Tourist Association, TDC. Cruises with Cruise Muhibah, every 14 days between Port Kelang-Singapore-Kuching-Kota Kinabalu or Kuantan-Kota Kinabalu-Kuching-Singapore. Information: **Feri Malaysia**, Block E, Lot 33, Jl. Tunku Abdul Rahman, Tel: 082-418330.

Accommodations
LUXURY: **Holiday Inn**, Jl. Tunku Abdul Rahman, Tel: 082-423111. **Holiday Inn Damai Beach Resort**, Tel: 082-411777. **Hilton**, Jl. Tunku Abdul Rahman, Tel: 082-248200. **Hilton Batang Ai Loghouse Resort**, Tel: 082-248200. *MODERATE:* **Riverside Majestic**, Jl. Tunku Abdul Rahman, Tel: 082-247777. **Metropole Inn**, 22, Jl. Green Hill, Tel: 082-412484. **Aurora**, Jl. McDoughall, Tel: 082-240281. **Fata**, Jl. Tabuan, Tel: 082-248111. **Long House Hotel**, Abell Road, Tel: 082-249333. **Borneo**, 30C-F, Jl. Tabuan, Tel: 082-241267. **Ferritel**, Tel: 082-484799.
BUDGET: **City Inn**, Lot 275-276 Abell Road, Tel: 082-414866. **Kuching Hotel**, 6, Jl. Temple, Tel: 082-413985. **Anglican Guest House**, Jl. Tun Haji Openg, Tel: 082-414027. There are other cheap, if not very clean, hotels in the old city, particularly on **Jl. Green Hill**.

Restaurants
INDIAN-MALAY: **Madinah Café**, Jl. India. **Duffy**, Jl. Ban Hock.
CHINESE: **Tsui Hua Lau**, Jl. Ban Hock. **Meisan**, Holiday Inn. **Hongkong Noodle House**, Jl. Tun Abang Haji Openg.
FISH is the specialty of **Rock Road Seafood Restaurant**, Jl. Rock. **KTS Seafoods Canteen**, 157, Chan Chin Ann Rd.

Museums
Sarawak Museum, Jl. Tun Haji Openg, Tel: 082-20620, Kuching, Mon-Thu 9:15 am-5:30 pm, Sat & Sun 9:15 am-6:00 pm, closed Fri and holidays.

Tours

Borneo Adventure, 55 Main Bazaar, Tel: 082-245175; trips to the Scrang and Batang Ai. **Asian Overland**, 286A Jl. Tabuan, Westwood Park, Tel: 082-251162, tour to Sungai Engkari.

Shopping

Numerous shops around the bus terminal. **Groceries:** Market, Jl. Masjid, Jl. Gambier on the river. **Furniture and jewelers:** Jl. Carpenter. **Textiles, tailors, household**: Jl. India. **Shopping centers:** Sarawak Plaza, Wisma Phoenix, Kuching Plaza. **Sunday Market** is on Jl. Satok. **Souvenirs:** Museum, Karyaneka Handicraft Shop, Jl. Satok, Sarawak Batik Art Shop, Jl. Temple.

Immigration Authorities / Consulate

Immigration, Jl. Song Thian Cheok, Kuching, Tel: 082-25661. **Indonesian Consulate**, 5a, Jl. Pisang, Kuching, Tel: 082-241734.

Hospital

Normah Medical Specialist Center, Lot 937 Section 30 KTLD, Jl. Tuan Haji Abdul Rahman, Kuching, Tel: 082-2440055.

Tourist Information

Sarawak Tourist Association (STA), Airport Kuching, Tel: 082-456266, Square Tower, Pengkalan Batu, Jl. Gambier, Tel: 082-20620. **TDC Sarawak**, AIA Buildg., Jl. Song Thian Cheok, Tel: 082-246575. **Sarawak Tourist Information Centre**, Tel: 082-248088. **Parks & Wildlife Office**, Kuching, Tel: 082-410944.

SANTUBONG
Accommodations

BUDGET as well as more comfortable lodging in **government bungalows.**

BANDAR SRI AMAN
Accommodations / Restaurants

BUDGET, clean hotels: **Alishan Hotel**, 4, Jl. Council, Tel: 083-322578. **Hoover Hotel**, 139, Club Road, Tel: 083-321985. Good Chinese meals in **Alishan Hotel** or at cookshacks.

SARIKEI
Accommodations

BUDGET: **Sarikei Hotel**, 11, Wharf Road. **Ambassador Hotel**, 54, Repok Rd.

KAPIT / BELAGA
Accommodations

KAPIT: *BUDGET:* **Guest House**, Missionsstation. **Rajang Hotel**, 28, New Bazar. **Kapit Longhouse**, Berjaya Road.
BELAGA: *BUDGET:* **Belaga Hotel**, Marketplace. **Resthouse**.

SIBU
Accommodations

MODERATE: **Premier Hotel**, Jl. Kampong Nyabor, Tel: 084-323222. **Tanah Mas Hotel**, Jl. Kampong Nyabor, Tel: 084-333188. **Li Hua Hotel**,

Long Bridge Commercial Centre, Tel: 084-324000. *BUDGET:* **Traveller's Hotel**, 9, Workshop Rd., Tel: 084-311677. **New World Hotel**, 1-3, Jl. Wong Nai Siong, Tel: 084-310311. **Sarawak Hotel**, 34, Jl. Cross, Tel: 084-333455. **Zuhra**, 103, Jl. Kampong Nyabor, Tel: 084-310711. Phoenix Hotel, Jl. Kai Peng, Tel: 084-313877.

Restaurants

SEAFOOD: **Wong Sha Wong**, Jl. Maju.
CHINESE: **Jhong Kuo Rest.**, 13, Jl. Wong Nai Siong.

BINTULU

(Overpriced because of the oil and gas industry.)

Accommodations

LUXURY: **Li Hua Hotel**, about 2.5 miles (4 km) out of town in Kemana, Tel: 086-35000.
MODERATE: **Sun Light Hotel**, 7, Jl. Pedada, Tel: 086-32681. **Royal Hotel**, 10-12, Jl. Pedada, Tel: 086-32166. *BUDGET:* if you can't find private accommodations, **Lodging Houses** are the cheapest places to stay.

Restaurants

Cookshacks in the marketplace or Lien Hua Cafe, 94, Jl. Abang Galau. *WESTERN/CHINESE:* In the restaurants of the **Kidurong Club, Regent Hotel, Li Hua Hotel**.

MIRI
Accommodations

LUXURY: **Park Hotel**, Kingsway, Tel: 085-414555.
MODERATE: **Cosy Inn**, 085-545547, Jl. South Yu Seng, Tel: 085-415522. **Gloria Hotel**, 27 Brooke Rd., Tel: 085-416699. **Million Inn**, 6, Jl. South Yu Seng, Tel: 085-415077.
BUDGET: **Fatimah Hotel**, 49, Brooke Rd., Tel: 085-32255. **Tai Tong Lodging House**, 26, China Street, Tel: 085-411948.

Restaurants

There's good food in the restaurants of the better **hotels**, or fast food in **Wisma Pelita**. Chinese restaurants on **China Street**, Malay dishes at cookshacks by the **fish market** and evenings at the **Night Market** on Brooke Street.

LIMBANG
Accommodations

BUDGET: **South East Asia Hotel**, 27, Market Street. **Australia**, Bank Street.

NATIONAL PARKS
Accommodations

BAKO NATIONAL PARK: as well as in the simple Hostels of the headquarters at **Telok Assam**, you can stay in two **Rest Houses.** Tel: 084-246477.
GUNUNG MULU NATIONAL PARK, NIAH NATIONAL PARK: reserve places in the hostels there through the **National Park Office**, Miri, Tel: 085-36637.

THE LAND TO WINDWARD

SABAH
KOTA KINABALU
MOUNTAIN OF THE GODS
JUNGLE ADVENTURES
THE SOUTHEAST
PULAU LABUAN

SABAH

Sabah is even more different from the other Malaysian states than Sarawak is. Once known as North Borneo and, with its 29,685 square miles (76,115 sq. km), almost twice as large as Switzerland, it is the state which lies furthest away from the Federation's capital. From the state capital of Kota Kinabalu, it's just as far to Hong Kong, 1,178 miles (1,900 km) away, as to Kuala Lumpur. Nowhere in the country is there such a low proportion of Malays in Sabah, the second-largest state. Here they make up just 8 % or so of the 1.2 million population. Alongside the Malays come 30 national minorities, who together add up to almost two-thirds of the Sabahans: these include the Kadazan or Duzun, the largest group, followed by the Murut and Bajau. Most of the non-*bumiputra* are Chinese, predominantly Hakka, at 20 %. Their forefathers landed on Sabah as early as the 15th century. Indians, Indonesians, Filipinos and Europeans also live in Sabah. The demographic situation does affect the political administration. Sabah is the only Malay-

sian state to have a Christian government; and this asserts, not always without tension, its opposition to K.L. The Prime Minister, Dr. Mahathir, is supposed to have himself described the political culture of Sabah as the "Wild East."

The distance from the rest of the federation is reflected in the prices. Sabah is one of the most expensive destinations in Southeast Asia for tourists.

As far as landscape is concerned, the state can chalk up an unrivalled high point: Mount Kinabalu has an altitude of 13,407 feet (4,100 m), and is therefore the highest mountain in Southeast Asia.

From the earliest times seafarers appreciated the north of Borneo; lying near the typhoon belt, which stretches from the Philippines via Taiwan to the Chinese mainland, it offered shelter from the frequent storms in the region. They called the area the "land to windward," which did not include necessarily protection from the pirates, who are still a danger today.

In Search of Sabah's Treasures

One of the outsiders who wanted to get rich in North Borneo was Kublai Khan (1215-1294). The Mongol ruler landed here in 1260 on his quest for the "Golden Jade." Neither he nor the traders who fol-

Preceding pages: The tropical rain forest on Mount Kinabulu is still by and large intact. Left: Bajau women in the market at Kota Belud.

lowed him succeeded in tracking down the sources of this mysterious precious stone, which they traded from the forest-dwellers. The Chinese first made permanent settlements on the coast around 1424. From the 16th century – following the crews of Magellan – Europeans started arriving more frequently. They, too, were hindered by the jungle in their push into the interior of the island. At this time, Sabah was under the dominion of the Sultan of Brunei, who did, however, pay proceeds from Sabah to the Sultanate of Sulu. The British East India Company had tried to gain a foothold in North Borneo in 1763 after they had acquired a piece of land from the ruler of Sulu. Fighting for their independence, the native inhabitants, who had already defied the sultans, initially managed to keep the whites, as well, at bay.

Roughly 100 years later, in 1865 to be precise, Baron von Overbeck, Austrian

Right: Kota Kinabalu, the progressive harbor town in North Borneo.

consul and opium dealer resident in Hong Kong, clambered into North Borneo by purchasing it from the Sultans for 12,000 dollars. Thenceforth he was entitled to call himself Maharajah of Sabah. Unlike the White Rajahs in Sarawak, he had little success in North Borneo. The mineral riches eluded him, Kaiser Franz Joseph in Vienna was not interested in a new colony, and thus he was compelled to sell his share to the English brothers Edward and Alfred Dent in 1881. Supported by their government, the Dents founded the North Borneo Company. London had now acquired yet another base in the Malayan archipelago. Connections with the Straits Settlements on the peninsula become closer, until Sabah, together with Sarawak and Brunei, became a British protectorate in 1888.

The brutal rebellion led by Mat Salleh in 1895, equally brutally suppressed, threatened the colony for a good five years; another, later, blow was the Japanese invasion in 1942. Even after independence in 1963 and entry into the

Malaysian Federation, Sabah remained a critical territory. Neither Indonesia nor the Philippines recognized the state, as they themselves laid claim to parts of it. A regular border war with Indonesia did not stop until 1966, when that country's President Sukarno was removed from power; as for the Philippines, the governments of Aquino and Ramos have not yet officially renounced their country's claims to Sabah. Finally, there was violent unrest in Sabah after the Christian Kadazan won the elections in 1985.

It is not difficult to see why Sabah's neighbors and inhabitants fight so obstinately over the state: the reason is its rich resources. "Black gold," vast reserves of oil and natural gas, the forests (now suffering badly from overlogging), and enormous, hardly-tapped mineral reserves: all these make Sabah the economically most important state in Malaysia. However the profits hardly make any impact on a local level. Sabah is at the same time one of the most backward regions of the country. The call for complete local autonomy, even independence, finds support, albeit reservedly, from most residents of Sabah, given the unequal distribution of wealth.

KOTA KINABALU

The capital of Sabah is a rapidly-growing administrative and commercial center with a population of around 200,000. From the tourist's point of view the town is only moderately attractive. In the 19th century, its residents still called it *Api Api*, which means "fire" and recalled the many conflagrations it suffered at the hands of pillaging pirates. The English, who in 1897 moved their settlement from the offshore island of Gaya to the mainland, named this sprawling outpost Jesselton in honor of Charles Jessel, a director of the North Borneo Company. With independence the town was renamed Kota Kinabalu which is generally shortened to K.K.

The colonial heart of the town was destroyed by Japanese bombs; today, modern bank and department store buildings shape the city's appearance. In the north, at Likas Bay, the 30-storey futuristic glass tower of the **Sabah Foundation** looms over the town. The city foundation accommodated in this suspension-structure building strives to improve the living conditions of the Sabahans, a third of whom live below the poverty line. To this end, the foundation administers under a 100-year contract more than 2.5 million acres (a million hectares) of forest, "careful" logging of which is intended to convert the profits in the country into benefits for the people. It's a praiseworthy institution; but all the same, 90% of logging companies in Sabah are foreign-owned.

Also modern is the **Sabah State Mosque**, built in 1977. The mosque, one of the largest in Malaysia, can hold 5,000 people. Nearby, on slightly higher ground on Jl. Penampang, is the **State Museum** of Sabah, which was built in 1983 in the style of a Rungus longhouse. Exhibits cover the ethnography, history and natural environment of the state. Difficult to miss is a slice of the largest tree ever felled in Sabah; this wooden disk, 8 feet (2.45 m) in diameter, has been set up in the entrance hall. Another museum sensation is the collection of human skulls, the *Bangkavan* collection. In 1972, the Kadazan made publicly accessible these relics of their head-hunting past. The Kadazan's principal place of worship today is the Roman Catholic **Sacred Heart Cathedral** on Jl. Tuaran, which is worth a visit.

If the rotating restaurant in the Sabah Foundation tower has not yet reopened, the best view over the town will be from **Signal Hill**, to the southeast. The best ascent begins at **Town Padang** behind the **Old Post Office**, the only surviving colonial building.

Right: A fishing village of pile houses off the island of Gaya.

Like other larger towns in Borneo, K.K. also has its **Kampong Air**. In the "water village" of pile dwellings opposite the main road Jl. Tunku Abdul Rahman live thousands of Filipinos. Around 400,000 immigrants from the neighboring country have come to Sabah, most of them illegally. They have also settled on the offshore islands and have been blamed for the rapid increase in crime in the town; in 1993, the government threatened to repatriate them all.

The **Night Market** between Jl. Tun Fuad Stephens, Jl. Datuk Chong Thain Yun and Lorong Jesselton is a nightly playground for the Filipino traders. So, too, the **Central Market**, which is set up along Jl. Tun Fuad Stephens. A third market is the **Pasar Minggu**, which springs up between Jl. Pantai and Jl. Gaya on Saturday evenings. The bustle peaks early in the morning and late in the afternoon on the water side of the **Fish Market**, to the right of the Central Market, when the fishing cutters discharge their glistening and slippery cargo.

Outside K.K.

Not far from the Kampong Air are the outskirts of the satellite town of **Tanjong Aru**, which stretches as far as the airport 3 miles (5 km) away. This is also the length of the well-tended beach edged with parks. K.K. residents like to unwind here or have a bite to eat in one of the restaurants or eating stalls. Spectacular sunsets and fishing boats at sea round off the romance of the view. Guests at the **Tanjong Aru Beach Hotel** can enjoy the hotel's privileged location on a spit of land.

The hotel adjoins the **Tunku Abdul Rahman National Park**, which since 1974 has been protecting five islands and 19.5 square miles (50 sq. km) of ocean. Only on the largest island, **Pulau Gaya**, are there actually fisher families living. At the park headquarters, on **Pulau Manukan**, there are a number of tourist

chalets. On both of these islands, paths wind through lowland forest and mangrove swamp, where sea eagles, hornbills, macaques and varans make their home. Attractive, too, are the little sandy coves and coral reefs of Gaya, Manukan, Sapi, Mamutik and other islands.

For would-be Robinson Crusoes, however, the park is hardly suited: the Tanjong Aru Hotel sends tourist boats over to the island beaches every day. Between December and May, when underwater visibility is better because of the calmer weather, is a particularly good time for scuba divers and snorkelers to visit.

Anyone who'd like the grisly thrill of examining genuine skull trophies, these in family possession, should make his way to the "House of Skulls." Located in **Kampong Monsopiad**, around 8 miles (13 km) south of the State Mosque of K.K., near Putatan, is the house of the Moujings, direct descendants of the famous head-hunter Monsopiad, for whom the village is named. From the living-room ceiling dangle 42 skulls and a thighbone, supposedly 300 years old. Mr. Moujing is happy to put on Kadazan costume, including the keen sword of his ancestor, decorated with human hair. Monsopiad, who was venerated almost as a god when he was alive, is buried in a rice field close by – in one piece, as his enemies could not agree on who should possess the famous head. (The TDC, the Sabah Tourism Promotion Corporation or the hotels will be able to provide exact directions for how to get there.)

KINABALU, MOUNTAIN OF THE GODS

Its jagged pinnacles tower threateningly through the clouds. The Kadazan call this mountain *Aki Nabalu*, seat of the gods, ghosts and spirits of their ancestors. Once the 13,410 foot (4,101 m) Mount Kinabalu, part of the Crocker range, was taboo to them. As Dalrymple reported more than 230 years ago, they believed the peak area also to be the entrance to paradise; it was guarded, however, by a

firedog, which attacked any virgins who might happen to be approaching. The Englishman Sir Hugh Low was certainly not the first person to climb the mountain, much less to "discover" it – though he is famed for having done both in 1851. The Kadazan ancestor Gunting Lagadan is supposed to have reached the peak long before that, when he lost his way while out hunting.

The highest mountain in Southeast Asia and the national park surrounding it are the destination of many tourists. Every year over 15,000 visitors struggle to climb the mountain as part of a tour which may last two days at most. Because of the congestion, would-be visitors should obtain a permit in good time from the park administration. Most often you will need to overnight in a hut at an altitude of around 10,800 feet (3,300 m), and here there is only room for 220 people.

Above: The Kadazan call Mount Kinabalu Seat of the Gods. Right: Weird tropical vegetation in the National Park at Kinabalu.

Southeast Asia's Roof

The steep path leading to the peak is only one of the possibilities in this 294-square-mile (754 sq. km) park. Tropical vegetation covers the slopes of the mountain, but at the top you can expect temperatures around the freezing point. Your equipment should be selected accordingly: pullover, hiking boots, clothing offering protection from wind and rain, and also a flashlight for the storm that begins up there before the sun goes down. Experienced Kadazan guides are absolutely essential, particularly for the final stage. Even climbers who are only in average condition will manage it to the top with these guides. The march, however, does not begin at the foot of the mountain, but at the power station 2.5 miles (4 km) away from park headquarters, which can be reached in a drive of two hours or so from Kota Kinabalu and which is itself at an elevation of 6,180 feet (1,890 m).

This is also the settlement boundary of the Kadazan, who do not feel at ease any higher, due to the thin air and the spirits of their ancestors – except, of course, when they are taking tourists up the mountain and earning money from their love of the heights.

Despite all the hardships you may experience slogging along these slippery paths, drenched in rain and swathed in mist, you can still be entranced by the plant world. Occasionally you may need to slow the guide down. Ten species of carnivorous pitcher plants thrive on Kinabalu alone, and 26 rhododendron species and 1,200 varieties of orchid have been counted. If you are lucky you will see the largest bloom in the world, that of the *Rafflesia*, about 23 inches (60 cm) across. Nearly all of the almost 600 species of bird and some orangutan live in the park. Zoologists suspect that it may still house some of the last members of the virtually extinct breed of Sumatra rhinoceros.

After leaving the **Laban Rata Resthouse**, which was the first day's goal and where rescue helicopters can be called in by radio in an emergency, you continue on the second day upwards to **Low's Peak**. The last 1,000 feet (300 m) is a struggle over granite boulders to the summit at 13,123 ft (4,101 m) where sunrise reveals a unique panorama. The view extends out over the mountains and forest as far as the distant islands.

JUNGLE ADVENTURE

One especially rewarding excursion from the national park is to **Poring** which is reached via the small town of **Ranau**, otherwise a place of transit on the Kota Kinabalu-Sandakan route. Here, beautiful jungle paths have been laid out that to waterfalls and caves inhabited by mysterious bats.

A special experience is touring the forest at a lofty height above ground. In 1990, the American Illar Muul installed a system of platforms and hanging bridges

about 1,800 feet (550 m) long at a height of 100-130 feet (30-40 m) in the treetops where 75% of the mammals, 85% of the birds and 95% of the insects in the forest are to be found. This **canopy walkway** is the second of its kind in the world – the first was a similar project in French Guiana – and conveys the nature of the rain forest from a perhaps dizzying but certainly optimal perspective.

The other attraction here are the **hot springs** which the Japanese enclosed to make "hot tubs" during World War Two. With some luck you can admire the flowers of the *Rafflesia* here between June and September.

The inhuman side of the occupation is commemorated by the **Death March Monument** at **Kundasang**. In 1944, 2,400 Allied prisoners were forced to make a death march through the jungle from Sandakan to Ranau. Only six survived the ordeal. Today this town, about 3.5 miles (6 km) from the national park, is the center of Sabah's vegetable-cultivating region.

Sandakan and Sepilok

Sandakan, until 1947 the capital of Sabah, lies about 185 miles (300 km) to the east of K.K., almost at the eastern end of Malaysia. William Pryer founded the town in 1879 and called it Elopura. At that time, there was already a settlement called "Kampong German," about 12.5 miles (20 km) from the present town, where the Scotsman Cowie and a number of Germans lived. They were soldiers in the service of the Sultan of Sulu.

Cowie is supposed to have given the name *Sandakan* to this hamlet. In the Sulu language this means "the place which was pledged." Now numbering 30,000 inhabitants, it is a center for export goods such as rattan, hardwood and palm oil. During the war it was entirely destroyed and, like K.K., rebuilt after the war on a gridiron pattern. Many thousands of Indonesian and Philippine immigrants live here, too. The protected bay and numerous islands have attracted smugglers and settlers since time immemorial. Out in the Sulu Sea, pirates practice their often bloody trade, virtually unaffected by the coast guard stationed in Sandakan.

Tourists make a visit to Sandakan at least on the way to Sepilok, but there is not a lot to see. The old harbor of **Pengkalan** is certainly interesting, and there's also the **Pasar Besar**, or town market. Unfortunately the **Orchid Gardens** at Town Padang opposite the old post office are in a sad state of neglect. Around 2 miles (3 km) north of the center, there is a **Chinese temple** on Jl. Singapura; its terrace commands an impressive view over Sandakan, the neighboring Moslem water village of **Sim Sim** with its great mosque, and the offshore islands.

The visitor's main destination in this region is the **Sepilok Orangutan Reha-bilitation Center**, about 20 minutes by car west of Sandakan. Over 150 of these anthropoid apes, once held in illegal captivity in Malaysia, Indonesia and worldwide, are prepared here for a free life in the protected forests. A male orangutan named Hein was even repatriated to Sepilok around 20 years ago from Frankfurt Zoo and still swings through the trees here. The young learn by imitating their elders, something essential if they are to survive in the jungle. It is not an easy matter, either for the animals or for their human trainers, as animals which have been in captivity exhibit behavioral disturbances very quickly, and are not able to build shelters or find food independently. It takes between 7 and 9 years before an orangutan student finally becomes what his name means: a "man of the forest." The scientists at Sepilok have for this reason set up a platform on the 9,000-acre (4,000 ha) site, where the apes can find additional food laid out for them.

This project tries to reach a compromise between tourism and conservation. At Sepilok you will not find animals performing tricks, nor snack bars, nor souvenir shops. Instead, excellent and informative wildlife trails lead you through lowland forest and mangrove woods. The exhibition at the **Nature Education Center** provides information on Sabah's flora and fauna. Souvenir shops and restaurants have been relegated to the entrance of the park.

Only around 3,000 orangutans still live in Sabah, while on Sarawak, Indonesian Kalimantan and on Sumatra there are a total of about 35,000. They are fascinating creatures, as they are so similar to man. But it is precisely man who is threatening them unremittingly by hunting and by destruction of the forest. Carbonized bones found in the Niah caves show that humans were already eating orangutan 40,000 years ago. Although orangutans today are no longer killed as trophies by western hunters, as they were

Right: This orangutan came out of his reha-bilitation course well.

in the 19th century, they are still compelled to lead sad lives in zoos around the globe. In the end, this will be the only place to find them once the tropical rain forest, has disappeared.

Buses connect Sandakan to Sepilok. You can also see other animals such as snakes, occasionally an elephant or rhinoceros. Visiting permit are available at the arrival station. Showing up on time gives you the chance (10 people / one group per day) to also take a small guided hike to see the adult animals in their natural habitat after watching the feeding of the young. There is no overnight accommodation.

On the way back, you should stop at the **Crocodile Farm** about 9 miles (15 km) from Sandakan to watch these reptiles lying lazily about the edge of a pond.

Caves and Tortoise Islands

The largest of the 27 cave systems of Sabah found to date is situated about 18.5 miles (30 km) south of Sandakan, on the other side of the bay. Getting there, either independently or by arrangement with one of the town travel agents, is not cheap – unless you can hitch a ride at the fish market on one of the boats taking the salangan nest collectors to their perilous work. You will have to climb a 3-mile (5 km) path up to the cave. The permit to the underworld of the **Gomantong Caves** is issued by the **Wildlife Office** in the Government Complex, about 6 miles (10 km) from Sandakan. Formerly the caves were considered sacred, as they were used as burial grounds. Now on numerous occasions during the year they are the destination of the intrepid acrobats who climb rickety bamboo scaffolding up to 300 feet (90 m) high in order to harvest the nests of the salanganen swifts for the bird's-nest soup which originates in Sarawak. But this enormous cave is worth visiting for the innumerable birds and bats alone.

Off the coast, directly on the border with the Philippines, lies **Turtle Island Park**. Its 6.5 square miles (17 sq. km) en-

compass and protect the islands of Selingan, Bakungan, Kecil and Gulisan. In the Turtle Island Sanctuary of **Selingan**, rangers watch over the Green Turtle (*Chelonia mydas*) so prized by predatory animals and, as an ingredient for soup, by man. The turtle broods can hatch without being disturbed and then be released under protection. The sea turtles, which also include the hawksbill turtle (*Eretmochelys imbricata*), prefer to come ashore in the bright light of the full moon, between August and October.

The Bajau – Sea Nomads and Cowboys

The second-largest ethnic group in Sabah after the Kadazan are the Bajau. They live for the most part along the west coast between Papar and Kudat. Scientists believe that their ancestors, nomadic sea gypsies, settled here from the Philip-

Above: "Cowboys of Borneo" is the nickname of these Bajau hard riders.

pines around 2,000 years ago. For their part, the Bajau assert that they originated in the vicinity of Johor. A surprise attack on their fleet by Brunei soldiers was the cause of their restless peregrinations around the waters of southeast Asia. There is no doubt that a number of the piratical activities of past centuries, which did not spare even inland areas, can be credited to their account. But often they were blamed for the misdeeds of others, as gypsies still are in Europe.

Since that time the Moslem Bajau of Sabah have become peaceful farmers and stockmen, which has earned them the nickname of the "Cowboys of Borneo." When during festivals they gallop by on their wiry horses, dressed in their colorful costumes and turbans, they recall not the lasso-swirling cowpunchers of the prairies but rather the Asiatic riders of the steppes. They have not entirely abandoned their passion for the sea, as is evidenced by the pile village of **Mengkabong**, which projects out into the sea at Tuaran in a picturesque bay north of K.K.

Tamu – Weekly Peace Markets

An institution typical of Sabah is the *tamu*, a lively weekly market, where men and women from the different ethnic groups dressed in their finest meet to trade and haggle, to buy and sell cattle, but also to play games and music, to gossip and to show off in sports such as buffalo-racing, arm- or finger-wrestling.

This old custom derives from the times when land acquisition was not always peaceful and so attempts were made to settle conflicts by negotiations on neutral ground. *Tamu*, which is the Malayan for visit, became a permanent institution, which the colonial masters also diligently cultivated in order to strengthen their relations with the local chiefs. The current *tamu* schedule is displayed in the tourist offices, and the market day is shown for each major location. Important, because very well attended, *tamu* are held in **Tuaran** and **Kota Belud**. More rustic markets are found in smaller locations, such as that held every Wednesday at **Tamparuli,** about 3.5 miles (6 km) from Tuaran; there, the participants are almost exclusively locals. **At** Tamparuli, you can also swing on the longest suspension bridge in Sabah which crosses the **Sungai Tuaran**.

In the North

The town of **Kudat** with its 40,000 inhabitants, located on the peninsula of the same name which thrusts like a wedge into the South China Sea, lies within the settlement area of the Rungus. A very small part of this subgroup of the Kadazan still lives in longhouses, surrounded by coconut palm groves, rice fields and banana plantations. Apart from them, what was once uniformly a longhouse village of the Kadazan is now a mixture of modern kinds of dwellings. The Rungus women appear particularly graceful when they don rich pearl and brass jewelry in addition to their embroidered black sarongs. The Rungus hold their large *tamu* every Sunday in **Sikuati**. Unfortunately the fabulously beautiful and truly unfrequented beaches cannot really be enjoyed by less adventurous visitors: they are remote and offer no accommodation. The beach paradise of **Pulau Banggi** comes over better here. Boats cross over to this jungle island at irregular intervals. Visitors who can manage to speak a little Malay can arrange overnight accommodation with the villagers. Kudat's own beach, **Bak Bak**, is located 6 miles (10 km) from town, so you have to take a taxi to get there.

The Sabah Hinterland

Some 7.5 miles (12 km) south of Kota Kinabalu, communities of Kadazan live in traditional and attractive villages at **Penampang**. The pile dwellings are roofed with palm leaves; sago and coconut palms grow all round about. Just 31 miles (50 km) to the south is the little town of **Papar**; many Murut live nearby. These former nomads were pushed further and further inland by the Kadazan. Their settlements extend into the mountain regions bordering on Indonesia. Many of them live in longhouses. The Murut still hunt with blowpipes, which makes them interesting for tourists.

An unforgettable experience for travelers in this region is the railway journey between **Beaufort** and **Tenom**. Neither town is special (except for the Sunday *tamu* in Tenom), but the ride provides an unforgettable impression of the landscape of the hinterland. Very slowly, hugging the rock walls, the train edges through the **Padas Gorge** in the Crocker mountains with a forest river rushing far below. The train rocks to the clacking of the rails, everything is redolent of yesteryear, and these two or three hours will turn out to have been too brief after all. Another, and faster, stretch of railway links Beaufort with Tanjong Aru.

18.5 miles (30 km) northeast of Tenom lies **Keningau**, also a place to begin trips to the Murut settlements. Herds of cattle and ponies graze in the broad meadows between the rice fields; it is a peaceful landscape.

Tambunan, 31 miles (50 km) northwest of Keningau, evokes the memory of Mat Salleh, the notorious resistance fighter. The ruins of his fortress and the graves of his followers can be seen here. Not far off are the settlements of the Hill Kadazan, who live in bamboo houses around **Sinsuron**.

THE SOUTHEAST

The three larger towns in the southeast of Sabah can only be reached by air or, with a great deal of trouble, by road. **Tawau** is cocoaville par excellence: the entire town and its surroundings lives on

Above: The weekly markets in Sabah are popular meeting-places. Right: The Rungus women make their own beaded jewelry.

this pod fruit, which is shipped out worldwide as a raw material for chocolate. But Tawau is also a trading center for dried coconut (or copra), high-grade timber and rubber. Nature remains undisturbed on **Tuwau Hill**, where there is a protected park with hot springs and jungle.

Close to the border with the Philippines lies **Semporna**. The offshore islands with their miles of coral reefs will be of interest to divers and snorkelers. The best diving is around **Pulau Gaya** and **Pulau Sipadan**; the **Semporna Ocean Tourism Center** can assist in arranging the expensive boat trips out to these areas. The K.K.-based agency of Borneo Divers & Sea Sports maintains its own diving base on Sipadan.

An enchanting underwater world is also offered 62 miles (100 km) to the north by the islands around **Lahad Datu**, the trading town on the north edge of Darvel Bay. Despite a number of hotels there are very few visitors to be seen here, which may have something to do

with the frequent pirate attacks. Facing the bay are the Philippine Sulu Islands, a notoriously unsafe area.

Since 1986, the **Danum Valley Field Center** between the Danum and Segama rivers has been a refuge for flora and fauna. The Sabah Foundation has reserved here 172 square miles (440 sq. km) of its almost 3,900 square miles (10,000 sq. km) of logging operations area as a research and conservation area. Most of the plants native to Sabah grow here, and planners hope to make it into a habitat for threatened species such as orangutan, the Sumatran rhinoceros and the elephant. A resthouse is available for visitors, who must first have registered with the foundation in K.K.

PULAU LABUAN

Off Brunei and Sabah lies the 39-square-mile (100 sq. km) island of **Labuan**. Since 1984 it has been a Federal Territory and thus an autonomous administrative area. It has a free port and coal deposits which aroused the interest of the Royal Navy in the 19th century. To be able to bunker fuel here for the British ships, Captain Mundy acquired the island in 1846 from the Sultan of Brunei in exchange for assistance in fighting the pirates. The next, but not the last, owner of Labuan was the North Borneo Company. In 1906 the island was placed under the Straits Settlements; and in 1942, it was occupied by the Japanese. After the war, to which the Australian **Soldiers' Cemetery** and the **Commonwealth War Memorial** bear witness, it became once again part of British North Borneo; since independence, it has belonged to Sabah.

At present, the Malaysian government has great plans in store for Labuan, which, as a free-trade zone, is to attract investors and capital. Certainly it's already attractive enough to oil-rig workers from Brunei; while alcohol is forbidden there, in Labuan it flows copiously and duty-free. This clientele can also afford the pricey hotels in **Victoria**, the island's only city.

193

Adventure Trips

The impassable interior of Sabah holds many a fascinating route in store for the traveller seeking adventure. For example, you can fly to **Sapulot** and there join organized trips to visit the Murut; or push into Indonesian territory on the **Sungai Sembakung**. This illegal form of immigration will have no consequences provided you leave the country by the same route you entered. Experienced paddlers can embark on whitewater trips down the **Padas Gorge**. There are also many hiking routes through the jungle, all guaranteed to provide unique experiences, whether in the region lying between Kinabalu Park and Sandakan, or from **Sindumin**, southwest of Beaufort along the border with Sarawak to **Long Pa Sia**. In addition to all this, there are over 40 caves in Sabah, many of which can only be reached after days of tramping.

Above: Jungle trekking in Sarawak can be a real adventure.

STATE OF SABAH

KOTA KINABALU
Getting there / Transportation

BY AIR: **MAS** has flights between Kota Kinabalu and Kuching, Kuala Lumpur, Johor B., Keningau Kudat, Labuan, Lawas, Miri, Sandakan, Sibu Tawau. Internat. Flights to and from Singapore, B Seri Begawan, Manila. Flights between Sandakar and Kudat, Semporna, L. Datu, Tawau, Pamol. Tomanggong – L. Datu, Semporna.

BY BOAT: regular connections to Kuching, Kuan tan, P. Klang, Info: **Feri Malaysia**, Tel: 088-215011.

TRAIN: Daily trains from Kota Kinabalu via Beaufort to Tenom. Kota Kinabalu's Main Station is or Tanjong Aru.

BUS / OVERLAND TAXI: The bus and taxi termi nal is on Jl. Balai Polis.

Accommodations

LUXURY: **Hyatt Kinabalu International**, Jl Datuk Salleh Sulong, Tel: 088-221234. **Tanjong Aru Beach**, Jl. Aru, Tel: 088-241800. **Shangri-La**, 75, Bandaran Berjaya, Tel: 088-212800.

MODERATE: **Capital**, Jl. Hj. Saman, Tel: 088 231999. **Jesselton**, 69, Gaya St., Tel: 088-223333.

BUDGET: **The Town Inn**, 31-33 Jl. Pantai, Tel 088-225823. **Hotel Holiday**, Jl. Tun Razak, Tel 088-213116. **Nam Xing**, 33-35, Jl. Hj. Saman, Tel 088-239388.

Restaurants

INTERNATIONAL: Restaurants in the Hotels **Hyatt**, **Tanjong Aru**, **Shangri-La**. **Gardenia Restaurant**, Jl. Gaya, Tel: 088-54296.

MALAY: **Sri Melaka Restaurant**, Jl. Laimar Diki, Tel: 088-224777. **Sri Pinang Restaurant**, Jl Padang, tel: 088-216059. **Kampong Air Restaurant**, Jl. Merdeka. **Peoples Food Center**, Ka ramunsing complex.

CHINESE: **Nan Xing Restaurant**, Jl. Haj Saman, Tel: 088-239388. **Diamond**, Jl. Mawas, Lot 1, Luyang Phase (also seafood).

INDIAN: **Shiraz House of Moghul Food**, Jl Kampong Air, Tel: 088-225088.

KADAZAN CUISINE: **Hongkong Seafood Restaurant**, Jl. Penampang, Tel: 088-718390. There are many cookshacks, particularly **around the Night Market**.

Museums

Sabah State Museum, Kota Kinabaru, Jl Penampang, Tel: 088-225503, open daily except Fr 9:00 am-5:00 pm.

Shopping

Center Point Shopping Complex, Jl. Centre Point. **Wisma Merdeka Complex**, Jl. Haj Saman. In Wisma Merdeka (Tel: 088-239258/87) souvenirs at **Borneo Handicrafts**, **Rafflesia Gift Center**. **Sabah Handicraft Center**, Bandaran Berjaya, Tel: 088-221231.

Hospitals

Queen Elisabeth Hospital, Jl. Penampang, Tel: 088-218166. **Sabah Medical Cent**er, Jl. Yayasan Sabah, Tel: 088-424333.

Car Rental

Adaras Rent A Car, Wisma Sabah, Jalan Haji Saman, Tel: 088-222137. **Travel Rent A Car**, Wisma Sabah, Jalan Haji Saman, Tel: 088-222708.

Police / Consulate / Immigration

Police: Jl. Karamunsing, Tel: 088-212222.
Indonesian Consulate, Jl. Karamunsing, Tel: 088-54100.
Immigration Office: Jl. Laiman Diki, Tel: 088-216711.

Tourist Information

TDC, 1, Jl. Sagunting, Tel: 088-248698. **Sabah Tourism Promotion Corp. (STPC)**, Jl. Gaya, Tel: 088-212121.

TUNKU ABDUL RAHMAN PARK

A group of 5 islands about a half-hour boatride northwards off Kota Kinabalu. Basically, only the main island of **Manukan** offers the possibility of lodgings in comfortable chalets. Food and drink supply is also guaranteed. A sea-side holiday can also be had on the other islands, but you'll have to bring a tent and supplies. For reservations: Sabah Parks in Kota Kinabalu, 088-21188.

KINABALU NATIONAL PARK

Registration: **Sabah National Parks Headquarters** in K. K., Jl. Tun Fuad Stephens, Tel: 088-211811. *BUDGET:* **Old Fellowship Hostel** and **New HosTel: Kinabalu Lodge**. On the mountain: several huts. In **Poring**: Camping, two huts (**Old** and **New Cabin**), **hostel:**

RANAU

MODERATE: **Mt. Kinabalu Perkasa** (outside of town), Tel: 088-79511.
BUDGET: **Mountain View**, Kandasang, Tel: 088-889518. **Kheng Lok Hwa**. **Ranau Hotel**.

SANDAKAN

LUXURY: **Renaissance**, Km 1, Jl. Utara, Tel: 089-213299. **Ramai**, about a mile (1.5 km) out of town, Jl. Leila, Tel: 089-216988. **Hsiang Garden**, Jl. Leila, Tel: 089-43191. *BUDGET:* **Kin Nam**, 51, Jl. Tiga. **New Sabah**, Jl. Singaporea, Tel: 089-218711. **Malaysia**, 32. 2nd Avenue, Tel: 089-218322. **Paris**, 45, Jl. Tiga, Tel: 089-218488.
Restaurants: Two seafood restaurants near the bus terminal. **Apple Fast Food**, next to the NAK Hotel,

Jl. Pelabohan, also has Asian dishes. Chinese restaurants on Jl. Elopura & Leboh Lima: **Kheong Soon**, **Ming Shing**; Malay restaurants nearby.

KOTA BELUD

BUDGET: **Kota Belud**, 21, Jl. Francis, Tel: 088-976576. **Government Rest House** (out of town).

KUDAT

BUDGET: **Kinabalu**, No1, Block C, Sedco Complex, Tel: 088-613888. **Kudat**, Little St., Tel: 088-616379. **Yun Nyen**, Sedco Complex, Tel: 088-61386. **Sunrise**, Tel: 088-61517. **Resthouse**, Tel: 088-61304.

BEAUFORT / TENOM

BEAUFORT: *BUDGET:* **Foh Lodging House**, at the train station (very simple, often crowded). **Padas**, between the fish market and the bus terminal, Tel: 088-211441.
TENOM: *BUDGET:* **Kin San**, Shophouse No. 58, Tel: 088-735485. **Sri Jaya**, Main Street. **Sabah**, opp. the police station, Tel: 088-735077. **Tenom Hotel**, Tel: 088-736077. **Resthouse**, Tel: 088-7353477.

KENINGAU / TAWAU

KENINGAU: *BUDGET:* **Perkasa**. Cheaper: **Rai**, **Alishan**, **Hiap Soon**.
TAWAU: *LUXURY:* **Marco Polo**, Tel: 089-777988. *MODERATE:* **Emas**, Jl. Utara, Tel: 089-762000. **Royal**, Jl. Belian, Tel: 089-773100. **Far East**, Jl. Mesjid, Tel: 089-773200. **Oriental**, 10, Jl. Dunlop, Tel: 089-761601. *BUDGET:* **Malaysia**, 37, Jl. Dunlop, Tel: 089-772800. **Wah Yew**, 117, Jl. Chester, Tel: 089-771300. **Foo Guan**, 152, Jl. Chester, Tel: 089-771700.

SEMPORNA

MODERATE: **Island View**, Tel: 089-781638. **Floating Hotel**: *BUDGET:* **Guest Houses**.

LAHAD DATU

MODERATE: **Mido**, 94 Main Street, Tel: 089-881800. **Perdana**, Jl. Bajau, Tel: 089-881400.
BUDGET: **Ocean**, Jl. Timur, Tel: 089-81700. **Lahad Datu**, Jl. Kemboja, Tel: 089-81100. **Rest House**, near the airport, about half a mile (1 km) out of town, Tel: 089-81177.

LABUAN ISLAND

LUXURY: **Labuan**, Jl. Merdeka, Tel: 087-412311. *MODERATE:* **Victoria**, Jl. Tun Mustapha, Tel: 087-412411. **Emas-Labuan**, 27-30, Jl. Muhibbah, Tel: 087-413966. *BUDGET:* **Kim Soon Lee**, 141-2, Jl. Okk, Awang Besar.

THE RICHEST
COUNTRY IN ASIA

**BRUNEI
DARUSSALAM
BANDAR SERI BEGAWAN**

BRUNEI

From history, we know Brunei as a powerful kingdom. Today, the Sultanate is shrunken and very few people could actually locate its precise position on the globe. Brunei, however, is often cited as the perfect example of comfortable affluence and incredible wealth flaunted before the eyes of impoverished neighbors. Jammed in between Sarawak and Sabah and just 2,248 square miles (5,765 sq. km) in area, it lies on the northwest coast of Borneo, divided in two by a region of Sarawak which extends to the sea on either side of the Limbang river. 85% of the country is covered by jungle. Apart from the coast road which leads from Sarawak into the capital, there are very few paved roads in the country.

The Sultan has 300,000 subjects, of whom around 60 percent are Malay and the rest European (mostly British), Chinese and minorities. Add to this the thousands of men and women here as guest workers, such as 60,000 Chinese and an equal number of Europeans, who produce the country's riches in return for

Preceding pages: The sources of Brunei's wealth lie off the coast. Left: The splendid mosque in the capital of Bandar Seri Begawan.

handsome salaries.

The oil and natural gas wells off the coast, which have been pouring out their bounty for the last 70 years, supply 99 percent of the exports and make the inhabitants of Brunei the richest people in Asia. Their Sultan was, up until a few years ago, the richest man in the world. The Malay Bruneians, predominantly in the police, armed forces and government offices, can devote themselves to idleness without any pricking of conscience. Totally free of foreign debt, with no income tax and with an average annual per capita income of US $17,500 (1993) the Bruneians are loyal to their feudal lord even though his conservative Islamic regime doesn't give much stock to notions such as parliamentary democracy or western freedoms.

The present Sultan, who was born in 1946, is the 29th scion of a dynasty which was founded 400 years ago by the legendary seafarer and pirate Bolkiah. Once the power of Brunei extended over all Borneo – from which the sultanate takes its name – as well as broad swaths of present-day Indonesia and the south Philippine islands.

As early as the 6th century, Brunei is mentioned in Chinese writings; 800 years later, it belonged to the Javanese empire of Majapahit. After the Rajah of Brunei,

Awang Alak ber Tabar, married a princess from Malacca and converted to Islam in the 15th century, ties between the two feudal realms strengthened.

Magellan's chronicler Pigafetta described the royal court of Brunei back in 1521. He also noticed a large town built out over the water where the women travelled around in sampans. Sultan Bolkiah, who was ruling at that time, and his successor Hassan helped Brunei to reach the height of its power. Relations with Portugal were extremely cordial, and Brunei developed into a base for ships on the Malacca-Macao route.

Up until 1645 the Spanish repeatedly attempted to get control over Brunei, but in vain. Nor had the Dutch occupation of Malacca been able to weaken the country. All the same, the golden age of the Sultans was approaching its end. Their influence over their vassals was shrinking; the pirates were getting more

Above: For the time being, Brunei's children can still look forward to a carefree future.

and more powerful. Finally Brunei's rulers gave away what was left of their empire to the Europeans: Sarawak to the White Rajahs, Sabah to the North Borneo Company. The remainder of Brunei became a British protectorate in 1888, was absorbed into the Straits Settlements in 1906 and later placed under the governor of Sarawak. Just as the rest of Malaya and Borneo, Brunei was under Japanese occupation from 1942 to 1945.

In accordance with the desire of the British colonial masters, Brunei, like the other states, could have become independent and also a member of the Malaysian Federation. Rumor has it that the newly-discovered oil reserves induced the Sultan at that time, Sir Haji Omar Ali Saifuddin, to break off negotiations. He did, in fact, prefer to reap the benefits of the black gold for himself and his people alone, under British protection.

Three years after the constitution was ratified in 1959, the Sultanate had to master its most serious crisis yet with the help of London. Controlled from abroad – at least, this is the official version – parts of the army mutinied. The success of the opposition party in the elections was so impressive that the British saw no choice but to intervene. Political parties were rapidly disbanded, Parliament dissolved, and a state of emergency proclaimed.

In 1967, Omar Ali Saifuddin abdicated in favour of Muda Hassan Bolkiah, one of his four sons. Under the young Sultan, whose full name and title is Duli Yang Maha Mulia Paduka Seri Baginda Sultan dan Yang Di-Pertuan Sir Muda Hassanal Bolkiah Mu'izzaddin Waddaullah, the first constitution was revised in 1979 and Britain's responsibility recognized solely in foreign affairs and defense. The Sultanate of Brunei Darussalam has been fully independent since 1984, and has also in the meantime become a member of ASEAN, the Association of Southeast Asian Nations. In this way any desires for expansion that neighboring countries

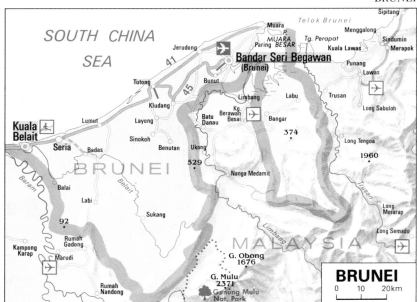

might entertain have been, for the time being, neutralized.

The reserves of oil and natural gas, on which the economy of Brunei is founded, are expected to last until the year 2015. In fact it will be longer than this, however, as new fields have already been discovered off the coast.

Brunei's social welfare institutions are generous in the extreme when compared with those of other countries. Health care and education are free of charge to all citizens; and people have been able to draw pensions without paying into a pension fund beforehand since 1955. There are grants available for studying abroad, and interest-free loans for purchasing a car. If a foreigner's dog has to go to the vet – pious Muslims, believing dogs to be unclean, don't keep them as pets – it is treated free of charge. Malnutrition and other illnesses of developing countries are for the most part unknown here, while the complaints of the industrialized world, such as heart and circulatory ailments, are on the rise. 80 percent of foods are imported, even fish, of which there's such an abundant supply right off the coast. This is what happens when work becomes a hobby, as it is for the Bruneians. Chinese, who industriously keep business and trade moving, can only become citizens after taking a pernickety examination. If they were all to leave Brunei one day, this promised land would seize up and cease to function.

The state-owned Royal Brunei Airlines carries mainly diplomats and businessmen, who stand in line at court to get their slice of the big oil cake. Tourists are still rare birds. This expensive sultanate can only attract relatively well-off visitors, and considering the few sights it has to offer, the 14 days' stay which is the maximum allowed without a visa should be completely adequate.

BANDAR SERI BEGAWAN

Even on the road from the airport, you can see where the Sultan is investing his petrodollars. In a town district on the

north bank of the **Sungai Brunei**, a government quarter, a shopping and business center, and hospitals have sprung up in recent years. The city center is dominated unmistakably by the **Mesjid Sultan Omar Ali Saifuddin**, inaugurated in 1958. The architect was Italian, the work force came from the Philippines and other countries. In Brunei people like to compare this imposing edifice of Shanghai granite and Carrara marble with India's Taj Mahal. The mosque rises from an artificial lake on the banks of the river and is joined to a ship of stone, a replica of a royal boat from the 16th century. Visitors can tour the mosque outside the hours of prayer and take an elevator up the 144-foot (44 m) minaret for an impressive panoramic view from the top.

From here, the eye falls on the **Kampong Air**, a giant village on the Brunei river where over 30,000 people live in pile dwellings. It is no slum – every

Above: Detail of the Sultan Omar Ali Saifuddin Mosque in Bandar Seri Begawan.

house has electricity and running water. The cars parked on the nearby roads belong to the residents of this water village, and a television aerial pokes out from every rooftop. Private boats or taxi boats take the children to school. Only under the jetties does rubbish pile up at low tide: no modern technology has yet been designed to remove it. Many of the villagers craft objects out of brass, bronze and silver, which, together with mats and woven articles, they offer for sale on stalls around Kampong Air.

Fruit, clothes, audio cassettes and magic charms are sold in the **market** between Jln. Sungai Kianggeh, Jln. McArthur and Jln. Sultan. It is debatable whether the antiques occasionally on sale there are genuine, in view of the great demand for these by Brunei's foreign community in the past.

To the north are the grandiose government buildings: the Royal Ceremonial Hall, or **Lapau**, and Parliament, which the Bruneians call **Dewan Majlis**. Nearby is the **Sultan Hassanal Bokliah**

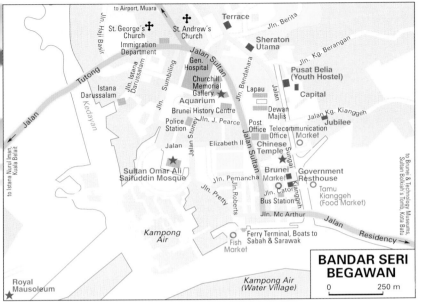

BANDAR SERI BEGAWAN

0   250 m

Aquarium with a very respectable selection of tropical fresh-water and salt-water fish. Next door, the **Churchill Memorial Gallery** attests to the Anglophile attitude of Brunei's rulers. It is certainly worth visiting if you are interested in the slightly eccentric lifestyle of this famous politician. On the other side of broad Jln. Sultan is the **History Museum**, which deals with the recent history of the country; more extensive coverage in this area is provided by the **Brunei Museum**, which is around 3 miles (5 km) out of town in the direction of Kota Batu. This expensively fitted-out building, standing where Pigafetta was so impressed by the Sultan's palace with its elephants and cannons 470 years ago, exhibits archeological finds from the Sultanate. Foreign relations, the history of oil production and the life of the Iban and Murut peoples who live in the western half of the country, **Temburong**, are other themes presented by the museum.

Close at hand is the **Malay Technology Museum**, where traditional techniques of gold- and silversmithing are demonstrated and promoted. If you follow the riverbank a few hundred yards you will come to the **Mausoleum of Sultan Bolkiah**, who, as the fifth ruler of Brunei led the country to its heyday.

The present Sultan has unquestionably constructed for himself a memorial in his own lifetime with the **Istana Nurul Iman**, built in the mid-1980s by the river in the western part of the city. With almost 1,800 rooms and a dining hall wherein all 6,000 princes and princesses of Brunei can dine at once, this new palace is on a scale with Versailles. It numbers among the largest personal residences in the world and cost a trifling sum somewhere in the neighborhood of 800 million U.S. dollars. A battalion of Nepalese Gurkhas watches over the safety of the royal family. Visitors are only permitted a glimpse of a tiny part of life within the Istana, if even that much. Occasionally entrance is granted to non-employees and normal mortals, but only on the Sultan's birthday, July 15th. Infor-

mation may be obtained from the **Government Tourist Office** (GTO). The palace is particularly impressive early in the evening when it reflects in the Brunei river alongside the golden dome of the family mosque.

On the occasion of his Silver Jubilee in October, 1992, the Sultan had another place of devotion built, the **Masjid Wagaf**. He intended this mosque to be used by himself, his two consorts, his nine children, and the rest of his numerous relatives.

Away from Pomp and Splendor

Paradise on earth will also include certain beautiful sandy beaches. The favorite is **Muara Beaches**, about 17 miles (27 km) northeast of the capital. To the southwest, near **Tutong**, is the beach resort of **Pantai Seri Kenangan**.

Above: A jetty at Kampong Air, the giant village on the Brunei river.

After 31 miles (50 km) along the coast, a forest of oil well derricks and pumps announce **Seria**, which like its neighbor **Kuala Belait** is a center of the oil industry. The first drilling was started here back in 1880, and in 1929 the earth released its bounty of black gold upon which Brunei has founded its wealth ever since. Foreign geologists, divers, seamen and workers work flat out here for the Sultan, the oil multimillionaires and the crowded expressways in their homelands. Off-duty, they can relax in their luxurious bungalows, play golf or polo, and, in their own enclave, need not go without their long drink at sundown.

How long the reserves will last is not clear. The latest discoveries will indubitably secure Brunei's prosperity into the next millennium. Enjoying the benefits of good advice, Sultan Muda Hassanal Bolkiah is thinking ahead. He wants to invest billions in the education sector and build a second university. Chemicals and high-tech factories are to be established as a stand-by for "drier" times.

SULTANATE OF BRUNEI

BANDAR SERI BEGAWAN

Getting there

BY AIR: Various international airlines fly to Bandar Seri Begawan, including **MAS**, office: 144, Jln. Pemancha, Tel: 02-224141. **Singapore Airlines**, Tel: 02-227253. **Philippine Airlines**, Tel: 02-222970. The office of **Royal Brunei Airlines** is in RBA Plaza, Jln. Sultan, Tel: 02-242222. **Flight information:** Tel: 02-331747. Airport taxes: for flights to Malaysia and Singapore: BR$ 5; for other international flights: BR$ 12.

Transportation

BUS: **Terminal** for overland trips, including those to Sarawak via Seria and K. Belait: Jl. Cator, near the Brunei Hotel.

BY BOAT: Daily ferries to Labuan (about 2 hrs.), from there to Kota Kinabalu. You can continue on to Sabah, first by boat to Punang, then by bus to Lawas or via Limbang.

CAR RENTAL: **Avis Rent-a-Car**, Block 4, Hasbullah Building, Tel: 02-242284. **Avis**, Hotel Sheraton Utama, Tel: 02-244272. **National Car Systems**, No 2, 1st Floor, Hasbullah 4, Jln. Gadong, Tel: 02-224921. **Hertz Rent-a-Car**, Ang's Hotel, Tel: 02-243553. As in Malaysia, driving in Brunei is on the left.

Accommodations

LUXURY: **Sheraton Utama Hotel**, Jln. Bendahara, Tel: 02-244272. **Riverview Inn Hotel**, km 1, Jln. Gadong, Tel: 02-238238.

MODERATE: **Brunei Hotel**, 95, Jln. Chevalier, Tel: 02-242372. **Ang's Hotel**, Jln. Tasek Lama, Tel: 02-243553.

BUDGET: **Capital Hostel**, Jln. Berangan, Tel: 02-221561.

APARTMENTS: **Service Apartments**, Plaza Abdul Razak, Jln. Kubah Makam DiRaja, Tel: 02-241536.

Restaurants

CHINESE: **Phongnum Restaurant**, 56-60, 2nd Floor, **Teck Guan Olaza**, Jln. Sultan, Tel: 02-229561.

INDIAN: **Popular Restaurant**, Pap Haaiah Norain, Tel: 02-221375.

WESTERN: **Café de Paris**, Jln. Gadong, Tel: 02-443319. **Swensen's Ice Cream and Fine Food Restaurant**, Bangunan Halimatul Saadiah, Jln. Gadong, Tel: 02-445083. Budget meals are available from the **cookshacks** on Jln. Sungai Kianggeh and along the river. There are other Chinese, Malay and Indian restaurants on Jln. McArthur and in Jln. Roberts. Because of the country's Islamic bent, pork is not served in any of the restaurants; and only at a very few bars, such as those in the international hotels, will you be able to find (moderately) alcoholic drinks.

Museums

Brunei Museum, open daily except Mon, 9:30 am-5:00 pm. Fri 9:30 am-11:30 am, and 2:30-5:00 pm. **Malay Technology Museum**, hours as the Brunei Museum. **Sir Winston Churchill Memorial Museum**, open daily except Tue, 9:00 am-12:00 pm and 1:45-4:45 pm.
Sultan Hassanal Bolkiah Aquarium, next to the Churchill Museum, open daily except Mon, 9:00 am-12:00 pm and 1:30-5:00 pm. Closed Fri 12:00-2:30 pm. **History Museum**, hours as the Churchill Museum.

Excursions

FREME Travel Service, Jln. Sultan (Hongkong & Shanghai Bank Building), Tel: 02-335025.

Diplomatic Representation

German Embassy, 6th Floor, UNF Building, 49-50, Jln. Sultan, 2085 Brunei Darussalam. Tel: 02-225547.

Holidays

National holiday on February 23. **Hari Raya Puasa** (End of the Islamic fasting month of Ramadan) im July; the exact date changes every year, depending on the state of the new moon. The **Birthday of His Majesty** the Sultan of Brunei, July 15th, is also celebrated with a great deal of pomp and circumstance.

Hospital

Health Clinic, Pertanyaan, Tel: 02-235331. **Hart Medical Clinic** (Privat), 47, Jln. Sultan, Tel: 02-225531.

Post / Police

General Post Office, Jln. Elizabeth Dua, Tel: 02-243101. **Emergency:** Tel: 02-222333.

Tourist Information

Tourism Section, Economic Development Board, Ministry of Finance, P.O. Box 2318, Bandar Seri Begawan 2011, Tel: 02-226557, 240243, 242595.

KUALA BELAIT
Accommodations

MODERATE: **Hotel Sentosa**, Jln. McKerron, Tel: 02-243561. **Hotel Seaview**, Jln. Seria.

SINGAPORE

HISTORY

SIGHTS

TRAVEL INFORMATION

THE HISTORY OF SINGAPORE

The old seafaring empires Srivijaya and Madjapahit already kept supply stations on the southern tip of the Malay Peninsula, because of the strategic position of this small group of islands. The shipping line in the narrows between Sumatra and Malaysia, which was later named the Straits of Malacca by the European colonial powers, had been one of the most significant trade routes in the world for ages. All goods being ferried between India and China sailed through this passage, a fact well-known to pirates, who found cover in the dense mangrove forests of the myriad islands of the Riau Archipelago. In fact pirates still ply the waters of the Straits.

A legendary prince in the 13th century coined the name *Singapura*, meaning the Lion City. He allegedly saw animals on the island he thought were lions. After the Dutch took over the Indonesian islands, Singapore's significant position along the main shipping routes gradually diminished. The Dutch put a stop to the spice trade of other peoples and sailed on

Preceding pages: View of Singapore over Sentosa, the island for recreation, and over the giant container harbor. Left: A peek inside Thian Hock Keng Temple in Chinatown.

a more southerly route to Java. When the Netherlands entered the French camp during the Napoleonic era, the British, who had always been the arch-rivals of the Dutch in this corner of the world, seized what they called their "East Indian" colony. Their stay was short-lived, however. The Congress of Vienna, held in 1815 after Napoleon's final defeat at Waterloo, granted the Dutch their old possessions again.

Stamford Raffles, a highly talented gentleman who had served as the British governor of Java during the interregnum from 1811 to 1816, was sorry to lose strategically well-situated Batavia, as it was known, and set about looking for a substitute.

On January 29, 1819, Raffles landed along the Singapore and, skillfully applying the old tactic of divide and conquer to a conflict of succession in the Sultanate of Johor, hammered out an agreement with the *Tumenggong*, the local strongman. The British East India Company was to pay him 5000 Spanish dollars per annum and the Sultan another 3000 for the right to set up a trading post.

The Treaty of London subsequently sealed British ownership of Singapore, at the time a town of 11,000, which was already on the good side of the profit margin. As a free port, Singapore attracted

209

not only many entrepreneurial types, but also throngs of poor immigrants, notably from overcrowded China. Turnover for 1860 was already registered at 10 million pounds sterling. Tin mining in Malaya, the growing no pun intended plantation economy, and the opening of the Suez Canal further boosted Singapore's wealth at the end of the 19th century.

The exotic, somewhat dreamy atmosphere in which colonial officers and businessmen continued to lead their British lifestyle so far from the green hills of home was well described by several literary figures of the early 20th century. This pleasant colonial way of life, which affected only a part of the population, might have continued indefinitely had it not been for the brutal arrival of the Japanese in 1942. On February 15, they marched into the city after landing in

Above: "Shop until you drop" is the motto of Orchard Road. Right: Sir Thomas Stamford Raffles, the founder of Singapore in effigy on Boat Quay on the Singapore River.

Kota Bharu and driving the British army through all of Malaya.

After the two atom bombs dropped by the Americans and subsequent Japanese capitulation on August 21, 1945, the British felt it to be a moral right that they retake their former colonies. In the eyes of the Asians, however, they had lost face as a nation, as they had allowed a massive military tragedy to take place against a numerically inferior enemy. Moreover, a new generation of politicians educated in Europe rejected colonialism out of hand. Their aim was to throw off the colonial yoke once and for all.

The British tried to delay the process in 1946 by dividing the Straits Settlements into two Crown colonies, the Malayan Union and Singapore. In 1957, a new constitution was negotiated in London which, however, was only ratified by the British Parliament two years later. Elections in May 1959 gave the People's Action Party (PAP) 53 percent of the votes and 43 of the 51 seats in the Parliament. The General Secretary of the Party, Lee

Kuan Yew became Singapore's first Prime Minister. Yew, a lawyer with a degree from Cambridge University, steered the affairs of the city-state with a strong hand until 1990. The 1963 unification with Malaysia in the Malaysian Federation was revoked on August 9, 1965. This date serves as the day the Republic of Singapore was founded, and is the city's national holiday.

In spite of dire predictions, the change in the generational guard has been gone without a hitch in this country of 59 islands, 225 square miles (580 sq. km), and boasting a population of 3 million. Lee Kuan Yew is still operating as Senior Minister. The executive style of Goh Chok Tong, the new Prime Minister since 1990, is hardly any different from that of his predecessor.

THE SIGHTS

Orchard Road is the main street of contemporary Singapore and the sole destination for many a tourist, thanks to the virtually inexhaustible amount of consumer goods offered by the highly modern **shopping malls**. The underground stations alone are sights to see: **Orchard Station** has department stores, restaurants and an aquarium. The newest, the most chic, the most expensive in the world can be seen in the display windows between the Hilton and the National Museum.

A special little gem is the **Peranakan Museum** in the middle of Orchard Road. The *Peranakan* are the descendants of the early Chinese immigrants from the 16th century, who married Malay women and thereby created a special cultural combination. Right next to it, located among restored houses in "Straits Baroque" on Emerald Hill Road, is one of the nicest beer gardens in the city. And the **Istana**, the President's palace, stands a good way to the north on Cavenaugh Rd. Its gate is protected by uniformed guards.

Serangoon Road, the heart of **Little India**, can be reached from Orchard Road via Dhoby Ghaut and Selegie Roads. The aroma of jasmine flowers, incense sticks and curry wafts through the area, and Indian costumes abound, dhoti or lunghi for the men and a sari for the ladies. Southern Indian vegetarian dishes are still served on banana leaves here.

Bugis Street, once the sinful playpen of the sailors stopping off in Singapore, has had its act cleaned up in every which way. The average person can now stroll about freely here in the evening, keeping an eye out for copy watches or sample some sweet-and-sour fish in one of the sidewalk restaurants. The transvestite shows in the Boom Boom Cabaret are quite popular.

Arab Street, lined with shops selling batik and silk cloth, gold jewelry and handicrafts, is the aorta of the Muslim quarter. The bulk of the population here is made up of Indians, Malays and Arabs. The shimmering gold dome of the great **Sultan Mosque** built in 1928 can be seen

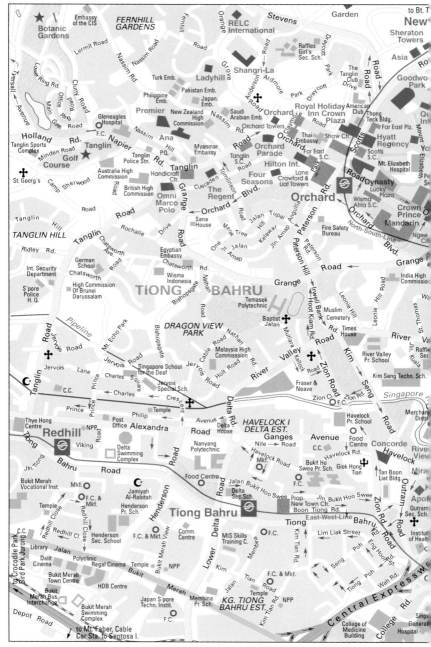

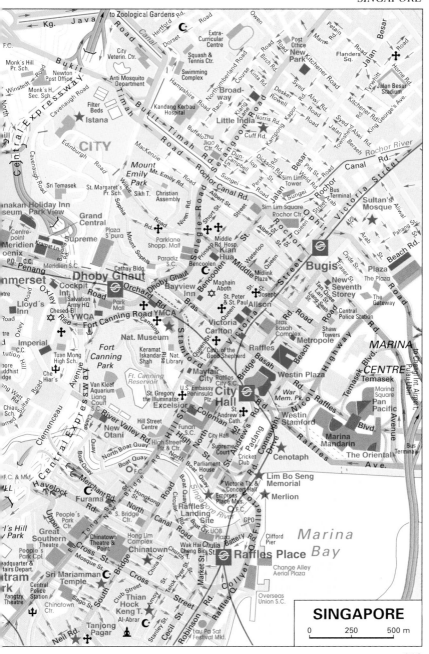

SINGAPORE

0   250   500 m

from afar. The best restored shophouses are at the **Jalan Besar**.

Of all the worthy old gastronomic institutions from the colonial days, the most famous in all Asia is the **Raffles Hotel** on Bras Basah. It was started by three Armenian brothers (the Sarkies) in 1889, and soon housed so many famous writers including Somerset Maugham and Hermann Hesse, that it ultimately found a place in world literature. Worldwide protest in the early 1980s prevented the Raffles from being torn down to make room for the blockbuster project called Raffles City. In 1987, it was declared a national monument, and then underwent thorough restoration until 1991. The birthplace of the *Singapore Sling* thus remained, though the drink is available elsewhere at much lower rates.

The **Raffles City Centre**, a Garden of Eden for consumers, begins opposite the Raffles Hotel on Bras Basah Road. The 73-story high **Westin Stamford**, the world's tallest hotel, rises above it. The restaurant all the way at the top is called **Compass Rose** and offers not only a fine food, but also a panoramic view of the city.

War Memorial Park lies before Raffles City, with a monument consisting of four pillars each representing one of the four ethnicities of Singapore: Chinese, Malayan, Indian, Eurasian.

The largest of Singapore's shopping centers, **Marina Square**, sprawls nearer the coast on land gained from the sea. Next to it stands the new Congress building.

St. Andrew's Cathedral, an edifice shining in pure white from a stand of trees whispers its message "Don't shop until you drop." It was consecrated in 1862. The dark blue vaulted ceiling inside does indeed suggest heavenly feelings, and services in various languages are held here several times a day. 400,000 Christians live in Singapore.

The most important buildings from the colonial age are to be found along the **Padang** a word that comes from Malay and means "large green space." In 1942, the Japanese herded Singapore's remaining Europeans together on this spot before sending them to the Changi internment camp.

The **Supreme Court** surmounted by a large dome and bearing a pillared faade suggesting antiquity, was completed in 1927. The representative steps of the **City Hall**, built in 1929, were the site of many a historic event: On September 12, 1945, the Japanese general Itagaki turned the city over to the British here, and in 1959, Lee Kuan Yew declared Singapore's independence from England. Nowadays fresh graduates and newly-weds like to use it as a backdrop for being photographed.

The old **Cricket Club** on the Padang once symbolized the continuance of British lifestyle in distant climes, and still maintains its old set of strict rules.

Singapore's oldest house was designed as a private residence, but served as a courthouse after its completion in 1827. It's been used as the city **Parliament** since 1963. The bronze elephant in front of it was a gift from the Siamese king Chulalongkorn in 1871.

Victoria Theatre and Concert Hall is the residence of Singapore's Symphony Orchestra. The statue of Sir Stamford Raffles standing before it is the original one cast by Thomas Whooner in 1887. A copy has been placed a few steps away along the Singapore River where Raffles is thought to have landed in 1819 to found the city. Next to it (downstream) is the **Empress Place Museum**, a neo-classical building built in 1854. Its focus is on Chinese culture.

Majestically enthroned at the mouth of the river is Singapore's hallmark, the **Merlion**, which, as its name suggests, is a kind of water-spouting feline symbolizing the city born from the sea.

Upstream on **Clarke Quay** and on the opposite bank of the Singapore River, **Boat Quay**, the old trading houses and warehouses have been renovated. A long series of bars and restaurants were then opened along the riverside promenade, creating a surprisingly attractive place to stroll about, a very fine addition to an evening out for Singaporans and visitors.

Singapore's oldest church stands on Hill Street, **Saint Gregory the Illuminator**, the former church of the Armenians, built in 1835 by Coleman, Singapore's most important architect. He is buried there beside the Sarkies brothers and Agnes Joaquim, after whom the national flower was named.

Between Hill Street and Clemenceau Avenue lies the **Bukit Larangan**, the erstwhile "forbidden mountain." Once upon a time, the palaces of Singapore's Malayan rulers stood at this strategically advantageous location. Iskandar Shah, the city's last Sultan, is allegedly buried here.

Raffles had little respect for the old commandments and built his own residence on the site, which was renamed Government Hill. **Fort Canning**, erected by the British in 1860, is no longer extant. Instead there is a park by the same name and a water reservoir.

The **National Museum** is a typically neoclassical colonial construction, 1887 vintage. A set of dioramas here illustrates the city's history. In addition to the wedding customs of the various ethnic groups, Peranakan (Chinese) culture is documented by perfectly furnished living quarters. The museum's jade collection is world famous.

Chinatown and the Financial District

Large sections of Chinatown have had to make way for the office skyscrapers and banks (notably the *Standard Chartered* and the *Hong Kong & Shanghai*) of the Financial District. Whatever is left has to be carefully nursed so as to keep its local color as a tourist attraction. The old *Telok Ayer Market* in Victorian style, was cast in England and shipped in 1899 to

Singapore. In 1986 it was restored from top to bottom and renamed **Lau Pa Sat Festival Market**. Nowadays, its food stalls make it a nice place to visit in the evening. Street artists begin showing up around 7 pm. The market provides a nice counterpoint to the surrounding bank buildings, which rise to heights of up to 700 ft (280 m).

Telok Ayer Street, accessed via canyons of houses with stark facades of polished granite, was once right on the coast. During the early British period in Singapore, Chinese immigrants from Fukien built a temple there to thank the sea goddess Ma Chu Po for their safe boat journey to Singapore. It was later expanded, and in 1842 completed and named thenceforth **Thian Hock Keng Temple**. The building materials came from China. Ma Chu Po is flanked by two divine admirals: The one can see for 500 li, the other can hear for 500 li (about 165

Above: Chinese mythology in the Haw Par Villa, formerly of the "Tiger Balm Brothers."

216

miles/264 km). To the left of the altar are wooden figures representing gossip spirits, who are clearly marked by the blows delivered by the victims of their gossip. There are also the statues of two brothers dressed in sacks: One was a bandit in life, the other a banker. Gamblers used to sacrifice opium to them.

Singapore's oldest Hindu temple rises in the middle of Chinatown. It was built in 1827 and consecrated to **Sri Mariamman**, the goddess of rain and the pox. The richly-colored Gopuram gate tower rising over the entrance is evidence of the Dravidian style of southern India. During the Thimithi Festival in October, the faithful walk over glowing coals without showing any signs of pain. The streets of old Chinatown in the vicinity of the temple have been restored and have their contingent of souvenirs on sale.

One of the most beautiful views of Singapore and the surrounding islands is up on **Mount Faber** (329 ft/106 m), but it is shared by huge throngs of tourists arriving in buses that jam up on the way. You can also pick up the cable car to the island of Sentosa from here.

Oases of Greenery

The **Botanic Gardens** spreads on a surface area of 104 acres (42 ha) between Holland Rd. and Cluny Rd. It was opened in 1859, and now boasts about 2,000 carefully labeled plant species and 250 types of orchid, including Singapore's heraldic flower, the Vanda Miss Joaquim orchid. More pristine is the **Bukit Timah Nature Reserve** arranged around the 518-ft-high (162 m) Bukit Timah. 198 acres (80 ha) of virgin jungle can be investigated on foot here. The **Zoological Gardens**, considered one of the finest in the world, was founded in 1973 and now has over 2000 species. Children inevitably thrill at the event "Breakfast with Orangutan." High tea can also be enjoyed in the company of these apes. The 99-acre (40 ha) **Night Safari** is a night zoo with fenced-in areas arranged according to the most modern standards, and open until midnight.

Southeast Asia's largest **bird sanctuary** is located in **Jurong**. 450 bird species live in the park, which also has a 5-acre (2 ha) aviary, rain forest, an artificial waterfall and the All-star Birdshow, where birds perform tricks.

The global trend toward creating artificial worlds is strongly reflected in Singapore. Ancient Chinese legends are presented in the **Haw Par Villa Dragonworld** using "walkable" creatures of fable and horror chambers.

The **Tang Dynasty City** cost about 60 million dollars. Visitors climb onto a rebuilt section of the Great Wall of China and look out over the replica of a typical imperial Chinese city from around A.D. 600. Scenes from everyday life and festivals, including battles between warriors, are reenacted daily. The buildings have been furnished in authentic style and may be visited. They are supposed to give a

good feeling of the Tang period, which is thought to have been a pleasant epoch.

The Island of Sentosa

Once a pirate hideaway, **Sentosa Island** has become a recreational park. As mentioned above, a cable car connects it to Mount Faber, but there is also a ferry that leaves from the World Trade Center. Cars are not allowed on the island, the various attractions can be reached using a little train. The **Dragon Tail** takes visitors on trips through the innards of mythical creatures. 4000 fantastical rock carvings can be inspected in the **Rare Stone Museum**. In **Butterfly Park** visitors keep a roving eye out for the 2500 species that flutter about; the **World Insectarium** shows countless samples of creepy crawlies. The **Coralarium** looks at life of the corals, shellfish and invertebrates. The major attraction, however, is **Underwater World**, with its 300-ft (100 m) tunnel running under two gigantic aquariums where tropical sea fauna flit about. To stand under sharks and ray fish is quite an experience, especially during feeding times at 11:30 am and 4:30 pm.

Scenes from the founding years and the Japanese occupation during World War Two using wax figures are exhibited in **Fort Siloso**. The traditional lifestyle of Asian peoples are displayed in the 20-acre (8 ha) **Asian Village**, which can be viewed from an elevated train. The latest events to come to Sentosa Island are **Fantasy Island** and **Volcanoland** with simulated earthquakes.

Finally, the island also offers the option to simply go swimming using the Monorail beach train to Siloso, Central, or Tanjung Beaches. **Siloso Beach** is too beautiful to be true. Indeed, Indonesia delivered 300 tons of golden, sterilized sand and 300 adult coconut palms to the site. Two beach hotels, the **Rasa Sentosa** and the luxurious **Beaufort** have also been added to the landscape.

SINGAPORE
Telephone area code 0065
Arrival
BY AIR: The international airport Changi Airtropolis has two terminals, connected to one another by the Changi Sky Train. Taxi rides into town last about 30 minutes. The station of the airport bus is under the airport building. A S$ 15,-- airport tax is levied on departures.

SHIP: Overseas travelers arrive at the new terminal near the World Trade Centre.

TRAIN: Railway lines connect to Kuala Lumpur and Bangkok right until Chiang Mai in northern Thailand.

Accommodations
Hotels with vacancies offer discounted rooms through the last-minute accommodation agency at the airport, Tel: 5426955.

LUXURY: **Goodwood Park**, 22 Scotts Rd., Tel: 7377411; elegant colonial edifice. **Hyatt Regency**, 10-12 Scotts Rd., Tel: 7381234, Fax: 7321696; with a beautiful pool and gardens. **Mandarin**, 333 Orchard Rd., Tel: 7374411, Fax: 7322361; a revolving restaurant on the roof, Asian specialties in the Coffee Shop Chatterbox. **Oriental**, 5 Raffles Ave., Tel: 3380066, Fax: 3399573; gigantic lobby and glass elevators, view of the harbor. **Raffles**, 1 Beach Rd., Tel: 3373644, Fax: 3397650; noble restaurant and extremely expensive. **Shangri-La**, 22 Orange Grove, Tel: 7373644, Fax: 7337220; the top hotel, with golf course, French restaurant, savvy disco and large garden. **The Beaufort**, Sentosa Island, Bukit Manis, Tel: 2750331, Fax: 2750228; exclusive, small beach hotel.

MODERATE: **Allson**, 101 Victoria St., Tel: 3360811, Fax: 3397019. **Amara**, 165 Tanjong Pagar Rd., Tel: 2244488, Fax: 2243910; with excellent Thai restaurant. **Bayview Inn**, 30 Bencoolen St., Tel: 3372882, Fax: 3382880, with swimming-pool on the roof terrace. **Carlton**, 76 Bras Basah Rd., Tel: 3388333, Fax: 3396866; centrally located. **Concorde**, 317 Outram Rd., Tel: 7330188, Fax: 7330989; at walking distance from Chinatown. **Crown Prince**, 270 Orchard Rd., Tel: 7321111, Fax: 7327018. **The Duxton**, 83 Duxton Rd., Tel: 2277678, Fax: 2271232; consists of 8 luxuriously restored Chinatown houses with stylishly furnished rooms, but no pool. **Excelsior**, 3/5 Coleman St., Tel: 3387733, Fax: 3393847. **Furama**, 60 Eu Tong Sen St., Tel: 5333888, Fax: 5341489; in the middle of Chinatown, with pool. **Garden**, 14 Balmoral Rd., Tel: 2353344, Fax: 2359730; 2 pools, quiet location, rooms with balcony. **Grand Central**, 22 Cavenaugh Rd., Tel: 7279944, Fax: 7333175. **Hilton International**, 581 Orchard Rd., Tel: 7372233, Fax: 7322917. **Holiday Inn Park View**, 11 Cavenagh Rd., Tel: 7338333, Fax: 7344593. **King's**, 403 Havelock Rd., Tel: 7330011, Fax: 7325764. **Ladyhill**, 1 Ladyhill Rd., Tel: 7372111, Fax: 7374606; quiet location in the exclusive, green residential area Fernhill Gardens. **Le Meridien Singapore**, 100 Orchard Rd., Tel 7338855, Fax: 7327886. **Lloyd's Inn**, 2 Lloyd Rd., Tel: 7377309, Fax: 7377847; quiet location, rooms in motel style. **Miramar**, 401 Havelock Rd., Tel: 7339222, Fax: 7334027. **Orchard**, 442 Orchard Rd., Tel: 7347766, Fax: 7335482. **Orchard Parade**, 1 Tanglin Rd., Tel: 7371133, Fax: 7330242. **Phoenix**, 227 Orchard Rd., 7378666, Fax: 7322024; Top location for shoppers, popular disco. **Riverview**, 382 Havelock Rd., Tel: 7329922; Italian management, on the Singapore River.. **Royal Holiday Inn Crown Plaza**, 25 Scotts Rd., Tel: 7377966. **Shangri-La Rasa Sentosa Resort**, 101 Siloso Rd., Sentosa Island, Tel: 2750100, Fax: 2750355; on the island, top furnishing and service. **Westin Plaza** and **Westin Stamford**, 2 Stamford Rd., Tel: 3382862, Fax: 3382862 (Plaza) and 3371554 (Stamford).

BUDGET: **International**, 290A Jalan Besar, Tel: 2939238. **Lido**, 54 Middle Rd., Tel: 3371872; large rooms, friendly personnel. **Mitre**, 145 Kiliney Rd., Tel: 7373811; a remnant of the colonial era, weather-worn, but with its own special atmosphere. **New Sandy's Place**, near MRT-Newton, Tel: 7341431; family-like guesthouse. **San Wah**, 36 Bencoolen, Tel: 3362428. **Mayfair City**, 40/44 Armenian St., Tel: 3374542, Fax: 3371736; central location, frequently has no vacancies. **Majestic**, Bukit Pasoh Rd., Tel: 2223377; small Chinatown hotel built of old materials in an up-coming quarter. **South East Asia**, 190 Waterloo St., Tel: 3382394. **Sloane Court**, 17 Balmoral Rd., Tel: 2353311, Fax: 7339041; small half-timber house with garden, Western cuisine. **Sun Sun**, 260-262 Middle Road, Tel: 3384911; clean, one of the best budget hotels. **Victoria**, 87 Victoria St., Tel: 3384911. **YMCA International House**, 1 Orchard Rd., Tel: 3366000, Fax: 3373140; central location, mid-range furnishings, pool, squash courts, reservations a must! **Metropolitan YMCA**, 60 Stevens Rd., Tel: 7377755, Fax: 2355528, a mid-range hotel rather than a youth hostel.

Restaurants
CHINESISCH: **Beng Hiang**, *Hokkien* cuisine, 20 Murray St., Tel: 2216684. **Chang Jiang**, *Shanghai,* Goodwood Park Hotel, 22 Scotts Rd., Tel: 7377411. **Canton Garden**, *Canton,* Westin Plaza, Stamford Rd., Tel: 3388585. **Cherry Garden**, *Szechuan,* Oriental Hotel, Marina Sq. Tel: 3380066. **Dragon City**, *Szechuan,* Novotel Orchid Hotel, 214 Dunearn Rd., Tel: 2547070, specialty: smoked duck, impressive desserts. **Fook Yuen**, *Canton* and

seafood, 290 Orchard Rd., Tel: 2352211. **Furama Palace**, Furama Hotel, 60 Eu Tong Sen St., Tel: 533888, specialty: shark's fins and abalone. **Grand City**, *Canton* and *Szechuan*, 11 Dhoby Gaut, Cathay Building 07-04, Tel: 3383622, elegant, a favorite with Chinese wedding parties. **Golden Phoenix**, *Szechuan*, Equatorial Hotel, 429 Bukit Timah Rd., Tel: 7320431, "Imperial Buffet" for 10 guests and upward. **House of Blossoms**, *Canton*, Marina Mandarin Hotel, Marina Sq., Tel: 3383388. **Imperial Herbal Restaurant**, *vegetarian*, Metropole Hotel, 41 Seah St., Tel: 3370491. **Jiang-Nan Chun**, *Canton*, Four Seasons Hotel, 190 Orchard Blvd., Tel: 8317220. **Li Bai**, *Canton*, Sheraton Towers, 39 Scotts Rd., Tel: 7376888, creative cuisine with western inspiration, unusual, expensive. **Miao Yi Vegetarian Restaurant**, Nr. 03-01/02 Coronation Shopping Plaza, Tel: 4671331. **Pine Court**, *Peking*, Mandarin Hotel, 333 Orchard Rd., Tel: 7374411, buffet. **Westlake Eating House**, Blk 4, Nr. 02-139 Queen's Rd., Tel: 4747283.

NONYA: **Luna**, Apollo Hotel, 405 Havelock Rd., Tel: 7332081, lunch buffet. **Nonya and Baba**, 262 River Valley Rd., Tel: 7341382, Specialty: Udang Kuah Nanas (scampi in pineapple sauce). **Peranakan Inn**, 210 East Coast Rd. **Ginas Peranakan Restaurant**, 49 Boat Quay, Tel: 5387764, excellent Otak-Otak (fish balls in banana leaves).

INDIAN: **Annalakshmi**, Excelsior Hotel, 5 Coleman St., Tel: 3399993. **Banana Leaf Apollo**, 56 Race Course Rd., Tel: 2935054. **Bombay Woodlands**, B 1-06 Forum The Shopping Mall, Tel: 2352712. **Casa de Goa**, Holland Village, 26 Lorong Mambong, Tel: 4622946. **Dehli Restaurant**, 60 Race Course Rd., Tel: 2964585. **Komala Vilas**, *vegetarian*, 76 Serangoon Rd., Tel: 2936980, inexpensive south Indian cooking, specialty: Idlis, Thali. **Moghul Mahal**, Colombo Court, 1 North Bridge Rd., Tel: 3386907.

MALAYAN / INDONESIAN: **Alkaff Mansion**, 10 Telok Blangah Green, Tel: 2786979, Stylish colonial bungalow in a pleasant garden, very chic, specialty:"East-West-Buffet" and rice dishes. **Aziza's**, 36 Emerald Hill Rd., Tel: 2351130. **Sanur**, Nr. 04-17/18 Centrepoint, Tel: 7342192. **Sukmainda**, Royal Holiday Inn Crowne Plaza, 25 Scotts Rd., Tel: 7377966. **Tambuah Mas**, Tanglin Shopping Center, Level 4, Tel: 7333333.

JAPANESE: **Hoshigaoka**, 175 Orchard Rd. **Inagiku**, Westin Stamford Hotel, 2 Stamford Rd., Tel: 3388585. **Keyaki**, 7 Raffles Blvd., Tel: 3368111. **Unkai Japanese Restaurant**, Ana Hotel, 16 Nassim Hill, Tel: 7321222.

THAI: **Chao Phaya Seafood Market and Restaurant**, Nr. 02-4272 Blk. 740 Ang Mo Kio Ave. 6, Tel: 4560118. **Tum Nak Thai**, 100 East Coast Parkway, East Coast Recreation Centre, Tel: 4420988.

VIETNAMESE: **Mekong Restaurant**, East Coast Parkway, Tel: 2424525. **Saigon Restaurant**, Cairnhill Rd., Tel: 2350626/7343891.

WESTERN CUISINE: **Baron's Table**, 25 Scotts Rd., Tel: 7377966. **J. P. Bastiani**, Clarke Quay, 30 River Valley Rd., Tel: 4330156, nicely situated on the main evening promenade along the Singapore River, outdoor tables, Mediterranean cuisine. **Compass Rose**, Westin Stamford Hotel, 70 Stock, 2 Stamford Rd., Tel: 3388585. **Dan Ryan's**, Tanglin Mall, 91 Tanglin Rd., Tel: 7382800. **Emmerson's Tiffin Rooms**, 51 Neil Rd., Tel: 2277518. **Fratini**, 51 Neil Rd., Tel: 3232088. **L'Aigle d'Or**, 83 Duxton Rd., Tel: 2271232. **Maxim's de Paris**, Regent Hotel, 1 Cuscaden Rd., Tel: 7338888, The Singapore branch of the famous Parisian venue, affordable luncheon menus. **Raffles Grill**, Raffles Hotel, 1 Beach Rd., Tel: 3371886, European prize chefs give "guest performances" here, exclusive, expensive. **Upstairs English Restaurant**, Tudor Court, 145a Tanglin Rd.

HAWKER CENTRES / FOODSTALLS: Collection of food stands that is one of the highlights for Singapore's visitors. **Lau Pa Sat** on Raffles Quay, till midnight, with street artists; the neighboring **Boon Tat Street** also becomes an inexpensive outdoor restaurant evenings. **Empress Place Food Centre**, on the Singapore River, frequented at lunch by white-collar workers and bankers, closed evenings. **Satay Club**, Connaught Drive, excellent chicken kebabs with peanut sauce in the evenings, enjoyed outdoors. **Newton Circus Hawker Centre**, at MRT Newton station, a favorite with tourists and locals alike, Food Centre is open till 3 am.

Nightlife

Brannigan's, in the Hyatt Hotel, 10-12 Scotts Rd., live music, international scene.

Hard Rock Café, 50 Cuscaden Rd., a licensed franchise of the international chain, live music sometimes by famous foreign bands.

Hotline, Orchard Rd. corner Cuscaden Rd., it the cellar of the Ming Arcade, bar and disco, both atmosphere and rock are "harder" than in Hard Rock Café.

Ginivy, Orchard Rd., Orchard Towers, American flair, Country & Western, "something for lonely hearts."

Top Ten, Orchard Rd., Orchard Towers, in-crowd disco, good atmosphere for stricking up conversations, expensive.

Somersets, 2 Stamford Rd., in the Westin Plaza, live jazz of the international scene.

In addition, you can take an evening stroll along **Clarke Quay** and **Boat Quay** and investigate the many restaurants and bars there.

Museums
National Museum, Stamford Rd., Tue-Sun 9 am-5.30 pm. **Empress Place Museum**, 1 Empress Place, daily 9 am-6 pm. **The Pewter Museum**, 49-51 Duxton Road, Tanjong Pagar, daily 9 am-5.30 pm. **Peranakan Place Museum**, 180 Orchard Rd., Mon-Fri 10.30 am-3.30 pm. **The Substation**, Armenian St., daily 11 am-9 pm, Galerie, Café, Theater; meeting place for young intellectuals.

Parks
Zoological Gardens, Mandai Lake Rd., 8.30 am-6.30 pm, Tel: 2353111, "breakfast or high tea with Orang," for reservations, Tel: 2693411. Getting there: Express from Orchard Rd, 8.30 am and 1 pm, Tel: 2353111; MRT to N10, then bus No. 138.

Night Safari (night zoo), adjacent to the day zoo, 7.30 pm-midnight, Tel: 2693411. Mosquitoes are also busy at night!

Botanic Gardens, Cluny Rd., 5 am-11 pm, buses No. 7, 106, 174. Old stand of trees, conifers and spice plants, orchid show.

Jurong Bird Park, Jl. Ahmad Ibrahim, MRT to W12, dthen buses No. 251, 253, 255. Largest collection of southeast Asian toucans, bird show with bird performances, a panorail train, nature-like aviary.

Bukit Timah Nature Reserve, Hindhede Drive (via Bukit Timah Rd.), 8.30 am-6 pm, MRT to N4, then buses No. 67, 170, 171. 198 acres (80 ha) primeval forest with apes, serpents, etc., located on Timah Mountain (518 ft/162 m), signposted hiking trails.

Haw Par Villa Dragonworld, 262 Pasir Panjang Rd., MRT to W7, then bus No. 200. Former villa of the Tiger Balm brothers Aw Boon, nowadays it's the world's largest theme park (22.5 acres/9 ha) for Chinese mythology, with walk-in creatures of fable and a roller-coaster. Favorites are the *Wrath of the water gods flume ride* and the *Tales of China boat ride*.

Tang Dynasty City, 2 Yuan Ching Rd., 9.30 am-6.30 pm, MRT to W11, then bus No. 240. Theme park, replicas of Chang'an (the capital of China's Tang dynasty, 7th-9th century A.D.), der the Great Wall of China (a section almost 1900 ft/600 m long), the famous terracotta soldiers of ancient China, and a typical marketplace as might have been seen on the Silk Road back then; performances of historic sword fights.

Shopping
SHOPPING CENTERS: **Far East Plaza**, 14 Scotts Rd., cheap clothing in the basement (Metro). **Lane Crawford**, Orchard Blvd., branch of the luxury department store chain from Hong Kong.

Galerie Lafayette, Liat Towers, 541 Orchard Rd., A branch of the famous luxury store of the same name in Paris. **Marina Square**, 6 Raffles Blvd. **Ngee Ann City**, Orchard Rd. This gigantic shopping complex houses the Japanese luxury department store **Takashimaya** and **Tangs Studio** (designer fashion), in addition to restaurants and swimming pools.

Paragon Sogo, Orchard Rd., exclusive men's fashions, pewterware, Sogo supermarket. **People's Park Complex**, 110 Upper Cross St. **Raffles City**, 250 North Bridge Rd. **Tanglin Shopping Centre**, 19 Tanglin Rd., taylor, Asian handicrafts, antiques, jewelry, rugs; you must haggle here!

Funan Centre, North Bridge Rd. / High St., an El Dorado for computer freaks. **Peninsula Plaza**, North Bridge Rd. / Coleman St., cameras and equipment.

Anything resembling a complete list of all shopping venues in the city would be too much for this book, so let us suggest you pick up the free brochure entitled *Singapore – a guide to shopping* and Y*our guide to good bargains in the Suburbs*. Shops carrying good quality wares and with good service are granted a white lion (a Merlion) on a red background by the Singapore Tourist Promotion Board (STPB), Tel: 2705433. If you feel you've been cheated, you can turn to the Small Claims Tribunal for a S$10,-- fee, Tel: 5309895.

Transportation
CAR RENTALS: **Avis Rent-a-Car**, 200 Orchard Blvd., Tel: 7371668. **Hertz Rent-a-Car**, 19 Tanglin Rd., Tel: 7344646. **Ken-Air Rent-a-Car**, 01-41 Specialist's Centre, Orchard Rd., Tel: 7378282 **Sintat Rent-a-Car**, 320 Orchard Rd., Tel: 2355855.

UNDERGROUND: **Singapore MRT**, safe, perfect and cheap: inner-city fare is 70 c, keep your ticket until leaving your destination (turnstile!).

BUS: The city buses of the SBS are cheap and comfortable; keep exact fare handy as there is no change. The Singapore Explorer Ticket costs S$ 5,-- and is good for one day.

TAXI: airconditioned and cheap. The drivers turn on their taxameters without any further ado – by no means self-evident in Asia. Night surcharge 50 percent from midnight-6 am. Radio taxis: 4525555, 2500700.

City Tours
RMG Tours, Tel: 2208722. **Grayline**, Tel: 3318244.

Harbor Tours
Embarcation on Clifford Pier; afternoon tours with high tea, evening tours with a buffet, sometimes on large, revamped Chinese junks. **Watertours**, Tel: 5339811. **Eastwind**, Tel: 5333432.

Excursions to the Islands

KUSU ISLAND: The sights on the little island of Kusu consist of a Muslim shrine and a Chinese temple with a turtle pond. A legend is told about the latter: A giant sea turtle once turned itself into an island in order to save to shipwrecked people – a Malay and a Chinaman. The beaches of Kusu and the top of its hill offer a magnificent view of the main island. The lagoon waters are ideal for bathing.

Ferries (30-minutes) from the Cruise Centre near the World Trade Centre. Departure at 10 am und 1.30 pm Mon-Sat as well as every 1 1/2 hours from 9.45 am to 5 pm Sundays and holidays. Tel: 3212198.

PULAU UBIN: The "Adventure Island" of Singapore is called Pulau Ubin: It is a welcome contrast to the noise and crush of the main island. Much of Singapore looked like this 40 years ago, thatched roofs, backyard gardens, dirt roads, a luxuriant vegetation and fishermen's huts, the so-called *kelongs*, standing on stilts over the water. Bats, apes and squirrels still run around freely here, and one of the main attractions is the *purple jungle fowl*, the bird from which all common hens in the world derive.

Other attractions are several Chinese temples (one of them was built in a cavern and is only accessible from the beach at low tide), a mosque in traditional architectural style, and a Buddhist meditation centre. A bicycle is a good way to get to the more remote parts of the island. An "Outward Bound" school is located there and several lobster and fish farms. Fish dishes are a specialty on Pulau Ubin. 10-minute ride from Changi Jetty.

ST. JOHN'S: Formerly a penal colony. This large, hilly island is a pretty vacation area with lagoons for swimming and white beaches, camping and picnic areas, hiking trails, B & Bs and soccer pitches, a favorite with the daytrippers. For ferries, see Kusu above.

PULAU HANTU, LAZARUS AND SISTERS ISLANDS

These tiny islets to the south are just the thing for those wanting to escape the maddening crowd of the city: casual manners, sand beaches and good swimming possibilities.

The sea around Lazarus and Sisters Islands is good for diving, but the currents are quite strong, so only good swimmers should risk it. Ferry connections from Jardine Steps (World Trade Centre) or Clifford Pier. At least 10-15 passengers are needed before the boat leaves. Crossing lasts 1 hour. Tel: 3211972.

GENERAL INFORMATION
Consulates

Australia, 25 Napier Rd., Tel: 7379311. **Canada**, 80 Anson Rd., Tel: 3253200. **Great Britain**, Tanglin Rd., Tel: 4739333. **New Zealand**, 391-A Orchard Rd., Tel: 2359966. **USA**, 27 Napier Rd., Tel: 4769100.

Drug Abuse

Death sentence for possession of over 15 g of heroin, 30 g of morphine, 30 g of cocaine, 500 g of cannabis, 200 g of haschisch or 1,2 kg of opium.

National Holidays

New Year's Day: Januar 1; Chinese New Year: January/February; Hari Raya Puasa: to end Ramadan; Good Friday: April; Labor Day: 1. Mai. Vesak Day: Mai; Hari Raya Haji: Pilgrimage Time; National Holiday: August 9; Deepavali: October/November; Christmas: Dezember 25.

Fines

For spitting and throwing garbage on the street (chewing gum, cigarette butts) S$ 1000,-- for the first offense, S$ 2000,-- for repeat offenders-; crossing a street up to 150 ft (50 m) from a pedestrian crossing: S$ 50,--; smoking in public buildings, hairdressers, and so on, restaurants with airconditioning, S$ 1000,--; for not flushing public toilets S$ 150,-- (repeat offenders: S$ 500--, 1000,-).

Credit Cards

American Express, Tel: 2998133. **Diners Club**, Tel: 2944222. **Master Card**, Tel: 5332888.

Medical Help

Singapore has many first-class state-run hospitals. **General Hospital**, Outram Rd., Tel: 2223322. **Ambulance**, Tel: 995.

Police / Emergencies

Police, Tel: 999.

Fire department, **Ambulance**, Tel: 995

Post / Telephone

General Post Office, Fullerton Building, Tel: 5338899. International prefix 005. Directory assistance 103. IDD-calls can be made from all large hotels. **Telecommunication Building**, 35 Robinson Rd.. **Telecoms**, 15 Hill St.

Tourist Information

Singapore Tourist Promotion Board (STPB), Raffles City Tower, Nr. 32-01, 250 North Bridge Rd., Singapore, 0617, Tel: 3396622, Fax:: 3390697, Mon-Fri 8.30 am-5 pm.

Tourist Information abroad

AUSTRALIA: Level 11, AWA Building, 47 York St., Sydney NSW 2000, Tel (o2-9290-2888, Fax: 02-9290-2882. *CANADA:* STPB, The Standard Life Centre, 121 King St. West, Suite 1000, Toronto, Ontario M5H 3T9, Tel: (1-416) 363-8898, Fax: (1-416) 363-5752. *GREAT BRITAIN:* STPB, 1st Floor, Carrington House, 126-130 Regent St., London W1R 5FE, Tel: (0171) 437-0033, Fax: (0171) 734-2191. *NEW ZEALAND*: STPB, 43 High St., Auckland, Tel (09) 358-1191, Fax: (09) 358-1196 . *USA*: STPB, 590 Fifth Avenue, 12th Floor, New York, NY 10036, Tel: (212) 302-4861, Fax: (212) 3024801. STPB, 8484 Wiltshire Blvd., Beverly Hills, CA 90211, Tel: (213) 852-1901, Fax: (213) 852-0129.

FLORA AND FAUNA IN MALAYSIA

Many visitors associate Malaysia with images of tropical rain forest and exotic life forms. It's questionable, however, whether these associations will still be valid in another 20 years. Considering the age of the jungle – over 130 million years – the tempo of its destruction is extremely alarming.

For the time being, the wealth of different animal and plant species in Malaysia is still impressive. Because most of them live in the tropical jungle, however, the number of species is declining rapidly. Thus, the ultimate task of the national parks will be to protect what remains of the irreplaceable fauna and flora, and to exhibit them as if in a museum.

There are over 40,000 types of flowering plants on the Malaysian peninsula and in Sarawak and Sabah. About 5,000 types of trees grow here, half of them on the peninsula and the other half in the northern part of Borneo. On Mount Kinabalu alone, there are 800 different kinds of orchids and 400 types of ferns. Some 200 mammal species, almost 700 species of birds and over 100 types of snakes can be found in this country.

The numbers, however, are constantly being reduced. It must be borne in mind that every day, worldwide, more than 100 species disappear from our planet forever.

One cause of the great natural diversity in Malaysia has been the relatively stable climate over millions of years throughout the region of Southeast Asia. In addition, some of Malaysia's natural areas encompass several different climatic zones, so that very different types of plants have

been able to evolve within a fairly restricted area.

Swamps and moorlands stretch along the coasts, especially in Borneo. Here mangrove groves, noticeable on the west coast of the peninsula, alternate with thickets of rattan palm trees and trunkless nipa palm trees. The groves of casuarina and coconut palm lining the beaches are typical of the east coast of the peninsula. From the lowlands up to an altitude of about 6,500 feet (2,000 m), *dipterocarpaceous* forests dominate the untouched landscape. Some 400 types of these trees, which can reach a height of up to 130 feet (40 m), have been found in Malaysia. On the next "floor" are mountain jungles, wrapped in fog. From here on up to an altitude of 11,500 feet (3,500 m) there is a realm of moss and lichen, ferns and orchids, seemingly endless ranks of rhododendron and bizarrely-formed pandanus palm trees (screw palm). Finally, the region of dwarf juniper and grasses gives way to rock; the peak of Mount Kinabalu, 13,455 feet (4000 m) in height, is a characteristic example.

The plantation business is dominated by para rubber trees (*Hevea brasiliensis*), a latex tree of the euphorbia family, and the oil palm tree *(elaeis guineensis)*, whose fruit and seeds yield palm oil and palm seed oil. Malaysia is the world's largest source of rubber, and produces 60 percent of the world's palm oil. In recent years, this latter industry has even started to overtake the rubber industry. The rain forest suffers the most from this competition, as its trees are felled to make room for these crop plants, which grow and are ready to harvest relatively quickly (rubber: seven years, oil palm: five years).

Giant Flowers and Insect Traps

A few examples here should illustrate the kinds of unique life forms threatened today by human irresponsibility, population growth and exploitation.

Left: The giant flower of Rafflesia can grow up to 2 feet in diameter.

Along with the many types of epiphytes, moss, ferns, orchids, strangler figs, saprophytic mushrooms and other parasitic plants found in the largely sunless rain forests, the best-known parasitic plant is the giant flower *Rafflesia*. The naturalist Dr. Joseph Arnold discovered it in 1818 in Borneo and named it after Sir Stamford Raffles, the founder of Singapore. The flower is indeed giant: its red, brown and white speckled blossom can grow to a diameter of about 2 feet (60 cm).

The *Rafflesia* has no leaves; it draws its energy from a liana creeping along the ground. It weighs around 20 pounds and lives for most of its life as part of the cell network in the trunk of the host plant, surfacing only when it begins to bloom. Five meaty, thick folds then unfold to make room for a calyx measuring a good

12 inches (30 cm) in depth. Its thorns give off a foul smell that attracts insects; it's these insects which, by carrying pollen from one plant to another, enable this jungle flower to reproduce and proliferate.

Less obviously striking, but far more commonly found in the tropical forests and jungles, is the pitcher plant *Nepenthes*. More than 25 types of this carnivorous plant, which specialized in eating insects, can be found on Kinabalu alone. Although it is found all over Southeast Asia, it's only in Borneo that species such as *Nepenthes rajah* attain impressive lengths of up to 14 inches (35 cm). Its leaves form a pitcher-like container, the bottom of which contains a fluid whose scent attracts insects. Alighting on the pitcher's waxy rim, the insects slip into the interior of the plant trap. There, they quickly dissolve and are digested.

Hugh Low, the Englishman who was the first to climb Kinabalu, discovered several different types of these plants.

Above: Pitcher plants in Bako National Park. Right: An agama, a member of one of Malaysia's many lizard families, lies in wait for its prey.

The *Nepenthes lowii* is named after him. This plant is an example of true beauty in nature; its baroque form, with a narrow waist and curved rim, can be seen hanging from tree trunks in the forests. Low was also the first to record the *Nepenthes villosa*, with its pink underside and glowing yellow rim, for science.

Fascinating Fauna

Hardly any other Asian country still contains as wide a variety of animal species as Malaysia. Aside from the orangutans (*Pongo pygmaeus*) in Borneo, the most threatened species of mammal include tigers; leopard; panthers; clouded leopards; tapirs; sundakoboldmakis (*tarsius bancanus*); dugongs, also called sea cows (*Dugong dugong*); and Sumatran rhinoceroses.

On peninsular Malaysia, several campaigns have been started to protect this latter animal, the *Dicerorhinus sumatrensis*. Its horn spells its doom, because for centuries it has been valued in powdered form in Asia as an aphrodisiac and fever medicine. Even in the large reservations, such as Taman Negara and Endau Rompin, you'll need luck to glimpse one of these pachyderms; there are fewer than 100 of them left. The Javan rhinoceros, once native to Malaysia, is already extinct.

Your chances of spotting elephants in the nature parks are considerably better. But tourism can also pose a danger to wild animals, as can be seen on the beaches of the east coast. At least the authorities have taken strong measures to put a stop to noisy spectators and flash photographers disturbing the green turtles (*Chelonia mydas*), hawksbills (*Eretmochelys imbricata*), and leatherbacks (*Dermochelys coriacea*) as they lay their eggs.

The snakes of Malaysia – 16 types of which are poisonous – can effectively protect themselves from human curiosity, but hardly prevent the destruction of their habitat. Nevertheless, many species benefit from their sacred status, such as

225

the Wagler's pit viper (*Trimeresurus wagleri*), which sends chills down the spines of the faithful in the Snake Temple of Penang. This viper is one of five snake species in Malaysia whose poison is also deadly to humans; the king cobra (*Opiophagus hannah*), the common cobra (*Naja naja*), the coral snake (*Micrurus fulvius*) and the striped krait (*Bungarus fasciatus*) are other dangerous reptiles.

One non-poisonous, yet constrictive, giant snake worthy of mention is the Indian python (*Python molurus*), which can reach a length of 32 feet (10 m).

Lizards, such as crocodiles, monitor lizards and dragons, live throughout the country. The most familiar, and least harmful, is the gecko; these little lizards can be found in every household, using their quick tongues to hunt common insects such as mosquitos, flies and cockroaches.

Above: An scaly anteater digs for dinner in the rain forest. Right: The hornbill, the heraldic bird of Sarawak.

Noteworthy among the apes, gibbons, and orangutans is the species known as *berok*. Man has assigned to these redbrown macaques a particular, and useful, function: the males are tamed and used to harvest coconuts. Like human farm laborers, they climb up ropes to the tops of palm trees and twist off the coconuts with their hands and feet.

Malaysia is important for entomologists, or students of insects. There are over 1,000 butterfly species known here. Most striking of these is the Rajah Brooke bird-wing butterfly (*Ornithoptera brookiana albescens*), discovered in Borneo by A. R. Wallace in 1855. The male is particularly striking for the brilliant metallic green stripes that spread across both wings; the wingspan can measure up to 6 inches (15 cm).

The green dragon-tail (*Lamprotera meges*) is a fascinating butterfly, up to 2 inches in size, which lives at altitudes of up to 5,000 feet (1,500 m). With its transparent forewings, its long, outstretched hindwings, and, above all, its wingspeed,

it looks very like a dragonfly when seen from a distance.

Other butterflies and moths boast such impressive names as Leopard (*Phalanta phalantha*), Courtesan (*Euripus nyctelius*), Batik-wing (*Cethosia biblis*), King's Crown (*Euploea phaenareta*), Dark Blue Tiger (*Tirumala septentrionsis*) or Chocolate Albatross (*Appias lyncida*). The largest butterfly in Malaysia is the Atlas moth, a night moth with a wingspan of up to 12 inches (30 cm).

Equally remarkable is the wide range of beetles, such as the Giant Rhinoceros Beetle (*Chalcosoma caucasus*), which can grow up to 5 inches (13 cm), or the shimmering rainbow-colored Jewel Beetle (*Chrysochroa ephippigera*). The dead-leaf praying mantis (*Deroplatys desicata*) is also unique, because – as its name indicates – it can camouflage itself extremely well by simply looking like a dead leaf.

Several species of scorpions also live in Malaysia; while their stings are poisonous, they are not fatal to humans.

On the east coast of peninsular Malaysia and on the beaches of Borneo you can occasionally see the horseshoe crab (*Xiphosura*), also related to the spider family, which has not fundamentally changed for the last 250 million years.

A World Under Water

That such a large number of ocean areas have had to be designated as "protected" is evidence of the degree to which Malaysia's underwater world is threatened. In the Marine Parks, you can get some idea of the erstwhile abundance of the coral reefs which used to abound along the coastline. Scuba divers can observe iridescent coral fish, sea bass, boxfish, sea cucumbers, starfish and shellfish.

Reef sharks, which are generally harmless, hunt for food; dolphins swim alongside the boats. At greater depths dwell whales, whale sharks, manta rays and various shoal fish, ranging from small flying fish to tuna measuring over a yard in length.

EATING IN MALAYSIA

The comparison with a melting pot is very appropriate in a discussion of Malaysian cuisine. For centuries, dishes, flavors, and ingredients have come together from many countries: Portugal, the Netherlands, England; Arabian lands and the Orient; China and India, Ceylon and Turkey; Pakistan, Thailand and Persia; Japan and Korea. Eating in Malaysia is like taking a culinary trip around the world.

Malay Cuisine

As in most Southeast Asian countries, rice forms the basis of every meal. It must be properly prepared, of course: not too dry, not too moist, just right to be picked up with the fingertips while eating in the traditional manner. It's served with beef,

Above and right: Meals in Malaysia are both international and taste delicious. Rice is served with every meal.

mutton, fish, chicken, crabs or other seafood, with vegetables or eggs.

While spices are never lacking from any dish, Malay cuisine is not overly hot. Depending upon the region, garlic, onions, pepper, ginger, curry, cloves, nutmeg, coriander, cardamom, caraway seeds, tamarind and cinnamon are used in varying degrees. In Penang, Kedah and Perlis, however, food can sometimes get rather hot for the unsuspecting – or untrained – Western palate. Cucumbers are always served on the side to help cool things down. Tiny, salty fish, called *ikan bilis*, are often an essential component of a meal.

Satay is without a doubt the country's most well-known dish. Small skewers with marinated beef, chicken or crab meat are grilled over a charcoal fire and dipped in spicy peanut sauce. These are also eaten with rice, called *ketupat*, which is passed around in a small basket made of palm leaves.

Another dish typical of Malay cuisine is *nasi padang*. This filling, spicy meal

consists of rice and various curry combinations. It was introduced from Indonesia, having originated in the city of Padang in central Sumatra. However, this meal is not really perfect until the *rendang*, beef curry made with coconut milk, is served. *Udang sambal* are hot, spicy crabs; *nasi lemak* is a rich dish of rice simmered in coconut milk, which is often eaten for breakfast with *ikan bilis* or eggs.

Nasi goreng, popular in Western countries as an exotic meal, is more of an everyday dish in Malaysia: fried rice prepared with peppers, onions, garlic, chicken and crabs in soy sauce. It is served with a variety of flavorful side dishes.

Mee goreng are fried, thin noodles. Noodles are also the main ingredient of *lakas Johor*; here, they're served with fish curry and fresh vegetables. The noodle dish *Mee Java* is pepped up with grilled prawns, *tofu* (soybean curds), and a hot sauce. *Soto Ayam*, a popular meal at the cookshacks because it is so hearty and

filling, is a chicken soup with rice and vegetables.

The main course is always followed by a dessert, such as *sago Melaka*, sago cooked in palm syrup (*gula Melaka*) – Malaysia's answer to Jello.

Chinese Cuisine

A visitor to this country can never forget the centuries of Chinese influence, which has left its traces everywhere in Malaysia, even in the restaurants. Time and again, the traveller is presented with opportunities of getting to know the differences between China's various regional cuisines.

Cantonese dishes tend to be mild, flavored mainly with ginger. A few drops of peanut oil give them their *je ne sais quoi*. In Peking, the noodles are made of wheat, rather than rice, flour. Hearty meat dishes – often including pork – are also popular. And the famous Peking Duck is prepared in Malaysia with the same care as it is in the Empire of the Sun.

is a dish consisting of chicken, sausages and vegetables. The ever-present rice is steamed in an clay pot.

The Chinese are especially fond of birds-nest-soup made from the gelatin-like strings of the salangane nests of Borneo. These are steeped in chicken broth and prepared with quail's eggs.

The "Steamboat" is one of the great culinary pleasures. This is a type of fondue pot. Guests are served individual portions of raw meat, fish, crabs and vegetables, which they cook themselves in the simmering broth and then dunk in various sauces.

A Chinese meal only tastes half as good if you do not use chopsticks. It pays to practice if you want to be able to enjoy more than the pale imitations and limited selection of dishes one generally knows from Chinese restaurants in European countries.

In Shanghai, food tends to be somewhat sweeter; and fish dishes are plentiful and popular. Szechuan cooks, by contrast, are as a rule more generous with hot spices such as the famous Szechuan pepper pods or garlic. Duck, when it is served, is usually smoked.

The Hokkien from southern China like to cook with soy sauce. A popular dish is Hainan chicken rice. The chicken, either steamed or grilled, is served with rice cooked in a chicken broth.

Cooks from Hainan, by the way, also love to play up the contrast between mild meat dishes and hot sauces. One of their delicacies is *chie pau kai*, chicken wrapped in paper. Chicken is marinated in ginger juice and rice wine, then wrapped in parchment paper and fried in oil. Frogs' legs, spiced with garlic and chili and fried in butter, are listed as "water chicken" on menus. *Ngah poh fan*

Nyonya Cuisine

The descendants of the Chinese who immigrated in the 18th and 19th centuries – for the most part men from Hokkien – formed their own ethnic group (*baba*) and married native women (*nyonya*). By identifying themselves as "Straits-born Chinese," they wanted to differentiate themselves from Chinese settlers that came later. The Baba and Nyonya communities thus created their own dishes, placing a great emphasis on spices and on the art of harmonizing their various flavors.

Laksa noodles are typical of Nyonya cuisine. With *curry laksa*, the rice noodles are refined with chicken curry, small mussels, soybean sprouts and other tasty ingredients. *Assam laksa* comes from Penang, where people prefer their rice noodles served with a fish sauce, cucumber salad, prawn purée and pineapples. *Blachan*, another specialty, is a paste made of dried prawns. It is used to enrich Nyonya, Malay and Chinese

Above: Europeans have long been attracted to the spices of Malaysia. Right: Cookshacks are popular throughout the country.

cuisine, as are *laos*, an aromatic root, or *serai*, lemon grass.

A few table manners round off the Nyonya art of cooking. *Nyonya* eat with their hands, whereas *baba* use forks and spoons. Eating with your hand – always use the right hand – takes practice; it supposedly makes food taste better. Rice and the other ingredients are rolled and pressed together, dunked in a sauce and put into the mouth using the thumb. This continues until your plate is completely clean. Children are told that they will get a rash if they do not finish everything on their plate.

Indian Cuisine

The menu of the Indians is also both tasty and diverse. In Malaysia, you can make a rough division between the cuisines of northern and southern India.

Northern Indians don't use spices to an excessive degree; and wheat, rather than rice, is the staple grain in their diet. Well-known internationally is *tandoori chicken*, chicken marinated in yoghurt, spices and lemon juice and cooked in a clay oven. Lamb cutlets with chutney are also a specialty of northern India.

Southern Indian cuisine centers around rice and many hot spices, which also make the vegetable dishes spicy. Vegetables are cooked with mustard seeds, fenugreek, curry and poppy seeds. Traditionally, meals are served on a banana leaf with rice and chutneys. There is no cutlery: here, too, food only tastes good when eaten with the fingers.

Other southern Indian delicacies include prawn curry, mutton mysore, and chicken biryani.

Eating at the Cookshacks

As in other Southeast Asian countries, you can find cookshacks throughout Malaysia. The *hawker* cuisine does not belong to any one ethnic group. Chinese

like to eat the meals cooked here just as much as Indians and Malays, as long as taboos concerning eating do not forbid them from eating certain dishes. The cookshack institution in Malaysia comes from the period of mass immigration, when one could feed, support, and employ an entire family with this relatively simple business.

A *hawker* is successful when he has the ingredients of the individual ethnic groups on hand and adapts them to the respective region. Thus, the white spring roll, *poh piah*, which is actually a Hokkien specialty, is also prepared at the cookshacks in an Indian version. The Indian *hawker* uses Chinese Hokkien noodles without hesitation, and at the Chinese cookshack you can smell the aroma of Malayan *laksa*.

In Malaysia, there are cookshack owners who become as renowned and sought-out as good restaurants in other parts of the world. It is not surprising that some of them have already "cooked" their way into a comfortable villa.

RELIGION

In Malaysia, the close coexistence of many different religions reflects, or corresponds to, the country's multi-ethnic society. Buddhist and Taoist temples are built in the immediate vicinity of mosques, Christian churches stand next to Hindu or Sikh temples.

Brunei and Malaysia are the only countries in Southeast Asia where the state religion is orthodox Islam and fundamentalist ideas are gaining ground. On the other hand, the constitution guarantees religious freedom. For the most part, diverse faiths are tolerated, but this does not prevent rivalries – mainly of a social or economic nature.

Animistic native tribes are still fair game for missionaries; Christians and Muslims compete for new members in

Above: The people of the east coast, in particular, are orthodox practitioners of Islam. Right: A center for Buddhists: the Kek Lok Si temple in Penang.

their congregations. But the Islamized Orang Asli or the Christianized Dayak often still maintain their faith in their traditional spirits. Even the Malays, animists themselves before Islam arrived in the country, still heed superstitions and taboos.

Islam

Arabic traders came to Southeast Asia as early as 1250. With the conversion of the Sultan of Malacca in the 15th century, Islam really took hold; over the ensuing 200 years, it spread quickly. Except in Buddhist Thailand, the new religion became very popular throughout the region. The simplicity of the belief in Allah, the one all-powerful god, was very attractive to the Asians, who were ready to turn away from the complex hierarchical systems of Hinduism. Islam's deep fatalism may also have appealed to the inhabitants of a tropical world who, then as now, are oriented toward the present and who live at the mercies of the powers of nature.

The structure of Islamic belief, which worships only Allah and the Prophet Mohammed, and demands a high degree of subordination from its followers, is clear and simple. Neither God nor the Prophet may be represented pictorially. Life forms, except for plants, should not be depicted either. This prohibition is the reason why Islamic art concentrates on developing and embellishing Arabic characters and ornamenting their arabesques. Old and modern mosques in Malaysia are testimony to the diversity of Islamic sacred architecture.

An irrefutable Islamic law stipulates that the Koran is the only true doctrine. The 114 suras (chapters) of the holy book were first compiled after the Prophet's death (571-632 A.D.); as well as statements on God, paradise and hell, they also contain laws and cultural commandments. Further requirements are the prayers to Allah, which should be said five times a day; a tax for the poor; and fasting during the day in the month of fasting called *Ramadan*, which Malaysians call *Puasa*. The ultimate experience of one's lifetime is a pilgrimage to Mecca, after which the believer has earned the title of *Hajji*.

Buddhism

Buddhist ideology reached the Malay peninsula long before Islam did. At first there were only sporadic influences, which came from India and the expanding Srivijaya kingdom of Sumatra between the 7th and 14th centuries. With the mass influx of Chinese immigrants into the country in the 19th century, Buddhism also spread to the southern part of the peninsula.

The teachings can be roughly divided into Mahayana Buddhism, also referred to as Great Vehicle, and Hinayana (Little Vehicle), or Theravada Buddhism. Mahayana Buddhism, which follows the teachings of Chinese Buddhism, con-

ceives of *bodhisattvas* (people on the way to Buddhahood), who are there to help enable others to reach *nirvana*, the obliteration of what is seen as the illusion of individual existence. Hinayana or Theravada Buddhism does not have such redeemer figures; in this system, everyone has to try on his own, throughout his life, to reach the stature of Buddha (the Enlightened One).

In Kedah, Perlis, Penang and Kelantan, formerly under Thai influence, the Hinayana teachings, which come the closest to the original forms of Buddhism, are widespread. The Chinese variant, on the other hand, is a mixture of Buddhism, Confucianism and Taoism.

Buddhism is a flexible religion. The many gods and goddesses, which were not part of the original doctrine but are utilized by believers, don't have specific established, set characteristics. Frequently, they are worshipped in different ways from one region to another. In Malaysia, for example, Kuan Ti, the god of war, is responsible in times of peace for

tion, places of prayer range from simple shrines to richly-decorated palaces, and they demonstrate a wide variety of manifestations of sacred art, in various hybrid forms adapted to the regions.

Hinduism

Over 2,000 years ago, Hinduism began to spread through Southeast Asia, adapting to specific local conditions. Although they accepted the world of gods and the power of the Indian Brahmans, the Southeast Asians never adopted the rigid caste system of India. In Malaysia, the earliest evidence of Hinduism found to date are the ruins in the Bujang Valley and at the mouth of the river Merbok in Kedah.

With the arrival of the plantation workers, who came into Malaysia from about 1850 to 1950, southern Indian Hinduism became dominant. The Tamils mainly worship the deities Mariamman and Subramaniam (Lord Murugam), an incarnation of the six-headed god of war, Skanda.

commerce, and symbolizes prosperity and good fortune. Kuan Yin, the goddess of mercy, evolved from the male *bodhisattva* Avalokitesvara. And the spirit of Admiral Cheng Ho, influential in the early 15th century in Melaka as the imperial ambassador, is worshipped today as Sam Po Shan, god of travelers.

As well as good spirits, the world of the gods also has evil demons who want to be pacified. In addition, the souls of the dead can exercise influences for both good and bad. The Chinese ancestor-cult developed out of this belief, and is very pronounced. The resulting tight family groups are a major contributing factor in the economic ambition and success of many Chinese families.

With more than 3,500 temples, Malaysian Buddhism is very much present. Depending on the wealth of the congrega-

Believing in the transference of the soul, hoping to end the cycle of reincarnation and to unite with *Brahman*, the basis of all existence, Hindus live in a predestined state of existence known as *dharma*. Good and bad deeds are weighed after death and, as *karma*, determine the next reincarnation. Divine incarnations of *Brahman* are Brahma, the Creator; Vishnu, the Protector – often portrayed as a four-armed, blue-skinned figure – and Shiva, the Destroyer. In temples of southern Indians, they are represented by *Shikara*, a symbol of the mountain of gods called *Meru*.

Followers of this religion don't believe in the idea of a mission or purpose on earth or other such dogmas. There are only the *Vedas*, holy revelations, which are said to have been brought to India more than 3,000 years ago by Indo-Aryan immigrants.

Above: The Thaipusam festival near Kuala Lumpur draws hundreds of thousands of visitors. Right: A Bisayan marriage ceremony in Sabah.

FESTIVALS AND HOLIDAYS

Malaysia's cultural diversity is reflected in its festivals and holidays. Hardly any other country on earth offers such a full calendar of ceremonies. Every religious community, every ethnic group, and, in addition, each state celebrates its own festivals and holidays. For such a relatively young national constellation as Malaysia, the national holiday celebrated on August 31 with parades is of particular importance; it aims to consolidate the national sentiment of this multi-cultural people.

Due to the fact that many of the events are not held on fixed, specific dates, the Malaysia Tourism Promotion Board (MTPB) publishes a schedule each year. A description of several of the most important festivals follows.

Islamic Holidays

According to the Islamic calendar, which starts with Mohammed's flight from Mecca on July 16, 622 A.D. and is based on the cycle of the stages the moon, each year consists of 354 to 355 days. The twelve lunar months have 29 or 30 days each. The Islamic New Year's festival *Ma'al Hijrah* thus falls on the day that the 13th new moon appears.

The most important Islamic festival – in Malaysia, with its state religion, every Malay is a Muslim – *Hari Raya Puasa* is celebrated at the end of Ramadan, the month of fasting. It usually lasts three days during the ninth month of the lunar calendar.

The faithful certainly have a reason to celebrate: during Ramadan (*Puasa*), a strict fast is observed between sunrise and sunset. This means everyone has to abstain from any form of eating and drinking, including water. Evil thoughts and wishes are forbidden during this time; in general, one should try to keep oneself as Muslim as possible in every respect.

The Prophet Mohammed, whose birthday is celebrated on *Maulidin Nabi*, is

supposed to have introduced Ramadan as an exercise in self-discipline and self-purification.

During *Hari Raya Puasa*, the breaking of the fast, meals are accordingly large and plentiful, and every member of the family receives new clothes which cannot be worn until the festival starts. For this reason, retailers and shop owners particularly look forward to this holiday.

Hari Raya Haji is also a festive day: on the 10th day of the 12th month, streams of pilgrims set out for Mecca by airplane.

The Chinese Festivals

The Chinese calendar is also based on the moon. The months have 29 and 30 days; every 30 months, an extra day is added. In the long term, the passage of time is reckoned in cycles of five times twelve years.

Above: Dragons play a big part in Chinese festivals: here, a dragon dance in Kuching.

Each of these twelve years has a designated animal whose characteristics are then transferred to individuals born in that year or more general social expectations. In the year 2000, the Year of the Dragon, the Chinese and everyone who believes in their calendar are hoping for prosperity and an economic upswing. Starting with the Year of the Dragon, which was last celebrated in 1988, the signs are dragon, snake, horse, goat, monkey, rooster, dog, pig, rat (1996), ox (1997), tiger and hare.

The *Chinese New Year*'s *Festival* starts on the first day of the first lunar month. According to the Western calendar, the day falls between the 21st of January and the 19th of February. Chinese who can afford it take a week of vacation. On the evening of the New Year's festival the family gathers for a lavish meal, the *reunion dinner*. New clothes are a must for the start of the New Year. Children and single adults in the family receive small, red envelopes with money as gifts, the *ang pow*. The Malays have adopted this custom; but their envelopes or small bags are green, the color of Islam.

The windows are opened before midnight to let in the New Year in the form of fireworks which last for at least two days. The following day is set aside for visiting relatives; for these visits, rich families may well travel to other cities and countries. New Year's trips are also often made to some "family-neutral" area where *ang pow* is no longer a requirement, as this custom can get to be quite expensive.

A special meal of *yee sang* (raw fish with salad) is served on the third or fourth day after New Year's Day. It is supposed to bring luck and success to everyone who eats it.

The *Tuan Wu Chieh* or *Dragon Boat Festival*, which is not a state holiday, takes place on the fifth day of the fifth month. It is held in remembrance of the poet Chu Yuan, who drowned himself in the 3rd century B.C rather than take a bribe. In different venues, such as Penang, races of artistically decorated dragon boats are held in his honor.

The *Feast of the Hungry Spirits* is celebrated in the seventh month. On this day, according to the Buddhist faith, the hungry spirits are allowed to leave the Hereafter in order to look for nourishment on Earth. The faithful help them by laying out offerings and lighting incense sticks.

The *Moon Cake Festival* on the 15th night of the eighth month is also not a legal holiday. This is to honor the successful rebellion against the Mongolians in the 13th century. Moon cakes – which are often savory rather than sweet, filled with meat and lard – are baked especially for this day. During the rebellion the Chinese smuggled secret messages inside the cakes. Chinese lanterns and other lanterns, now carried by children in parades on this festive evening in honor of the moon goddess, were also used for the same purpose.

Vesak Day is the festival in remembrance of Buddha's birth, his death and his enlightenment. It is celebrated on the sixth full moon, between April and May. Torchlight processions make their way through the streets. Buddhist monks sing holy verses the entire day, the faithful pray and are urged to do good deeds. Bird cages are opened in order to give the birds, symbols of imprisoned souls, their freedom. This day is celebrated differently from region to region. In Melaka, for instance, decorated vehicles parade through the streets.

The *Ching Ming Festival* is not a public holiday. Groups of relatives visit the dead in the cemeteries on the eighth day of the third month and tidy up the graves. They lay out offerings of food and light candles, burn incense sticks and even money as a sacrifice. Finally, the surviving family members eat the food offerings, from which the ancestors have already eaten their fill.

The *Festival of the Nine Emperor Gods* is celebrated on the ninth day of the ninth month in honor of the nine rulers of the heavens. Chinese operas and processions are part of the program; the central activity, however, is nine days of prayer. For the faithful, who have fasted before the festival for the same amount of time, the climax of this celebration takes place in some of the temples, when, in a trance, they walk across glowing coals.

Indian Festivals

Each year in February several thousand people meet at the Batu Caves, outside of Kuala Lumpur. *Thaipusam* has begun, the most spectacular of all the Malaysian festivals, which has been forbidden in India. For about 2,000 Hindus, this festival means self-castigation, pain and trances. One of these is Sundram. Yesterday, this Tamil taxi driver was standing smartly dressed in front of a luxury hotel in the capital, waiting for cus-

tomers. Now, in the early hours of the morning, he is standing, naked except for swim trunks, on the banks of a small river. His hands are folded, his head bowed. In front of him a guru, dressed in white, is singing religious chants to the rhythm of a drum. Helpers and musicians join in the song: "Vel, vel, vel...," which means "Spear, spear, spear..."

Sundram sways and the singing and drum beats get faster. Suddenly, the young man whips his arms up into the air and stands motionless. A woman, also dressed in white robes, steps up to the guru and hands him a spear. The priest takes it and holds back for a moment; then, quick as a flash, he sticks the spear through both of Sundram's cheeks. Sundram does not wince, not even when the guru carefully balances the spear, which is more than 6 feet long.

Above: Chinese baked goods for festive occasions. Right: During the Thaipusam festival, a practicing Hindu has his cheeks pierced with a spear.

Sundram swore to his favorite god Subramaniam that he would carry the *kavadi* during three successive *Thaipusam* festivals: to carry this spear, that is, thrust through his face, as well as a heavy altar, held in place by hooks pressed deep into his skin. The man is motivated to torture himself to show thanks: a few weeks previously, his wife gave birth to a healthy son.

The *Thaipusam* festival of Kuala Lumpur draws over 600,000 spectators, helpers and relatives in addition to the faithful who come prepared to subject themselves to pain. Also taking part are 10,000 musicians and gurus, as well as thousands of journalists, photographers, and tourists from all over the world, none of whom wants to miss this remarkable Hindu penitential pilgrimage. On the island of Penang, in Melaka, in the mining city of Ipoh and in Singapore, this festival in honor of Lord Subramaniam is also celebrated, but on less extravagant scale.

In order to understand the reverence, devotion, and disregard of pain which

many Indians demonstrate toward Subramaniam, one has to understand that the deity has a very special place in the hierarchy of the Hindu gods. Unlike Christianity and Islam, Hinduism has a multitude of gods. In addition, Hindus also worship the wives, children and grandchildren of the gods, as well as demons and spirits. At the top of the list, next to Brahma and Vishnu, is Shiva. With his wife, Durga, he sired Subramaniam in an extremely dramatic manner. When the demons threatened to defeat the gods, this divine pair appeared: fire shot out of Shiva's third eye, and his son Subramaniam emerged from the flames. With his help, the demons were quickly defeated.

The Hindus always call on Subramaniam, who inherited his father's good as well as his destructive qualities, when there are difficulties to overcome or wishes to fulfill. This god is believed to be helpful with everyday problems and sickness, when a test is impending or when a marriage has remained childless.

The *kavadi* carriers have prepared themselves for the torture for at least 16 days in the temple. Part of these preparations are sexual abstinence, avoidance of pleasures and unnecessary foods, and reading holy scripture under the direction of their gurus.

A guru does not have to be a scholar who has completed a course of study. Often, he is a simple man, who even used to be critical of religion, and who was then one day chosen by the gods to be a medium. Soon, the chosen one manages to surround himself with followers. God enters him, the medium, at certain intervals and enables him, or so his adherents believe, to heal the sick and to perform other miracles. He may not demand money for this. One of the tasks of the guru is to accompany his followers and to attend them when they want to carry a *kavadi* at the *Thaipusam* festival.

Some people don't find that carrying an altar fastened to their bodies with hooks and a spear through their faces quite fulfills their penance or vow. One

man cuts his tongue with a sword; another has his tongue pierced with a second spear. While these men slowly dance, those accompanying them sing softly.

The people around them also observe a number of symbolic procedures. A woman throws camphor into a small fire-pot, and shakes salt into the ashes. According to Hindu belief, the combination of fire and salt will burn away every sickness and disease. Others in the group cut up fruit and throw the pieces north, south, east and west. This is supposed to drive away evil spirits.

The guru chops up a pumpkin. This ritual is a modern stand-in for what was originally the sacrifice of a live goat. The animal's blood had to flow over the images of the gods.

Women and girls collapse; they have fallen into a trance. A girl jumps on a car-

Above: During the Thaipusam festival. Right: The painstakingly crafted festive jewelery of an Iban.

rier of a *kavadi*, digging her fingers into his hair. The girl would normally never dare even to speak to a man she does not know. During *Thaipusam*, however, everyday taboos are not in effect. Lord Subramaniam is in the people, he determines the type of dance, their ecstasy and trances.

At sunrise, the *kavadi* carriers suddenly leave their spots and move to the street leading to the temple in one of the caves, almost two miles away. They have to complete about 30 yards of vertical ascent over the uncertain terrain of steep, looming limestone. Once in the cave, the long procession still has to climb 272 steps, for only then are the vows fulfilled. During this extremely critical stage the gurus intensify their prayers and keep their charges under control with steady looks, while the cries of "vel, vel" become more and more intense. The *kavadi* carriers fight on; many of them appear to lose strength and courage during the climb.

At last they have reached the farthest corner of the giant cave. In a recess there is a golden statue of Lord Subramaniam. The taxi driver Sundram has made it. One last time he dances in front of the statue. His guru looks him deep in the eye and abruptly pulls the spear out of his cheeks. Another prayer and then the priest announces that Lord Subramaniam has accepted the penance. The *kavadi* carriers seem to be more relieved than exhausted. Back at the foot of the mountain, they pass out gold coins to waiting beggars. Hardly any blood has flowed, and their face bear no trace of any kind of wound, although the spear, a good half-inch thick, has been sticking through their cheeks for hours.

This, however, has nothing to do with magic, but rather with the gurus' excellent knowledge of human anatomy. The priests's swords pierce the cheeks directly behind the corners of the mouth. This is where the *Corpus adiposum buc-*

cae, fatty tissue without any nerves or blood vessels, are located. The tissue contracts immediately, as soon as the spear is removed; because of this, not even a scar remains.

The second most important festival for Hindus in Malaysia is *Deepavali*, celebrated between October and November during the Tamil month of *aipassi*. Once again, astrologers determine the date, which symbolizes the victory of light over darkness, good over evil. The god Rama triumphs over Ravana, the king of the demons. In several of the larger temples, believers walk through fire. After the festival has opened with prayers, people express their spiritual purification by putting on new clothes. Children, poor people and beggars receive gifts. *Deepavali* is also a family festival, and Hindus often hold "open house." They invite friends and neighbors to worship the goddess Lakshimi.

The *Hindu New Year's Festival* is usually in the middle of the month of April in the Western calendar; at this time, the Hindus start off the month of *sitthirai* with prayers at home and in temples.

Maha Shiva Rathiri is also celebrated with prayers and hymns. This holiday in honor of Shiva, which is not a state holiday, takes place at the end of February.

Lord Subramaniam, the fighter against evil, has another festival in his honor. *Kantha Shashti* lasts for six days and starts on the sixth day of the bright fourteen days in the Hindu month *aipassi*. On the last day, the climax of the battle between Subramaniam and Sooran is acted out in the temples. You can see this pantomime performance in the Kandasamy Temple in Kuala Lumpur, among other temples.

Christian Holidays

Christians celebrate Christmas in Malaysia, as well as Good Friday and the *Festa São Pedro, which* takes place on June 29th, especially in the Portuguese communities.

PREPARING FOR YOUR TRIP

Climate

The average daily temperature in the tropical countries of Malaysia and Brunei ranges from about 70F (21C) at night to 89F (32C) by day. In the highlands, however, it can be as cool as 57F (14C), and at the summits of the highest mountains the temperature hovers just above freezing. In lower areas, the heat of the day is compounded by humidity as high as 85 percent.

Monsoons have a decisive effect on the climate. The Northeast Monsoon blows from October to February, exposing the east coast of Malaysia to heavy rainfall and frequent flooding.

The west coast, with a few exceptions, is spared such extreme weather. In the time of the Southwest Monsoon, from March to September, there is a good deal of precipitation – particularly in the period between May and September.

When to go

While the west coast of the peninsula is fine for visitors year-round, you should aim to visit the east coast between the end of February and the beginning of October; for East Malaysia and Brunei, it's fine to go until the end of October.

Clothing

Because of the climate, light, loose clothes, preferably made of cotton, are your best bet. Hats and scarves are good protetion against the strong sun. In the evening, or in the air-conditioned interiors of luxury hotels, restaurants and shopping centers, you may want a light jacket. Formal occasions, such as an invitation to an "open house," will require appropriate clothing; make sure you have long trousers, a blazer, and a necktie in your luggage. It's also perfectly accept-able to go to a fancy occasion dressed, like a Malaysian, in a colorful batik shirt. Women wear appropriately decent dresses or blouses, preferably displaying less rather than more bare skin. See-through material or miniskirts can be offensive in an Islamic environment. If you're visiting a mosque, church, or other temple, you should demonstrate respect by dressing properly. Women are supposed to cover their arms and legs, while men have to wear long pants.

If you're planning to travel in the mountains, bring a warm pullover; even in the Genting Highlands, not far from Kuala Lumpur, this will do yeoman service. Anyone climbing Mount Kinabalu should be prepared for sudden changes of temperature; and around the summit, you'll need a warm, waterproof jacket. For jungle or mountain hiking, bring along sturdy, waterproof walking shoes or boots; and don't neglect to bring long pants and long-sleeved shirts as protection against mosquitos and leeches.

Visas

If you're on a business or pleasure trip lasting up to six months, can present a passport that's valid for at least another six months, and are a citizen of one of the following countries, you can enter Malaysia without a visa: Austria, Belgium, Denmark, France, Finnland, Germany, Italy, Iceland, Japan, Norway, Luxemburg, Sweden, South Korea. Members of Commonwealth countries (except India), the Netherlands, Pakistan, Ireland, Liechtenstein, San Marino, Switzerland and the United States do not need visas, either.

Members of other ASEAN countries (Brunei, Thailand, Indonesia, the Philippines and Singapore) can stay in Malaysia for up to a month without a visa. For Sarawak and Sabah, special conditions apply: citizens of Western European countries can only stay for one month without a visa. In Brunei, travellers from these countries can only stay for 14 days without a visa.

Immigration authorities are located in every Malaysian state, and can extend visas when necessary. The main office in Kuala Lumpur:

Immigration Department, Headquarters Office, Block 1, Pusat, Bandar Damansara, Bukit Damansara, Tel: 2555077.

Information at the **Malaysian Embassies**: In **Great Britain:** High Commission, 45 Belgrave Square, London SW1X 8QT, tel: 071/235 8033. In **Canada:** High Commission, 60 Botchler Street, Ottowa, Ontario, K1N 8Y7, Tel: 237-5182. In **Australia**: High Commission of Malaysia, 7 Perth Avenue, Yarralumla, Canberra ACT 2600, Tel: 273 1534/4/5. In the **United States**: *Washington*: Embassy of Malaysia, 2401 Massachusetts Avenue NW, Washington, DC 20008, Tel: (202) 328-2700; *Los Angeles:* Consulate General of Malaysia, 350 South Figueroa Street, Suite 400, Los Angeles, CA, 90071 Tel: (213) 621-2991, *New York:* Consulate General of Malaysia, Two Grand Central Tower, 140 E. 45th Street, 43rd Floor, New York, NY, 10117, Tel: (212) 490- 2722.

For information about **Brunei**, contact: In **Great Britain**: High Commission of Brunei Darussalam (England and Ireland), 19/20 Belgrave Square, London SW1X 8PG. In **Australia**: High Commission of Brunei Darussalam, 16 Bulwarra Close, O'Malley, A.C.T. 2602. In the **United States**: *Washington*: Embassy of Brunei Darussalam, Watergate Suite 300, 2600 Virginia Avenue NW, Washington, DC, 20037; *New York*: Permanent Mission of Brunei Darussalam to the United Nations, 866 United Nations Plaza, New York NY 10017.

Currency

The Malaysian unit of currency is the ringgit or Malay dollar (RM), which is divided into 100 sen or cents. There are coins with values of 1, 5, 10, 20, 50 sen and 1 RM. There are banknotes in denominations of 1, 5, 10, 20, 50, 100, 500, and 1,000 ringgit.

The Brunei dollar (100 cents) is issued in the same denominations. Its rate of exchange is closely allied with that of the Singapore dollar, while the ringgit is usually oriented to the U.S. dollar.

In 1996, you got 0.40 U.S. dollars for 1 ringgit; in the same period, the Brunei dollar equalled 0.63 U.S.dollars.

You can pay with the usual credit cards in large shops, restaurants and hotels. You'll get a better rate on your traveler's checks in banks, licensed exchange offices, hotels, and department stores; you need to show your passport whenever you use one. A fee is paid for each operation (not each check).

Kuala Lumpur has about 40 commercial banks, international and national. They are also open Saturdays from 9:30 am to 11:30 pm. Otherwise normal banking business hours are from 10:00 am to 4:00 pm.

Exchange bureaus (Money Changer), often offering a better rate of exchange, can be found on just about every street corner, but especially in department stores.

Health precautions

No inoculations are required to enter Malaysia or Brunei, unless you're travelling from a dangerous area. Nonetheless, you should check with a doctor or tropical disease center before your trip about the possible risks of infection with such diseases as cholera, typhus, and especially hepatitus.

It's a good idea to get a prophylactic injection against hepatitus if you're planning to stay in a rural area where the hygienic conditions won't always be exactly ideal.

Another danger which should not be underestimated in Southeast Asia is ma-

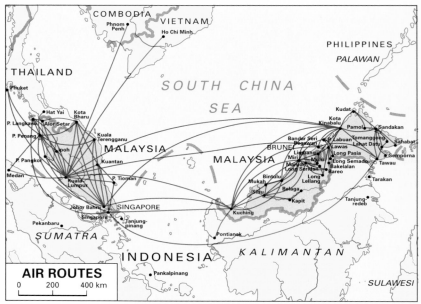

laria. It's only transmitted by female anopheles mosquitos, but these animals have built up a considerable resistance to many of the usual medicines, such as resochin, fansidar or lariam. A competent center for tropical disease control can tell you which medication to take.

In addition, it's advisable to protect yourself well with insect repellent, particularly in the evening and at night. Wear light-colored clothes that cover your whole body, and sleep under a mosquito net.

It's also important to get refresher shots against polio and tetanus. Surface cuts and scratches that at first seem harmless can easily develop into nasty tropical infections. Don't be shy about treating even a superficial scrape with antiseptic cream or solution. Don't swim in standing water, where there may be a variety of germs and disease-causing bacteria.

It's fine to walk barefoot on the beach, but in other areas it's best to wear shoes, or at least sandals, as protection against any number of parasites that dwell in the earth, such as hookworm (also to avoid cuts that could get infected.

Avoid sunbathing too long or too often on Malaysia's beaches, and make sure that you continue to use adequate sun protection even after you've gotten over your first sunburn. You'll be in even less danger of developing melanoma (skin cancer) if you keep your skin from getting red at all. Follow the example of the natives and avoid the midday sun. Give your body some time to get adjusted. This kind of careful approach is also good for your stomach and digestive system, especially if you aren't used to spicy cooking. Should diarrhea or stomach cramps persist for longer than three days, get yourself to a doctor. Usually the local doctors can take care of any problems that might arise. The modern pharmacies or dispensaries in the big cities are generally well-stocked. In addition, Chinese shops offer a large selection of medicaments and herbs which can exercise a fascination even on people in the prime of health.

Getting there:
Malaysia and Brunei

The national airline MAS (Malaysian Airline System) is one of some two dozen international carriers that serves Malaysia. The country's main airport is Subang in Selangor, near Kuala Lumpur. International flights also land at Penang, Langkawi, Tioman, Kuantan, Kota Kinabalu and Kuching. When you're comparing prices, take into account the fact that MAS often offers cheaper domestic fares (including Borneo), with one-price or stopover tickets when you buy an international ticket. Since August, 1993, the private airline Pelangi Air has flown shorter international routes, such as between Singapore and West Malaysia.

You can also enter Malaysia from Thailand or Singapore by train.

Boats to Malaysia run from Singapore to Port Klang, Kuantan, Kota Kinabalu and Kuching. Private boats run between Singapore and Pulau Tioman. There's also a regular route between Medan (Sumatra) and Penang. Froom Sarawak and Sabah, ships run along the coast to Brunei.

Continuing your trip / Leaving

If you fly within Malaysia, there's an airport tax of RM 5 for each domestic flight. For flights to destinations outside the country, including Brunei and Singapore, there's a departure tax of RM 20.

In Brunei, the charge for flights to Singapore and Malaysia is 5 Brunei dollars; for other international flights, 12 dollars.

TRAVELING AROUND

By air

Because of the low domestic fares, with discounts for groups, families, and students, air travel is perhaps the best way to get around the country. In addition to MAS, Pelangi Air serves a num-ber of domestic destinations. If you haven't already made reservations in advance, it's best to check around once you get to Malaysia for the cheapest fares.

Local **MAS offices** in major cities:

Kuala Lumpur: 33rd Floor, Bangunan AS, Jl. Sultan Ismail, Tel: 03-7463000/2610555. Ground Floor, Menara Utama UMBC, Jl. Sultan Sulaiman, Tel: 03-2305115. Lot 7A 3rd Floor, Pan Pacific Hotel, Jl. Putra, Tel: 03-4426759.

George Town: 3rd Floor, Kompleks Tun Abdul Razak, Penang Road, Tel: 04-2620011/2621403.

Melaka: 1st Floor, The City Bayview Hotel, Tel: 06-235722/3/4

Johor Bahru: Suite 1.1, level 1, Menara Pelangi, Jl. Kuning, Taman Pelangi, Tel: 07-3341001/3344701-2.

Ipoh: G 01 & Lot 108, Bangunan Seri Kinta, Jl. Sultan Idris Shah, Tel: 05-2514155/2530278.

Kuantan: Ground Floor, Wisma Bolasepak Pahang, Jl. Gambut, Tel: 09-555055/528816.

Kota Bharu: Ground Floor, Kompleks Yakin, Jl. Gajah Mati, Tel: 09-7447000/7483477.

Kuala Terengganu: 13, Jl. Sultan Omar, Tel: 09-6221415/622266.

Kuching: Lot 215, Jl. Song Thian Cheok, Tel: 082-246622/244144.

Kota Kinabalu: 10th Floor, Block C, Kompleks Karamunsing, Tel: 088-213555/239310.

By train and bus

Keretapi Tanah Malaysia is the name of the Malaysian Railway. The peninsula has such important export goods as tin, wood, and rubber to thank for its extensive rail network. There's a short railway line between Kota Kinabulu and Tenom over Beaufort in Sabah. In West Malaysia, the south line links Singapore with Kuala Lumpur via Johor, Melaka and Seremban. From K.L, you can go via Ipoh, Butterworth and Alor Setar to Bangkok, crossing the border at the towns of Padang Besar (Malaysia) and Haadyai (Thailand). The northeast line from Gemas (a branch line off the main tracks from Johor Bahru to Kuala Lumpur) leads through Jerantut, Kuala Lipis and Kota Bharu to Tumpat on the Thai border. From there, you can catch connections to Songkla in Thailand, where this line rejoins the north line to Bangkok via Haadyai. First and second class are very comfortable and air-conditioned, almost too much so, in fact. For night trains, you have to reserve a sleeping compartment in advance. If you have time, you should take the train from Singapore to Bangkok. The narrow-gauge track means a slower ride allowing for a good view of the variegated countryside as it goes by. Trains are cheap as well, and the compartments even in second class are meticulously cleaned by train personnel. Drinks and snacks are offered regularly. In this way, through local travel agencies or on your own initiative, you can explore three Southeast Asian countries by rail. It's important to reserve a seat in advance. A luxury train travels from Singapore to Bangkok via Kuala Lumpur, the *Eastern Oriental Express* (tickets from about 1100 - 4700 US$). Information: Singapore 0065-2910180.

The most effective, extensive system of ground transportation is the **bus**. Malaysia has some very good roads and a marvellously organized system of local and express buses. Express buses (*bas pesiaran*) run between all the major cities, are not expensive, and, in contrast to the local buses, have air conditioning.

By taxi, rickshaw, rental car

Only in the large cities will you find numerous and relatively affordable taxis. Although the driver is required by law to use a meter, it's a good idea to ask about the approximate price before you start the ride. At the airport and train station of Kuala Lumpur, you pay the price at a counter, which issues a coupon for the driver. In Penang and East Malaysia, you have to negotiate the price. The same is true of longer routes, such as a day tour through a given area. Shared taxis travel between the larger cities, departing from bus or train terminals. Passengers divide the lump sum for the route. **Minibusses** are common in Kuala Lumpur. They have a conductor and stop on request.

You also have to negotiate the price of a bicycle rickshaw (*trishaw*). They operate only in Melaka and Penang.

At least on the peninsula, the good roads are a temptation to many people to undertake the driving themselves. You can rent cars in the larger cities of Malaysia and Brunei at international and local car rental agencies, both with and without a driver. You can drive yourself as long as you can present a valid national driver's license from your own country and are between the ages of 21 and 65. Seatbelts in a car are mandatory, and helmets are likewise required for motorcyclists.

In Malaysia, Singapore, and Brunei, everyone drives on the left side of the road. The speed limit within cities is generally 50 kph, if not otherwise indicated, as on city expressways, with signs. On country roads, the limit is 50 mph (80 kph); on expressways, 70 mph (110 kph). After dark, great caution is advised. The roads, which are hardly lit in rural areas, are frequented by man and beast even in the night hours, and potholes or branches may block the way. Trucks take great risks when passing, relying on the principle of survival of the fittest. Opening of the north-south Highway has made travel from Singapore to Thailand easier.

PRACTICAL TIPS

Alcohol

Muslim restaurants, or the state hotels of the east coast states and Brunei, do not serve alcoholic beverages. There are several kinds of beer in Malaysia. Local spirits include *tuak* (palm wine), *arak* (palm brandy), *toddy* (lightly fermented palm beer), rice wine and brandy. Imported beverages such as wine, whiskey or cognac are extremely expensive, and are only officially consumed in Malaysia by visitors, Indians, or Chinese.

Bookstores

All of the cities have well-stocked bookstores – which can also be found in luxury hotels and airports – with English-language books and magazines about history, geography, art and culture of the country.

Shopping

The larger towns and cities have all been fitted out with modern shopping centers. There are duty-free centers at the airports in Kuala Lumpur and Penang, on Labuan in Sabah and in Langkawi. You should, however, be aware of prices back home, as electronic appliances, in particular, may not be any cheaper than they are in Europe or the U.S.A.

Prices are fixed in all the larger stores. At markets or in smaller antique or souvenir shops, however, bargaining is usual, even expected of you. By remaining friendly, smiling, and polite, you can generally make a purchase that's advantageous for both parties.

Specialties of the region, reasonably priced, are silver items, batik, and tinware, woven objets, and woodcarvings of the Orang Asli.

Electricity

In Malaysia and Brunei, the current is 220 volts. Plugs are, unlike the European norm, three-pronged. For appliances you've brought into the country with you, therefore, you'll need an adaptor.

Photographing

As is the rule throughout Southeast Asia, photographers will have no trouble finding subjects in Malaysia. People are generally glad to have their picture taken. Yet it's still necessary to have the proper respect. Adults, particularly older people, expect to be asked permission, even if you want to photograph their children. Great restraint should be exercised in houses of worship and private homes. Military facilities may not be photographed. In the cities and at every tourist center, you can buy all the usual kinds of film and equipment.

Opening Hours

Offices and public institutions are open Monday through Friday, 8:00 am-12:45 pm and 2:00-4:15 pm. Banks are open Monday through Friday, 10:00 am-3:00 pm, while post offices are open Monday through Saturday, 9:00 am-5:00 pm. Most shops are open on weekdays from 9:30 am to 7:00 pm, while supermarkets and department stores are often open until 10:00 pm. In the states of Kedah, Perlis, Kelantan, Terengganu, Johor, and Brunei, the weekend, according to Islamic custom, falls on Thursday and Friday. In the rest of Malaysia, Friday has an extended lunch hour lasting from 12:15-4:45 pm.

Weights and Measures

Malaysia, like most of the rest of the world, uses the metric system. Only occasionally, in rural areas, does one encounter units of measurement left over from British colonial days, such as inches (1 inch=2.54 cm), pounds (1 pound=0.45 kg), gallons (1 gallon=4.55 liters), miles (1 mile=1.61 km), or Fahrenheit (F minus 32 divided by 9 times 5=C). In markets the *kati* is often used (600 grams or over a pound) or the *biji* (by the piece).

Media

A small selection of international English-language media is available in large bookstores and luxury hotels.

The most influential of the more than 60 local newspapers are the New Straits Times and The Star, which are printed in English and which, like the tabloid Malay Mail and the Business Times, are controlled by the governing party, UMNO. Similarly, many of the Chinese and Tamil publications are owned by the Malaysian Chinese Association and the Malaysian Indian Congress, respectively.

Radio and television are state-owned, directly controlled by the Ministry of Information. Radio-Television Malaysia has two channels; a third is TV3, a private channel belonging to the investment division of UMNO. All of the stations broadcast news and entertainment shows in English. Like every other form of media, radio and television are controlled by the state censors.

Post and telecommunications

The postal system in Malaysia and Brunei is extremely efficient. An air mail letter takes only four to six days to reach Europe. Within Malaysia, a postcard costs 15 sen and a letter 30 sen. A postcard to Europe costs 50 sen, and an airmail letter (up to 90 g) costs 90 sen. Rates are more expensive in Brunei; there, an airmail letter to Europe costs 75 cents.

You can place direct-dial, international calls from any large hotel in Malaysia (country code: 60) and Brunei (country code: 673). Rates are cheaper, however, at official Telekom offices, such as STM (Syaricat Telecom Malaysia) and Kedai Telecom, which also have telefax and telex service. The official telecommunications office in Bandar Seri Begawan is next to the General Post Office on Jl. Elisabeth Dua, on the corner of Jl. Sultan, and offers 24-hour service.

Accommodations

Malaysia is working hard to attract tourism; 1994 saw the second official "Visit Malaysia Year" within four years. In keeping with this eagerness, the country offers accommodations in every price range. Luxury hotels provide a level of comfort and service that many comparable establishments in Europe can only envy. There are hotels like the E & O (Eastern and Oriental) in Penang, which, just as the famous Raffles in Singapore or the Oriental in Bangkok, can look back at a 100-year history. Prices are equally high-class (from 400 RM-2,000 RM for a double room). Usually tasteful, if not always cheap (150 RM-400 RM) are the state-subsidized First Class Hotels in tourist areas such as Penang, Langkawi, or on the east coast of the peninsula. The mid-range hotels offer perfectly acceptable comfort and cleanliness for reasonable prices (80 RM-200 RM). In simple chalets or bungalows, you can stay overnight for a mere 20 RM-60 RM with no trouble – as long as they're clean. In Kuala Lumpur, Cameron Highlands, Fraser's Hill, Kuantan, Penang, Kota Bharu, Port Dickson, Kota Kinabalu and on the island of Pangkor, there are also youth hostels open for visitors. The State Resthouses are as a rule provided for travelling officials. If rooms are free, other guests can also stay in them for a very reasonable 30 RM-50 RM. Cheap lodgings in the cities (10 RM-40 RM) are generally fleabags in which you can't be too particular about cleanliness.

Another option are the so-called Home Stay Packages, which involve a two- or three-day stay with a Malaysian family. These are organized by local travel agencies and cost about 300 RM, which includes meals.

Visitors to Brunei who can't avail themselves of private lodging can only turn to the expensive luxury hotels and beach resorts in and around Bandar Seri Begawan.

Security

Malaysians are proud of the country's relatively low crime rate. This doesn't mean that travellers can be lax about the necessary precautions. Valuables should be placed in the hotel safe or at least kept in a locked suitcase. There are pickpockets to be found in crowds of people the world over. In general, however, tourists don't need to feel threatened. Holiday centers and most of the large cities have tourist police offices.

For your own security, it's important to take the laws against drugs and drug dealing very seriously indeed. Breaking these laws can mean the death penalty, even for foreigners.

Time

Malaysia, Singapore and Brunei are 8 hours ahead of Greenwich Mean Time (GMT), 7 hours during daylight savings, 13 hours ahead of New York (EST), 16 hours ahead of Los Angeles, respectively, and 2 hours behind Sydney. Therefore, when it's midnight in Los Angeles, it's 3 am in New York, 8 am in London, 4 pm in Malaysia, and 6 pm in Sydney.

Customs

You can bring in up to 200 cigarettes, 50 cigars, 225 g of tobacco, one liter of alcohol, small gift items, cosmetics, electrical appliances and a camera for personal use without having to pay duty. For optical and electronic applicances, authorities may demand a deposit, which will be returned to you when you present your receipt as you leave the country. You may not bring in weapons, pornography, or illegal drugs. To take antiques out of the coutnry, you may need authorization

from the National Museum in Kuala Lumpur.

There are no limits to the amounts of hard currency and cash which may be brought in and out of the country.

ADDRESSES

Embassies in Kuala Lumpur

Australia: 6, Jalan Yap Kwan Seng, Tel:: 423122.
Belgium: Wisma Bunga Raya, Jalan Ampang, Tel:: 2485733.
Brunei: 112 A, Jalan U Thant, Tel:: 4562635.
France: 192-196 Jalan Ampang, Tel:: 24844235.
Germany: 3, Jalan U Thant, Tel:: 2429666.
Great Britain: 185 Jalan Ampang, Tel:: 2487122.
Indonesia: 233, Jalan Tun Razak, Tel:: 9842011.
The Netherlands: 4, Jalan Mesra, Tel:: 2431141.
Philippines: 1, Changkat Kia Peng, Tel:: 2484233.
Switzerland: 16, Persiaran Madge, Tel:: 2480622.
Singapore: 209, Jalan Tun Razak, Tel:: 2486377.
Thailand: 206, Jalan Ampang, Tel:: 2488222.

Embassies in Brunei

Australia: High Commission, Teck Guan Plaza, Jl. Sultan, Bandar Seri Begawan 2085, P.O. Box 2990, B.S.B. 1929.
Canada: Canadian High Commission (not resident in Brunei), 80 Anson Road, IBM Towers #14-00 and #15-00/01, Singapore 0207.
Germany: 49-50 Jl. Sultan, Bandar Seri Begawan (BSB), Tel:: 2-25547.
Great Britain: British High Commission, 3rd Floor, Hong Kong Bank Chambers, Bandar Seri Begawan 2085.

United States: Embassy of the United States of America, 3rd floor, Teck Guan Plaza, Jalan Sultan, Bandar Seri Begawan 2085.

Tourist offices outside Malaysia

Australia: Tourist Development Corporation of Malaysia (TDC), 65, York St., Sydney, NSW 2000, Tel:: 2-2994441. TDC, 56, William St., Perth, WA 6000, Tel:: 9-4810400.

Canada: Malaysia Tourist Information Center, 830, Burrard St., Vancouver, B.C., V6Z 2K4. Tel:: 604-6898899.

France: TDC, 29, Rue des Pyramides, 75001 Paris, Tel:: 1-42974171.

Germany: TDC, Roßmarkt 11, 60311 Frankfurt/M., Tel:: 069-283782.

Great Britain: TDC, 57, Trafalgar Square, London WC2N 5NU. Tel:: 071-9307932.

Singapore: TDC, 10, Collyer Quay, #01-03 Ocean Bldg. Singapore 01-04, Tel:: 02-5344466.

U.S.A.: Malaysia Tourist Information Center, 818 West 7th Street, Los Angeles, CA 90017. Tel:: 213-6899702.

GLOSSARY

Good morning . . . . . . *selamat pagi*
Good day (noon) . . *selamat tengahari*
Good afternoon . . . .
. . . . *selamat petang*
Good evening . . . . . *selamat malam*
Good night . . . . *selamat tidur*
How are you? . . . . *apa khabar*
Goodbye . . . . *selamat tinggal*
Bon Voyage . . . . *selamat jalan*
Welcome . . . . *selamat datang*
What's your name? . *siapa nama encik*
My name is . . . . *nama saya*
Can you help me? . . . .
. . . . *bolehkah encik tolong saya?*
What is this/that? . . . . *apakah ini/itu?*
How much does it cost? *berapa harganya?*

How far is it? . . . . . . *berapa jauh?*
What time is it? . . . . . . berapa jam?
How long does it take? . *berapa lama?*
Food/meal . . . . *makanan*
Drink . . . . *minuman*
I'd like to eat/drink . . . .
. . . . *saya mau makan/minum*
What would you like to eat/drink? . .
. . . . *makan/minum apa?*
I'd like the check . . . *saya mau bayar*
Have you got a room? . . . .
. . . . *adakah bilik kosong?*
Excuse me, I'm sorry . . . .
. . . . *saya minta maaf*
yes . . . . *ya*
no . . . . *tidak*
please . . . . *tolong/sila*
thank you . . . . *terima kasih*
where . . . . *di mana*
there . . . . *di sana*
why . . . . *mengapa*
how . . . . *bagaimana*
who . . . . *siapa*
I . . . . *saya*
you . . . . *anda, awak*
you (polite form, men) . . . . . *encik*
you (polite form, women) . . . *cik/puan*
Mr. . . . . *tuan*
Mrs. . . . . *puan*
we (not including the person
addressed) . . . . *kami*
we (including the person
addressed) . . . . *kita*
he/she . . . . *dia*
they . . . . *mereka*
good/okay . . . . *baik*
bad . . . . *jahat*
big . . . . *besar*
small . . . . *kecil*
little . . . . *sedikit*
lot . . . . *banyak*
cold . . . . *sejuk*
hot . . . . *panas*
expensive . . . . *mahal*
cheap . . . . *murah*
price . . . . *harga*
day . . . . *hari*
week . . . . *minggu*
month . . . . *bulan*

half	*setengah*
1	*satu*
2	*dua*
3	*tiga*
4	*empat*
5	*lima*
6	*enam*
7	*tujuh*
8	*lapan*
9	*sembilan*
10	*sepuluh*
11	*sebelas*
12	*duabelas*
20	*duapuluh*
30	*tigapuluh*
40	*empatpuluh*
50	*limapuluh*
100	*seratus*
500	*limaratus*
1000	*seribu*

Pronunciation

e . . . . between two consonants (setar, sebelas) is generally not spoken.

c . . . . as in "clap"

h inaudible at the beginning of a word; . . in the middle or at the end of a word . . . . . it is pronounced, but slightly.

AUTHORS

Karl-Heinz Reger is the editor of a daily paper in Munich, and the author of a number of books of popular science and history. In "Pepper from the Far East," for example, he traced the historic trade relationship between Germany and Southeast Asia. Since 1972, he has visited Malaysia regularly, and has published countless travel reports in newspapers and magazines about the country.

Albrecht G. Schaefer collaborated on this book as a Project Editor, editor and author. Thanks to his profession as journalist, photographer and ethnologist, he has had opportunity to get to know Malaysia inside and out. Southeast Asia has become something of a second home to him, something he's proven by editing and authoring the *Nelles Guide to the Philippine*.

Gerd Simon, editor, journalist and author, works for the publishing house of Simon & Magiera.

PHOTOGRAPHERS

Archiv für Kunst und Geschichte, Berlin 16, 21, 25, 32, 222
Bartl, Sibylle Ina 60
Beck, Josef 38, 115, 154
Bersick, Prof. Dr. G. 70, 95, 106, 117, 231
Cambridge University Library 24, 26, 27, 29, 31, 33
Deichmann, Günther (Mainbild) 137
Gessner, Werner 202
Hahn, Wilfried 73
Hellige, Wolfgang 71, 80, 166, 176, 187, 224, 225
Hinze, Peter 8/9, 48, 58, 64/65, 75, 76, 128, 136, 149, 178/179, 210, 215
Höbel, Robert cover, 15, 152/153, 156, 158, 160, 169, 173, 174, 175, 180, 183, 185, 186, 193, 194, 196/197, 226, 227, 229, 230, 235, 236, 241
Janicke, Volkmar E. 109, 119, 148, 198, 204, 206/207, 208, 211, 216
Karl, Roland F. 14
Malaysia Tourism Promotion Board 139
Müller, Kai-Ulrich 54, 99, 189
Reger, Karl-Heinz 140, 200, 234, 239
Riethmüller, Robert 104/105
Skupy, Hans-Horst 12, 19, 57, 144, 240
Schaefer, Albrecht G. 10/11, 17, 20, 22, 35, 37, 39, 44, 49, 52, 53, 55, 56, 66, 74, 79, 98, 101, 110, 111, 114, 118, 124, 126, 130/131, 132, 145, 157, 165, 167, 168, 190, 192, 228, 232, 233
Thomas, Martin 40/41, 82, 86, 88, 92, 96, 150, 238